r

social
roles

SOCIOLOGICAL OBSERVATIONS

Series Editor: **JOHN M. JOHNSON,** Arizona State University

"This new series seeks its inspiration primarily from its subject matter and the nature of its observational setting. It draws on all academic disciplines and a wide variety of theoretical and methodological perspectives. The series has a commitment to substantive problems and issues and favors research and analysis which seek to blend actual observations of human actions in daily life with broader theoretical, comparative, and historical perspectives. SOCIOLOGICAL OBSERVATIONS aims to use all of our available intellectual resources to better understand all facets of human experience and the nature of our society."

—John M. Johnson

social
roles
CONFORMITY
CONFLICT
AND CREATIVITY

LOUIS A. ZURCHER

SAGE PUBLICATIONS
Beverly Hills / London / New Delhi

For information address:

SAGE Publications, Inc.
275 South Beverly Drive
Beverly Hills, California 90212

SAGE Publications India Pvt. Ltd.
C-236 Defence Colony
New Delhi 110 024, India

SAGE Publications Ltd
28 Banner Street
London EC1Y 8QE, England

Printed in the United States of America

Library of Congress Cataloging in Publication Data

Main entry under title:

Zurcher, Louis A.
   Social roles.

   (Sociological observations ; 15)
   Bibliography: p.
   Includes index.
   1. Social role. 2. Role playing. I. Title.
II. Series
HM131.Z88   1983   302'.15   83-9548
ISBN 0-8039-2029-6
ISBN 0-8039-2030-X (pbk.)

Contents

To **Nora Breen Zurcher,**
whose creativity with social roles has
been an inspiration and a delight to me,
and
to **Susan Shrum Zurcher,**
her role model

Preface and Acknowledgments

For many years I have had a research interest in why and how people enact social roles. During my studies I was consistently impressed by the remarkable autonomy, versatility, and purposefulness of human beings as role enactors. They conformed to or modified established roles, created new ones, and employed all sorts of strategies to resolve any role conflict they were experiencing. They negotiated workable compromises between the behavioral expectations they had for themselves and the behavioral expectations they perceived others to have for them. They accumulated, organized, and enacted complicated sets of roles in a meaningful and satisfying manner. Even when a role was rigidly embedded in a highly structured setting, they found some way (unless completely incapacitated) to put their "mark" on it.

This book brings together a rewriting of those of my studies that best illustrate autonomy, versatility, and purposefulness in role enactment. The examples represent a variety of settings and roles: "boots" in a recruit training center; sailors aboard ship; fans and players at a college football game; "hashers" in a sorority house; passengers in an airplane; members of a disaster volunteer work crew; players in a poker game; Naval Reservists in weekend "drill" and on maneuvers in the field; an indigenous leader in a poverty program; priests in a protest movement; and felons in the parole system.

The guiding theoretical perspective for the book is symbolic interactionism, although the illustrative studies draw upon other theoretical notions about socialization, human personality, complex organizations, small groups, and social change. All of the studies involved qualitative research methods, usually some type of participant observation. A few of them also involved survey research methods. In the last two chapters, I offer a theoretical framework for analyzing social roles and a set of suggestions for how to study them in natural settings. I considered putting these at the beginning of the book, as introductory chapters, but concluded that they are more summaries than introductions. Furthermore, it seemed likely that they would make more sense to you after you had perused the illustrations of role enactment. None-

theless, you might want to skim the last two chapters after reading
Chapter 1 (Introduction) and before beginning the illustrations (Chapters 2 through 12).

I intend this book for undergraduate and beginning graduate
courses that wholly or in significant part feature the topic of social
roles in their syllabi. Depending on the focus of the course, it could be
used as a primary or a supporting text. Besides its appropriateness for
courses substantively concerned with roles, the book could be helpful
in teaching qualitative research methods.

The following journals and organizations generously gave me permission to use materials I had published under their auspices: *Sociological Inquiry, Social Forces, Symbolic Interaction, Qualitative Sociology, Human Organization, Social Psychology Quarterly, Genetic Psychology Monographs, Journal for the Scientific Study of Religion, Armed Forces and Society, Journal of Voluntary Action Research,* Human Sciences Press, and University of Texas Press. Complete acknowledgments are given at the beginnings of the appropriate chapters.

My writing the book was enabled by a presidential leave of absence
from a semester's teaching duties at the University of Texas—Austin,
and by a small grant from the University of Texas Research Institute. I
profited from and am thankful for the constructively critical comments
of Susan Zurcher, David Snow, Gideon Sjoberg, Ralph Turner, Ruth
McRoy, Kathryn Moss, and Michael Wood, and several of my graduate and undergraduate students, especially Roberta Thiessen, Catalina
Herrerias, Susan Pollock, and Dawn Gettman. Mary McNamara, my
editorial colleague in the stewardship of *The Journal of Applied
Behavioral Science,* not only coordinated and participated in the preparation of the manuscript, but consistently provided important suggestions on substance, style, and format. I am very grateful to her. I am
indebted to John Johnson, Editor of the Sage Sociological Observations series, for his insightful suggestions and unflagging support. Martha Williams, Dean of the School of Social Work, has administratively
nurtured a scholarly climate in which the writing of books is not only
an expectation but a pleasure.

1

INTRODUCTION

Learning and Enacting Roles

The term "role" has been used by social scientists in several different ways, depending on the focus of their studies (Linton, 1936; Parsons, 1951, 1970; Biddle and Thomas, 1966; Turner, 1968a; Newcomb, 1949). It typically refers to the behavior expected of individuals who occupy particular social categories. Those categories have included statuses (positions) in formal social systems, such as fathers in families, clerics in churches, and professors in universities. They also have included less formal statuses, such as member of a movie audience, jogger in a park, and customer in a supermarket. Finally, they have included statuses reflecting the cultural values of a society, such as a hard worker, concerned citizen, and hip Californian. One of the major differences in focus has related to the origin of the behavioral expectations constituting roles. Some scholars have concentrated on the way roles, as fixed components of established social structures or cultures, influence the behavior of people. Other scholars have concentrated on the way roles emerge in social settings, and on how individuals influence the character of behavioral expectations.

In this book, I will follow Heiss's (1981a: 95) broad conclusion that roles are behavioral expectations for what a person "should" do. The "should" comes from several sources: expectations associated with established and recognized roles, with roles in informal and emergent situations, and with the person's own self-concept and inclinations.

We learn roles in the process of socialization (Goslin, 1969; Clausen, 1968; Brim and Wheeler, 1966; Brim, 1968; Bush and Simmons, 1981;

Gecas, 1981; Turner, 1970). In many instances, others teach us the behavioral expectations they consider appropriate for the statuses we occupy or will occupy. Those expectations might be institutionalized in the society, organization, or group of which we are or want to be a member. For example, parents in our families, teachers in our schools, and supervisors in our workplaces instruct us about how to behave as sons or daughters, students, and employees, respectively. Sometimes the expectations are not institutionalized, but emerge from shared understandings we develop in temporary groups, as when we are members of certain kinds of crowds, or spectators at an auto accident, or riders in an elevator (Turner and Killian, 1972).

In everyday life, all of us routinely occupy many statuses, both formal and informal. Consequently, we enact complex repertoires of roles (Merton, 1957; Heiss, 1981a). We comply with and somehow coordinate, for example, the behavioral expectations associated with being an employee, a family member, a spouse, a parent, a citizen, a friend, a club member, a crowd member, and so on. How do we accommodate our many role obligations? Not easily, according to some researchers. We have problems integrating the roles not only with each other but into our self-concepts (Goode, 1960; Burchard, 1954; Gouldner, 1957; Toby, 1952; Gross et al., 1958; Gross and Stone, 1964). Other researchers have emphasized the beneficial aspects of role diversity. Sieber (1974) argues that an extensive role repertoire provides us with status security, resources for status enhancement or role performance, ego gratification, and personality enrichment. Turner (1978) observes that the network of roles we enact facilitates the development of what we are as "persons." Stone (1962) suggests that our role enactments provide us with a flexible identity specific to and situated in social settings. Sarbin and Allen (1968) note that the internalization of role expectations creates in us a functional self-concept, a versatile perception of ourselves.

Why do we enact roles in the first place? What "motivates" us to do so? One explanation, psychological in orientation, is that we are driven to enact roles because they help us satisfy specific primary (for example, hunger, sex) or secondary (such as approval, affiliation) needs that we have (Masden, 1968; Atkinson and Birch, 1978). Another explanation, sociological in orientation, starts with the observation that human beings by nature are active in their social environments (Dewey, 1922). The character of that activity, including the chàracter of role enactments, is determined in the social situation (Stone and Farberman, 1981; Scott and Lyman, 1968). Our role enactments are best understood not by linking them to specific physiological and psychological elements, but as products of our social interaction with other people. "Motives" and "needs" emerge in those interactions as vocabularies by which we explain or justify our role performances (Mills, 1940; Foote, 1951; Burke, 1962). This perspective on role enactment is part of the social-psychological orientation known as symbolic interactionism, an orientation that will heavily influence my interpretations throughout the book.

SYMBOLIC INTERACTIONISM

Among the basic assumptions of symbolic interactionism, the following are particularly pertinent to understanding how we learn and enact social roles (Stryker, 1981: 16-17; Heiss, 1981b: 23-24; Stone and Farberman, 1981: 1-2; Blumer, 1969: 2-3; Meltzer et al., 1975: 1-3; Turner, 1956: 316-318):

- We consciously and purposefully enact roles.
- We are active rather than passive role enactors. We not only conform to role expectations, we interpret, organize, modify, and create them.
- As human beings, we are unique in our ability to communicate by using complex systems of symbols, most notably, language. Because of that facility, we can develop, assign, and share with others the meaning of role expectations and enactments. Language also enables us to summarize roles with names or labels, thereby enhancing our communication about them.
- We develop our understanding of roles in social settings involving interaction with other people. The roles are specific to those settings. However, the accumulation of role enactments and the experiences associated with them shape our self-concepts, that is, the way we perceive ourselves (Hewitt, 1979; McCall and Simmons, 1966; Heiss, 1981a; Strauss, 1959). These self-concepts provide us with a sense of personal continuity as we enact roles in diverse social settings. Within each setting, we negotiate with other people both our own and their identities (Stone, 1962; Goffman, 1959; Strauss, 1978). Identities are compromises we effect between our own self-concepts and the demands of a role in a specific social situation. The compromises can influence us, and others with whom we are interacting, to modify self-concepts.
- Some roles, because they are embedded in social institutions and organizations, are not very flexible. Nonetheless, we usually find ways to enact even the most structurally rigid roles in a manner consistent with our own self-concepts and with our interpretation of the social setting. If we are expected to enact a role only vaguely defined in a social setting, we usually find a way, guided by our self-concepts and through interaction with others in the setting, to establish a workable role for ourselves.

- We consistently try to find ways to merge what we want to do with what is expected of us in specific role settings.
- The process of our interaction with others concerning role enactment precedes and shapes the content of the enactment.

The notion that we consistently are engaged in attempts to understand, interpret, and negotiate the relation between the behavioral expectations we have for ourselves and the behavioral expectations we perceive others to have for us is central to symbolic interactionism. Whenever we can, we conduct our role enactments as an effective balance between what Mead (1934) called the "I" and the "Me" (Karp and Yoels, 1979: 40-42; Meltzer, 1972: 10-11; Hewitt, 1976: 55-56; Kolb, 1942: 291-296). The "I" is the part of our self-concepts that includes the unique ways in which we have organized our social experiences. The uniqueness constitutes us as individuals. The "I" embodies our personal inclinations and impulses. The "Me" is the more socially conventional component of our self-concepts. It is that part of us which reflects our having conformed to the expectations of other people and to the institutionalized roles in those social organizations of which we are a part.

As individuals who learn from and organize our social experiences, we both "take" and "make" roles (Turner, 1956, 1962; Sherohman, 1977). When we take roles, we lean more toward conforming to the expectations we perceive others to have for our behavior in a given social setting, although we are purposefully engaged in interactions that clarify and shape those expectations. When we make roles, we lean more toward creating the roles in line with our own inclinations. This distinction between role taking and role making illustrates a major issue in social psychology. What is the relation between the individual and the social structures in which he or she functions (Argyris, 1957; Allport, 1961; Merton, 1940; Habermas, 1969; Weber, 1968; Littrell et al., 1983)? How do we arrange a satisfactory merging of our preferences with the preferences mandated by other people, those to whom we pay attention, in our social worlds?

There seem to be two opposing theoretical perspectives on role enactment. The structuralist view assumes that roles are givens in formal social structures. Individuals must in one way or another accommodate the roles. The structuralist position emphasizes the effect of historical factors, power distributions, and cultural values on role enactment. The symbolic interactionist view assumes that roles emerge from or are significantly shaped by interactions in specific social settings. I concur with those who have suggested that the difference between the two perspectives is only a matter of analytical focus, and that neither of the perspectives actually dismisses the views of the other (Stokes and Hewitt, 1976; Heiss, 1981a; Maines, 1977; Coulson, 1972; Stryker, 1980; Lauer and Handel, 1977; Handel, 1979; Shibutani, 1961; Wilson, 1970). Both describe important aspects of social reality, and should be acknowledged in any consideration of role enactment.

PURPOSE OF THE BOOK

The purpose of this book is to provide you with examples of situations in which individuals are called upon to enact roles in a variety of social settings. Some of those settings demand that the roles fully be "taken." Some of them provide considerable opportunity for the roles more elaborately to be "made." Some of them place individuals squarely in a situation where the enactment of the expected roles is at odds with personal preferences or with roles they have already enacted. All of the examples, regardless of the kind of setting or the complexity of the role expectations, are intended to demonstrate, following the symbolic interactionist perspective, how we engage roles with autonomy, versatility, and purpose. We conform to role expectations, but make efforts to protect our individuality. We create roles, but do so with a realistic sensitivity to relevant social structures. We resolve role conflicts, but are guided in that endeavor by our perceptions of a socially workable resolution. As healthy human beings, because of our cerebral equipment and capacity for elaborate social learning, we attempt to conduct ourselves competently in our environments (White, 1959; Murphy, 1947; Maslow, 1954; Douglas and Johnson, 1977; May, 1969; Schutz, 1967; Argyris, 1957, 1964; Heider, 1958; Festinger, 1957; Allport, 1955).

The examples I offer in the book will be keyed to four major social psychological notions: person, self-concept, identity, and social setting. The term "person" highlights the individual's inclination to be a processor and organizer of his or her social experiences and to be autonomous, purposeful, and versatile in role enactments. "Self-concept" refers to those perceptions of self that have become, within the individual's cognition, relatively stable operating compromises between own inclinations and the role-related lessons from social experience. "Identity" is the situation-based presentation of self that a person negotiates with other people in a specific social setting. "Social setting" refers to the pressures for role conformity put upon the individual by others (including groups and organizations) in a specific situation. I will expand upon the usefulness of these four notions for understanding role enactment in Chapter 13 (the theory chapter).

The symbolic interactionist perspective has been criticized for not giving enough attention to the influences of culture, history, and power on role enactment and for not considering the importance of feelings (emotion) in that enactment (Meltzer et al., 1975). The examples I offer will not completely offset the criticism, but they will show how culture, history, power, and emotion are involved in role behavior.

ORGANIZATION OF THE BOOK

Chapter 1, which you are now reading, is the introduction to the book. Chapters 2 through 12 present illustrations, each of which focuses on a particular aspect of role enactment: assimilating a role; developing an informal role; staging emotional role behavior; dealing with an unacceptable role; modifying a routine role; filling a role void; enjoying an ephemeral role; developing role balance; reacting to disruption of role balance; resolving role marginality; transforming an accustomed role. To some extent, the earlier chapters describe settings in which the actors (as I perceived them) manifested less, and the later chapters more, evidence of autonomy in role enactment. However, each illustration reveals how people purposefully enact roles whatever the demands of the setting.

Chapter 2 describes how role expectations are impressed upon young recruits in "boot camp," a quite demanding "total institution." Chapter 3 reveals how sailors aboard a Naval vessel, also a "total institution," enact informal roles within the ship's formal organization. In Chapter 4, the role behavior of football fans and players, including appropriate emotional expression, is shown to be influenced by the "staging" of the sports event. Chapter 5 illustrates how "hashers," male waiters in sorority houses, deal with conflict between the expectations they have for themselves as college men and the expectations the sorority women have for them as kitchen help. Chapter 6 documents how airplane passengers resist the expectation that they are to be passive compliants in "people pipelines."

In Chapter 7, volunteers in a disaster work crew are described as creating their own roles and their own temporary social structure after a tornado has voided everyday roles and structure. Chapter 8 shows how poker players both create and conform to roles in a "friendly game," and outlines the satisfactions the players derive from an "ephemeral" role. Chapter 9 presents the manner in which Naval Reservists innovatively balance military with civilian role expectations. Chapter 10 describes how the Naval Reservists cope with a disruption to the role balance they have effected. Chapter 11 outlines the dilemmas experienced by a neighborhood leader in a community helping program when he found himself torn between the role expectations of his followers and the role expectations of the program's officials.

Chapter 12 demonstrates how priests and parolees, each experiencing dramatic social change, attempt to transform their accustomed roles. In Chapter 13, a framework for analyzing role enactment is suggested. Chapter 14 offers some hints about studying role enactments in natural settings.

THE DATA BASE FOR THE BOOK

The examples given in Chapters 2 through 12 are based on field studies I have done in natural settings. The studies used qualitative research methods: participant observation, informal interviews, document analysis, and, in some instances, structured questionnaires. Whenever possible, the data were "triangulated" (Denzin, 1970). That is, data from different sources were compared as they related to the role enactment that was examined. Furthermore, each of the examples in Chapters 2 through 12 was analyzed and integrated in light of sociological and social psychological theory that either already was in the literature or emerged from the study (Glaser and Strauss, 1967). The specific examples presented should not be unduly generalized. Recruits do not all enact their roles in an identical manner, nor do all sailors, college football fans and players, sorority hashers, airplane passengers, disaster work crew volunteers, poker group members, Naval Reservists, indigenous leaders, priests, or parolees. The examples represent different and sometimes unique social situations. They were chosen because they illustrate the diverse strategies by which individuals maintain autonomy in their role enactments. The process of autonomy, not the particular examples of it, is offered for generalization. The illustrations might seem to be burdened with too much detail about the settings in which the role enactments occurred. That was deliberate, as my suggestions for studying role enactment in natural settings (Chapter 14) will argue. The social fabric into which role enactments are woven is very complex. Attention to detail is required.

I was to a greater or lesser extent involved not only as a researcher but as an actor in the field settings studied (Lofland, 1976; Johnson, 1975). The use of qualitative methods, especially when one is both researcher and actor, increases the possibility of a subjective or biased interpretation of what is going on in the setting. However, it also brings the investigator closer to the reality of role enactments than can the perhaps more objective techniques of experimental and survey research.

In this book, I take the stance that, when studying social roles, there is no substitute for "being there." Role enactments are part of everyday life (Garfinkle, 1967; Mehan and Wood, 1975; Blumer, 1969; Karp and Yoels, 1979). We can readily understand those enactments if we systematically examine the social world around us and our own behavior in it.

2

ASSIMILATING A ROLE
IN A TOTAL INSTITUTION
Recruits in Boot Camp

Among the organizations in which people might be members, total institutions are notable for the role conformity they demand. They include prisons, asylums, convents, monasteries, and, as I suggest in this chapter, Naval recruit training centers.

Goffman (1961a: xiii) has defined a total institution as a place "of residence and work where a large number of like-situated individuals, cut off from the wider society for an appreciable period of time, together lead an enclosed, formally administered round of life." The general characteristics of total institutions, as described by Goffman (1961a: 5), include:

- All aspects of life are conducted in the same place and under the same single authority.
- Each phase of the members' daily activity is carried on in the immediate company of a large batch of others, all of whom are treated alike and required to do the same thing together.
- All phases of the day's activities are tightly scheduled, with one activity leading at a prearranged time into the next, the whole sequence of activities

---

This chapter is a rewritten version of my previously published paper, "The Naval Recruit Training Center: A Study of Role Assimilation in a Total Institution," *Sociological Inquiry* 37 (Winter 1967): 85-98. Used by permission.

being imposed from above by a system of explicit formal rulings and a body of officials.

- The various enforced activities are brought together into a single rational plan purportedly designed to fulfill the official aim of the institution.
- There is a sharp split between the supervisors and the members, with social mobility between the two groups being highly restricted.
- Information concerning the fate of the member is often withheld from him or her.
- The work stucture in a total institution, geared as it is to a 24-hour day, demands different motives for work than exist in the society at large.
- There are usually real or symbolic barriers indicating a break with the society "out there."

The Naval recruit training center has the task of transforming civilians into sailors. The organizational structure of the center, the staff functions, and the educational program are wholly concerned with socialization of the sailor role. There is little slippage in the system, little opportunity for the recruits to enact other than that role. The earlier stages of recruit training seem constructed to dispossess the recruits of their civilian roles; the later stages to provide clarification of the sailor role to be enacted by the recruits. The clarification comes from classroom instruction, "real sailor" role models, contrasts with "outgroups" or role failures, and interactions among the recruits themselves as members of an increasingly cohesive recruit company.

The processes of social interaction during recruit training formulate and offer a new identity to the recruits—that of sailor. It is anticipated that the recruits will assimilate the sailor identity and, even better from the perspective of the Navy, will permit their self-concepts to be dominated by that identity. However, the degree to which the sailor identity is assimilated and self-concepts are modified is less important to the Navy than the degree to which the recruits enact the appropriate role behavior. It is possible for recruits to conform to role expectations in the training center, and yet not internalize them. Recruits differ in the manner in which they react to the dispossession of their civilian roles and in the extent to which they perceive themselves as sailors. Since the training center so strongly emphasizes role taking, there is little opportunity for the recruits creatively to make roles. The autonomy available to the recruits is very limited. They can choose to take the sailor role so completely that it engulfs them as persons. They can willfully refuse to enact the role in the expected manner and accept inevitable punishment. They can refuse repeatedly and thereby be discharged from the Navy, an outcome that they may prefer to enacting the sailor role. However, the most common way that recruits effect autonomy in the training center is to enact the appropriate behaviors as directed, while at the same time perceiving themselves as individuals independent from but conforming to the sailor role.

The quotes and illustrations in this chapter, and in Chapter 3, that are not referenced to other writers were drawn from my participant observation in the Navy and from interviews with Navy officers and sailors. I have been a recruit in a Naval training center, a sailor aboard ship (including the ship that is described in Chapter 3), and a Naval officer. While enacting those roles I kept a record of my observations in diaries, logs, and field notes. Though some of those data are now over twenty years old, I have updated them. With the exception of new technology and an all-volunteer military climate, the Naval recruit training process and life aboard ship remain fundamentally the same as they were twenty years ago. The proportion of women who are sailors has increased, as has their access to a wider range of Navy jobs. A few ships now have female sailors as crew members. The processes of recruit training for women, and their socialization experiences aboard ship, are essentially the same as for male sailors (Bachman et al., 1977; Goldman, 1973a, 1973b). Consequently, except where quotes from other researchers included them, I have avoided gender specifications throughout this chapter and Chapter 3.

ENLISTING IN THE NAVY

"Landlubber" civilians cannot go from the recruiting office directly to duty as enlisted sailors aboard a vessel or installation of the United States Navy. They must first spend nine weeks, sometimes less, depending on current Navy policy, at a Naval recruit training center. There they will undergo the "boot" indoctrination process that will, upon successful completion, qualify them for a place in the fleet. "Boot" is a slang term for recruit. It originates from the leggings, resembling boots, worn by recruits as part of their uniform. Naval recruit training centers are, consequently, called "boot camps."

All persons who join the Navy come to it with a set of values, beliefs, and expectations that influence their behavior. Always in peacetime, and largely in wartime, the Navy consists of volunteers. Thus it might be expected that individuals who enlist for a tour of active duty have already begun the process of enacting the sailor role. But they do not know the actual expectations of the Navy. The volunteers are civilian persons, see themselves as such, and enact their roles accordingly.

The day-to-day conduct of a civilian, guided as it is by relative freedom of decision, is not tolerated in a total institution. Therefore, the first major task of the training center is to "decivilianize" the entering individuals, to strip them of their civilian roles.

The enlistees, while going through the paper-processing stage of joining the Navy, will probably not notice any radical changes from their usual civilian interpersonal and organizational experiences. They will have several forms to fill out and some physical and mental examinations to take, but the officials treat them as civilians. The enlistees can still decide, for example, the time and day they wish to report for most parts of the enlistment process, and when they want to go on active duty.

When all the paperwork has been finished, and the scheduled day for formal enlistment arrives, the enlistees are shown into a room and, in the presence of an American flag, take the oath of service. After the oath has been completed, the transition is dramatic. Depersonalization has begun. The enlistees are not addressed as civilians, but as "boots," and are brusquely ordered about. Subsequently, they board transportation that takes them to the Naval recruit training center.

THE RECRUIT TRAINING CENTER AS A TOTAL INSTITUTION

The Naval recruit training center is a total institution. All aspects of the boots' lives are conducted in the same place (the center) and under a single central authority (the center commander or, more broadly, the U.S. Navy). The recruits do everything in the company of others, and the expectations for their recruit behavior are the same for all recruits. The day's activities tick off by the numbers, everything done at the proper time in the proper place, according to an elaborate plan of the day published and posted by order of the commanding officer. There is a single rational plan (to create sailors out of civilians) designed to fulfill the instrumental function of the center, to supply the fleet with personnel. The supervisors have their own quarters, mess facilities, and recreational facilities, are allowed to leave the training center, and cannot be approached by recruits without strict adherence to the chain of command and to military courtesy. Anyone who is not a recruit is a supervisor. Boots usually do not know what is in store for them from one moment to the next. They are told to fall in, to march, and find out their destination when they get there. The work structure is based on a 24-hour day of classes, drill, physical training, and watch standing. They are reminded that they belong to the Navy even when asleep. Fences and gates protected by armed guards separate the training center and the recruits from society at large.

CHALLENGES TO CIVILIAN
SELF-CONCEPTS AND ROLES

At the beginning of their first week in boot camp, the recruits are assigned to "R and O" (receiving and outfitting). In R and O the boots live and work, along with approximately sixty other members of their recruit company, in a set of buildings separated by chain-link fences from the rest of the training center. The "R and Os" (as they are called by the staff and by the more advanced boots) have their own mess hall, their own medical facility, and their own "grinders" (marching fields), and are not allowed access to the center at large. The ostensible purpose of this isolation is to prevent the spread of any contagious diseases the new recruits might be carrying, while at the same time issuing their clothing, giving them an extensive physical examination, administering General Classification Test batteries, giving them haircuts and shots, and getting them acquainted with the general rules, schedules, and marching as a group. But something more is happening than these obvious elements of organizational design. It is during the R and O phase that the challenge to the civilian self-concept begins in earnest.

From the point of view of the training center, boots have come through the gate with a civilian self-concept, a civilian frame of reference, and a set of values and expectations that are not compatible with the center's objectives. The adjustment problem for the recruits consists of reorienting their behavior from civilian to military standards. That adjustment is no easy task.

Some behavioral scientists have commented on the threat to self-concept posed by the military training center. The recruit is a "lone individual, hopelessly insecure in bewildering newness and complexity of environment," is "powerless," and is "subjected to shock treatment" (Stouffer et al., 1949: 411-412). He or she is taken "away from civilian life contacts and abruptly placed into a new routine, without customary individualistic responsibilities and dependent upon superiors for orders." In this context, "the recruit becomes depressed and disorganized" (Weinberg, 1944-1945: 272). The process of recruit training is "analogous to major crises in childhood, puberty, and adolescence." It involves "a strict discipline plus the end of opportunities for self-expression and impulse gratification" and engenders "mass frustration" (Janis, 1945: 159). The method of indoctrination in training centers is one of "feudalistic discipline" (Rose, 1946: 363-364). The fact that the institution is "governing the life of the individual" even when "not on actual work duty" contrasts with "normal civilian social controls." "Aspects of daily life considered by civilians to be solely within the realm of private discretion are regarded as fit subjects for regulation" (Anonymous, 1946a: 366). The training center not only requires of its recruits a "lapse of civilian occupations and avocations, but also involves the increasing decline of the social controls of the family and the neighborhood." "There is a knifing off of past experiences." "Nothing in one's past seems relevant." The recruit is "thrust into a completely alien role," and "experiences feelings of isolation, impersonality, and personal degradation" (Brotz and Wilson, 1946: 373-374). During the first part of recruit training, "so much happens to the person in such a short time that reactions tend to be confused." "The perfectly trained member of the military organization is one who has had his civilian initiative reduced to zero" (Hollingshead, 1946: 440).

Dornbusch (1955: 317), writing about the assimilation of the new cadet into the U.S. Coast Guard Academy, reports that the "swab" (the academy's equivalent of "boot") is, for the first two months after arrival, not allowed to leave the base or to engage in social intercourse with noncadets. This process provides, within a short period of time, a "clean break with the past" and a "loss of identity in terms of preexisting statuses." The individual is "softened up" and made receptive to the role expectations of the organization in which he or she is a recruit.

The pressures of the recruit training center, especially in the R and O phase, challenge, as Goffman (1961a: 237-238) has suggested, four areas of boots' lives that have influenced their understanding and acceptance of themselves as "civilians," and that have provided a foundation for their self-concepts: (1) autonomy of action (self-determination, responsibility for their behavior, feeling free to express themselves and to make choices, feeling personal integrity); (2) personal economy of motion (feeling free to move spontaneously toward, away from, or against a given experience according to their preferences, able to set their activity pace, to control and vary their rate of locomotion); (3) privacy (having opportunity for physical and mental privacy, having places to be alone and "get away from it all"); (4) perception of self as a physical person (seeing themselves in their usual choice of clothing, degree of neatness, and tonsorial demeanor). The following are some examples, taken from my field notes, of challenges to the new recruits' civilian self-concepts.

Challenge to Autonomy of Action

- New recruits find that they cannot choose the people with whom they experience everyday life. They must be "shipmates" to anyone assigned to their recruit company.

- Times for sleeping, eating, using the "head" (toilet facilities), personal hygiene, smoking, and other previously autonomous actions are now rigidly scheduled.
- Recruits are told that they will write letters home each week; thus a measure of control is established over their interactions with their families.
- All clothing, all bedding, and all personal items must be stored in exactly the prescribed manner. Any individual deviations result in punishment for the entire company of recruits. In controlling the condition and position of the boots' personal effects, the center authority strengthens its control over the boots themselves, who routinely have invested some element of themselves in their belongings.
- "You have been issued five pairs of shorts. Put one pair on each shoulder, one pair in your teeth, and hold one pair in each hand. Now, do you have a pair of shorts on each shoulder, in your teeth, and in each hand? Good! Put them in the sea bag. Next, you have been issued six pairs of stockings . . . " The recruits' ability to account for their own belongings is questioned.
- Every morning, all the R and Os must stand personnel inspection. One of the positions assumed during the inspection procedure is a rigid stance at attention, the left hand holding the hat bottom side up at elbow's length, the thumb of the right hand hooked underneath the collar of the "skivvy shirt" (undershirt), turning the material outward, so that the inspector can check both hat and shirt in one quick glance. Thus the recruits' responsibility for personal cleanliness is challenged.
- "Forget your name! All you have to remember is the number of the square on which you are now standing. I'm going to let you fall out, then have you fall back in. Return to the same numbered square. Understand? Ready? Fall out!" The recruits' identity is reduced to a numbered square.

Challenge to Personal Economy of Motion

- "When I give the command 'Attention!' you will bring your heels together sharply, toes at a 45 degree angle. Your hands will be by your sides, in a natural position, with your thumbs lined up with the seams in your trousers. You will pull your stomach in, push your chest out, keep your shoulders back and your body straight. I don't want to see any daylight between your knees. Keep your head and eyes forward at all times. And keep your mouths closed. If I haul ass out of here for a weekend liberty while you're at attention, you had better be in that same position when I get back!"
- "When the Captain comes by your position for inspection, don't blink and don't breathe! Make that uniform look good!"
- Everywhere boots go, they must march in formation. If for some administrative reason they must go somewhere alone, they will be given a "walking chit" (permit), stating point of origin, destination, a time limit, and who has given them permission to walk independently.
- The boots constantly are kept active and moving. The pace never seems to slacken. "You're not standing around on corners now!" They cannot pause for rest unless the company is ordered to fall out or stand at ease.

- "When they walk, when they sit, sailors are tall!"

Challenge to Privacy

- "There's a folder up in the administration office. We know more about you than you do!"
- "Remove all of your clothes, sit over there on that bench, and wait until you are told to line up facing the doctor."
- "You with the dreamy look in your eyes! What are you thinking about!"
- "Hey, mate, throw me your soap, will you?"

Challenge to the Individuals'
Picture of Themselves as Physical Persons

- Within a matter of hours after arrival at boot camp, new recruits are told to remove all of their civilian clothes and personal effects and place them into a shipping box. They stand nearly nude and wrap and address the boxes containing the accouterments of their civilianity. When finished, they proceed through a line in which they are issued their Naval attire.
- There is nothing distinctive about the clothes the recruits now put on. The blue dungarees and blue chambray shirts (R and Os are not allowed to wear the Navy blues or whites they have been issued), the underwear, the hats, the socks and shoes, look exactly like everyone else's. The clothing is untailored, and will remain so for about two weeks. "It's not that the clothes don't fit you, boot. You don't fit the clothes! We'll shape you up!"
- The haircut takes about thirty seconds. Full-length mirrors are conveniently placed around the barber shop. The reflection of the shorn head (or closecut hair for women), the baggy clothes, the drawn features, make their point: You are a boot!
- "You boots with the lard tails will knock off at least twenty pounds, and you beanpoles will gain at least twenty, before you get off these grinders!"
- "You're going to discover muscles you never knew you had before!"

Assault after assault is made on the new recruits' civilian self-concepts. Many of the responses to situations that had worked well in civilian life are now inappropriate or ineffective. The recruits seem unable to do anything right. Everywhere they go, everyone they must deal with, reminds them that they are not individuals but R and O boots, the lowest of the low. Even other recruits, those who are on the other side of the isolation fence, shout derisions about their clumsiness, appearance, and confusion. The new recruits' company is marched over to the end of the isolation area facing the main drill field. There they stand in their ill-fitting, stiff dungarees, arms still burning from shots, heads and shoulders itching from the haircut, tired, lonely, and lost. On the main drill field, company after company of sharp-stepping, cadence-singing seventh- and eighth-week recruits parade smartly to the thundering drum rolls of the center band. The company commander (himself an enlisted man) points to the experienced recruit companies and expresses doubt that the miserable R and Os in his or her command will ever look that good. The role is being defined. The expectations are becoming clearer. The recruits think to themselves, as they watch through the chain-link fence, "Someday, maybe . . . "

In the society at large, civilians compartmentalize their roles. They can be student, son or daughter, lover, part-time grocery clerk, and they understand a set of reciprocal expectations for each of those roles. Similarly, they expect compartmentalized authority over them. The professor may be able to set down limits for classroom perfor-mance, but the professor cannot tell the student what, where, and when, for example, to eat.

In the Naval recruit training center, boots have a single role; the authority over them is not compartmentalized. Any member of the staff can correct them for any offense at any time.

LEARNING THE SAILOR ROLE

During the R and O phase of recruit training, the boots have been pushed, pulled, and badgered from five in the morning until ten at night (and they are awakened from sleep to stand watches). They have been challenged in their previous expectations of autonomy of action, personal economy of motion, privacy, and perceptions of themselves as physical persons. They have found that the confidence they had in themselves as civilians is no longer supportive, that in the training center environment their previous patterns of behavior leave them powerless, isolated, and in conflict with the sanctioned norms, and make most of the center's day-to-day events appear meaningless. In short, if the purposes of the center have been realized, the recruits' civilian identity has been muddled, the comfortable feeling of knowl-edge of themselves has been taken away, and they begin to reject their former self-concepts and civilian expectations as ineffective. If the R and O process is fruitful, boots should be depersonalized and role-dispossessed shells, searching hungrily for the security and certainty of a sanctioned role they can enact.

During the R and O phase, the role of sailor has been constantly presented—in the physical environment, in the example of the com-pany commander, in the glimpses the R and Os get of advanced recruits. But the center's emphasis was on role dispossession; and the

major result, from the point of view of the recruits, is confusion about
rather than enactment of the sailor role. Hollingshead (1946: 442)
points out that in the training center, though the opportunity to attain
military status is present, the meaning of military status does not grow
clear for some time. When recruits realize that they are in a military
situation and that their civilian lives are behind them, that they are "in
the Navy now," the "self will begin to appraise itself in relation to the
new situation, and to adjust, or to figure out ways to evade the situation" (Hollingshead, 1946: 447).

BECOMING AN ADVANCED RECRUIT

It would not be correct to say that for all boots the R and O phase
(first three weeks) represents depersonalization and role dispossession,
and the advanced recruit stage (last six weeks) represents a clear presentation of the center's role expectations meant to fill the gap. Rather,
role dispossession and role enactment exist on a continuum, varying in
time and degree for each recruit. However, examination of the structure and scheduling of the two phases of recruit training reveals the R
and O period of the process to be functional largely in decivilianizing
the recruit, while the advanced period is functional largely in defining
the expectations of the sailor role.

DEVELOPING GROUP COHESION

Upon the completion of R and O, the recruits move to new
quarters in the main area of the training center, shed their dungarees
for blue or white uniforms (depending on the time of year), and are
issued a colorful company flag. Their company is now in official competition with the advanced recruit companies for the weekly honors
awarded with great ceremony at the Saturday brigade review. The
boots begin to see themselves in a different light. Where before there
was confusion, clumsiness, individual isolation, and general uncertainty, now there are "the recruits of Company 123." The company
becomes the center of orientation. Hollingshead (1946: 440) observes
that during recruit training a group substitute replaces the shattered
civilian self. Brotz and Wilson (1946: 374) note that "the complete
severance of accustomed social relations finds compensation in part in
the acquiring of 'buddies.'" To the recruit, the term "buddy" applies to
every person in the company. The hours of drilling and exercising
together, the constant exhortations to "move as one," work as a unifying discipline. Marching may be joked about, Warren (1946: 205)

points out, but let another recruit get out of step as the company passes in review and the in-step recruit "curses under his breath."

The low status of the recruits in R and O makes the new uniforms, the company flag, the new quarters in the main part of the training center, and a place among the advanced recruits seem like a significant increase in prestige. Dornbusch (1955: 317) observed a similar phenomenon in the Coast Guard Academy, where the assignment of low status to the "swab" was "useful in producing a correspondingly high evaluation of successfully completing the steps in an Academy career."

DEFINING "OUTGROUPS"

The recruits find themselves united with their company mates in efforts to "bilge the other companies" for the weekly honor prize (which is symbolized by a streamer or star affixed to the company flag. The flag is carried by the guideon bearer, who marches at the head of the company). One observer (Anonymous, 1946b: 378) describes that "we feeling" in infantry training:

> By sharing experiences, they have a feeling of closeness and begin to feel that they form a select group. This esprit de corps reinforces their new conceptions of themselves because the rifleman gets collective support from the sense of belonging with others.

Members of the Air Force are "airedales" and "flyboys." Marines are "jarheads" and "sea-going bellhops." Members of the Coast Guard are "fresh-water sailors" and "lighthouse keepers." Soldiers are "dog-faces" and "grunts." But *we* are sailors. Heels pounding in cadence unison, company flag snapping in the breeze, Company 123 now takes its turn marching fiercely past the R and O company standing in ragged lines on the outside of the chain-link fence:

> Got no lover, got no dough,
> But at least I'm not in R and O.
> Sound off! Sound off!
> Cadence count!

KNOWING THE SYSTEM AND SPEAKING THE LANGUAGE

Goffman (1961a: 51) reports that members of total institutions regain stability of self when they learn the institutional system. In the

Naval recruit training center, that system is presented by formal training (classroom and field) and informal instruction (examples set by staff and more advanced recruits or in "bull" sessions within the company). The recruits are thereby given a clearer understanding of the role expectations involved in being a sailor.

As advanced recruits, the boots attend daily classes in Naval tradition and customs, gunnery, first aid, seamanship, Naval history, military conduct, and shipboard organization. They are encouraged to be proud of their new knowledge and to demonstrate their prowess in such sailor skills as knot tying, flag signaling, and the use of weapons. Warren (1946: 205) reports similar behavior in Naval officer candidate schools, where trainees were "competing with each other on shipboard knowledge during their off-duty hours." Boots are members of a boat crew, a fire-fighting team, a rifle squad, and a watch section, in each of which they are taught what is expected of them and what they can expect of their shipmates. They learn Naval argot (a vocabulary unique to a social group) and find that they can communicate with the "real sailors" who are their instructors. Automatically now the floor is a "deck," the ceiling is "overhead," the flight of stairs a "ladder." It is not right and left but "starboard and port," not front and back, but "fore and aft." The boots become familiar with argot terms for many of the physical objects around them that previously had civilian names. Various events and sequences of behavior unique to the military are now understood by the recruits in single terms such as "taps," "AWOL," "liberty," "square away," and "field day." The recruits' acceptance of military language patterns, according to Elkin (1946), reflects an image of solidarity and an admission of a break with civilian society.

The routine use of obscene expressions by recruits has been described as representing freedom from some restraints of civilian culture. The most significant feature of such expressions is that they give "a unique universe of discourse which helps distinguish him (the member of the military), and thus they become a binding-in-group force" (Elkin, 1946: 414). Some authors have vividly described the obscene language of members of the military, and explain it in terms of expression of aggression, traumatic regression to an earlier level of impulse gratification, negativism, and need to express virility in a predominantly masculine society (Janis, 1945: 172-174). But a more useful explanation is that the words become part of the language of a social group. There seems to be no one emotion expressed by a particular obscene term. A given word can be used positively, negatively, or as a neutral expression. Sometimes the obscenity will be an adjective

("What a shitty drill"), sometimes a noun ("What is this shit?"), sometimes a verb ("Don't shit me"), and sometimes an expletive ("Oh,
shit!"). Such terms may come at the beginning of sentences, at the end
of sentences, between words, or even between syllables of words. Much
if not all of the original meaning of the word is lost in its versatile use.
A sailor is expected to swear. Boots, then, observing the language
habits of "real sailors," and having a need to communicate with them,
pick up the routine use of obscenities along with such terms as "bulkhead" for wall and "scuttlebutt" for drinking fountain or rumors.

As the boots progress through the advanced training phase, the
ceremonies and rituals become less strange to them and more a part of
everyday life. The company commander seems less "different" and less
fearsome. The boots' feelings of isolation and confusion diminish as
group cohesion in the recruit company develops. The formal and informal instructions the boots receive, the examples they see in nonboot
members of the center, and their interactions with other boots clarify
role expectations. "You boots keep it up," the company commander
comments, "and you just might turn out to be sailors!"

ACCOMMODATING THE RECRUIT ROLE

Boots come to the recruit training center with relatively unique
self-concepts based on organization of their past experiences. Each
recruit has a different facility for enacting roles, a different degree of
tolerance for change in self-concept. When pressured to dispossess
their civilian roles, the recruits, in accordance with their perceptions of
the sailor role they are supposed to enact, will attempt to work out
some sort of adjustment.

Goffman (1961a: 61-63) has described four ways in which individuals who are undergoing role dispossession-repossession within a total
institution might react: (1) situational withdrawal, (2) intransigence,
(3) colonization, and (4) conversion. These reactions can be observed
among boots in the Naval recruit training center.

Some boots meet the center's challenge to their civilian self-concept
by retreating within themselves. They shut themselves off from the
threat of depersonalization. Such individuals might be administratively discharged from the Navy during the R and O phase. If not, they
usually suffer internal torment for the first three weeks of boot camp.
Then, as the rest of the company members enact their new roles in the
advanced phase, they suffer additional torment as ostracized outsiders.
They become scapegoats, and are assigned such pejorative labels as

"scumbag." Ironically, the ostracized recruits serve as negative role models for the other recruits, and thereby facilitate the socialization process.

Intransigent recruits vociferously verbalize their discontent with the Navy and its ways. They often become, in fact, deeply involved in the total institution. Their careful study of institutional expectations in order to protest them contributes to their enactment of the very expectations they are admonishing.

Colonized recruits "find a home in the Navy." Their experience with civilian society has been marked by relative deprivation. Navy life provides them with the first real security they have known. As one chief petty officer put it:

> I left the cotton fields and joined this man's Navy. They gave me a place to sleep, good clothes, and all I could eat. Then one day they *paid* me. I thought they were crazy!

Recruit converts become "gung ho" and "red hots." They completely accept and perform the sailor role in accordance with the expectations of the training center. They wear their hats at the same angle as the company commanders, emulate their jargon, gestures, and perhaps even their seamanlike gait. Converts are sometimes rewarded with minor positions of authority within the recruit company.

It is difficult to determine how much the sailor role has been internalized, how much it has become part of the recruits' self-concepts. It is quite possible, for example, that recruits could overtly be converts and covertly be laughing at or distant from the whole recruit process. If they are only "playing at" the role of sailor, they provide themselves with some reason or rationalization for doing so. The following are examples of rationalization observed in the recruit training center:

- Well, you see, I really didn't want to get married . . .
- The job situation on the outside was lousy.
- I'll be darned if I was going to let the Army draft me!
- It was a way to get away from being hassled by my parents.
- Me? I want to see the world.
- I didn't join the Navy, I bought the G.I. Bill!
- I figure I had to do it sooner or later. I'm just putting in my time.

The training center staff, and the Navy in general, is not concerned about the recruits' rationalization for performing the sailor role, so long as they perform it. As Janowitz (1960: 174) has observed, when officers give orders, they do not care why their subordinates obey, just that they do obey.

GRADUATING FROM BOOT CAMP

After successfully completing the course of training in the center, the recruits graduate. The commencement ceremony is dramatized by a massed parade of recruits with a band, a drum and bugle corps, flags, banners, and an attentive audience of officials, families, and friends. Stirring speeches are given by senior Naval officers, and "Anchors Aweigh" is played or sung. Splendid in their pressed dress uniforms, arms heavy with the two new stripes indicating they are no longer seaman recruits but are now seaman apprentices, they are ready to leave the training center and to go "down to the sea in ships."

CONCLUSION

Total institutions demand more complete and extensive role taking from their members than most other organizations. Typically, they have been operating for many years and thus have a long history of socializing individuals into role conformity. They are by definition powerful organizations, their purposes being legitimized by the cultural values of the society in which they function. Nonetheless, people in those institutions find ways to maintain at least a modicum of autonomy.

In the Naval recruit training center, which is a total institution, boots seemed to have little opportunity to do other than be dispossessed of their civilian roles and then to embrace the sailor role, defining themselves accordingly. During their period of training in the center, all of the boots' time and energy was consumed by scheduled activities. Even sleeping and the very limited amounts of "free time" were scheduled. The recruits' civilian self-concepts and roles were challenged as being irrelevant to or inappropriate in boot camp and in the fleet. Autonomy of action, economy of motion, privacy, and perception of self as a physical person were especially challenged (Goffman, 1961a: 237-238).

The sailor role was offered to the recruits as a replacement for their civilian roles. Boots saw that role in the example of supervisors, in classroom instruction, and in the military activities they had to conduct as individuals and as members of a recruit company. The emergent group cohesion in the company, deliberately encouraged by center supervisors, was a powerful pressure for recruit role conformity. Feelings of belonging, predictability, and pride were offered as replacements for feelings of isolation, uncertainty, and shame. Though the role dispossession and resocialization in boot camp was intense, and though there was almost no opportunity for role making, recruits still had options for autonomy. They could withdraw from the situation or become intransigents, colonizers, or converts (Goffman, 1961a: 61-63). Though those strategies had different consequences and reflected different degrees of conformity, each involved a willful act, a choice of how best to respond in the setting. Situational withdrawal could lead to discharge from the Navy and an end to sailor role socialization. Colonizing or conversion could lead to a career of enacting the sailor role. Those outcomes generally were precisely what the recruits wanted.

The most typical manner in which recruits maintained an element of personal autonomy was to "play" the sailor role and successfully complete boot camp without letting the sailor identity completely dominate their self-concepts. They learned and adequately performed the sailor skills, spoke the appropriate sailor language, demonstrated their ability to function with others in a task-oriented group, yet protected a sense of themselves as individuals. The center supervisors did not know what the recruits really thought about the sailor role, and generally did not care, so long as the role was correctly and fully enacted.

Human beings are gifted with the cognitive ability to perceive themselves as objects (Mead, 1934; Strauss, 1956). Consequently, they can reflect about and assess the roles they are enacting or are supposed to enact. They can choose, for example, to let a role engulf their definitions of self or can accommodate the behavioral expectations without at all defining themselves in terms of the role (though observers of their behavior might). Even the most controlling of total institutions cannot, short of using mind-altering drugs, torture, or other disabling means, deprive individuals of the autonomy involved in reflecting about roles and in keeping self-concepts distanced from role enactments.

3

DEVELOPING AN INFORMAL ROLE IN A FORMAL ORGANIZATION
Sailors Aboard Ship

Though the Naval recruit training center (see Chapter 2) and subsequent specialty schools prepare boots for their jobs in the fleet, those individuals are further "sailorized" when they report aboard their first ship, which, like boot camp, is a total institution. New crew members are presented with two sets of shipboard role expectations, one by the ship's formal organization (official procedures, rules, and regulations determined by Navy supervisors) and one by its informal organization (unofficial expectations for sailor behavior determined by the interacting crew members). Sometimes the two sets of expectations complement each other; sometimes they conflict. It is not uncommon that informal expectations for sailor behavior are incorporated into or are tolerated by the formal organization, especially when that behavior advances the organization's purposes.

New crew members are exposed to the formal role expectations in their assignments to shipboard jobs and to a place in the ship's hierarchy of official authority. They are exposed to the informal expectations in a series of initiations conducted by experienced crew members,

This chapter is a rewritten version of my previously published paper, "The Sailor Aboard Ship: A Study of Role Behavior in a Total Institution," *Social Forces* 43 (March 1965): 389-400. Used by permission.

in "getting the word" from those crew members about how the system really works, and in becoming part of the ship's informal network for exchanging goods and services.

New crew members find that, although there are considerable pressures on them to take roles in both the formal and informal shipboard organizations, there is much more opportunity for them to make roles than they had in the recruit training center. They have at least some latitude to be innovative in their formal shipboard tasks, although the innovation must have prior approval from appropriate higher authority. They have considerable latitude to create or experiment with informal role behaviors aboard ship, although they cannot violate the standing expectations of the informal organization.

THE NAVAL VESSEL AS A TOTAL INSTITUTION

Like the Naval recruit training center described in Chapter 2, the Naval vessel at sea is a total institution. All aspects of life are carried out within the limits of bow to stern, beam to beam, and bilges to foretruck. Authority of captains is absolute, by law and by custom. They have total responsibility for their ships and sailors. Their influence spreads over all activities of the crew. As Homans (1946: 295) notes, captains are the *logos*, the "word." Nothing they say or do is taken impersonally. Sailors salute other officers aboard ship only the first time they meet them during the day. They salute captains every time they pass them.

It is virtually impossible for the sailors at sea to be alone. They go through each day's routine in close company with their shipmates. They work with them, eat with them, shower with them, participate in recreation with them, and sleep in compartments with them.

Each day is tightly scheduled by a plan of the day, which is mimeographed and posted on bulletin boards throughout the ship. The plan of the day specifies all activities from reveille until taps: what and when ship's work will be done, what uniforms will be worn during which time of the day, what time meals will be taken, who will be on duty and who will be at liberty, what the evening's entertainment will be. At the bottom of the plan of the day are listed by name those individuals captains have seen fit to promote and those whom they have seen fit to punish.

The official purpose of the ship, the unifying goal of the formal organization, is identical with the general purpose of the military—to provide defense during, or a deterrence to, war. The demands made of personnel by the formal organization are justified in this light. But there is another goal, an informal one that is closer to the crew—to sail "our ship" safely somewhere for some particular purpose.

The ship's formal purpose of national defense is reflected in the formal shipboard organization (chain of command, plans of the day, standard operating procedures, regulations) and articulates with higher authority throughout the Navy. The informal goal of "bringing the ship through" is reflected in the informal shipboard organization that is specifically concerned with *our* ship (unwritten, personalized, traditional, and social expectations). As we shall see, however, the informal structure is sanctioned at least tacitly by the formal organization, insofar as the informal goal helps to advance the formal purpose.

There is a clear distinction between supervisors and members, each individual clearly identifiable by uniform and insignia. The officers live in their own section of the ship. That section is painted green (the rest of the spaces are painted white or gray) and is called "officers' country." The chief petty officers have their own living area, called "chiefs' quarters." No enlisted sailor may enter those compartments without expressed permission, and then only with hat in hand. The officers eat in their "wardroom," the chiefs in the chiefs' mess. If the size of the vessel permits it, first-class petty officers have food brought from the general galley to their own eating compartment, and second-class petty officers have the privilege of going to the head of the general chow line. All enlisted sailors below the rate of chief petty officer sleep in assigned living compartments situated throughout the ship. Watch assignments, liberty, and work details vary as a function of rate and seniority. Social contact between officers and enlisted sailors is formally discouraged and in practice highly limited. The social distance between chiefs and lower-rated petty officers is less rigid, but still maintained, as is the social distance between petty officers and nonrated seamen and seaman apprentices.

Sailors often do not officially know the destination of their ship until well out to sea. They are, similarly, often not formally aware of when and where they are to be transferred until handed their orders.

The ship at sea is totally isolated from society at large. In port there are also barriers separating the vessel from the outside world. The gangway of the ship is guarded by armed watches who check the credentials of all persons who board or leave. No civil authority, even when conducting official business, can come aboard without the expressed permission of the captain.

FORMAL ORGANIZATION OF THE SHIP

The formal organization of the Naval vessel is described in the ship's published regulations, which conform to orders from higher authority in the Department of the Navy. With modifications to suit the size of the ship, the number of personnel aboard, and the function of the ship, all Naval vessels follow a similar organizational structure (Homans, 1946: 295). The formal role of the sailor aboard ship is determined by:

- rate (pay grade) and rating (job specialty);
- shipboard assignment during working hours;
- the Watch, Quarter, and Station Bill (assignment for collision, fire, special sea and anchor detail, atomic, biological, or chemical attack, and general quarters);
- the Uniform Code of Military Justice (legal articles of conduct, discipline, and punishment);
- the plan of the day;
- the Captain's policy (as executed by the executive officer); and
- the department and division policies.

Sailors' enactments of the role expectations presented to them by the formal organization can be called primary adjustments (Goffman, 1961a: 188-189). Primary adjustments occur when members of a total institution cooperatively contribute the required activities to an organization. They give and get what has been systematically planned for, whether it fits much or little with their self-concepts.

A good start on primary adjustment, the *how* and *what*, is provided to sailors in the Naval recruit training center. But the complexity of shipboard operations cannot be duplicated in a training situation. Furthermore, the role expectations associated wih the informal organization cannot be understood until sailors become members of the ship's company. Warren (1946: 206) has observed that despite the training received in officer candidate school, new ensigns were bewildered when they reported aboard and took part in the activities of a ship. Dornbusch (1955: 321) reports the same phenomenon in newly graduated officers from the Coast Guard Academy. He describes it as "reality shock," a sudden realization of the disparity between the way a job was envisaged before beginning work and the actual work situation. Sailors must accommodate the role expectations of the formal organization. If they do not, they are not "doing their duty" and will be punished according to established military law.

INFORMAL ORGANIZATION OF THE SHIP

An informal organization is a spontaneous friendship and interest group that develops around the formal organization and that tends in varying circumstances to aid, limit, and redirect the performance of formally assigned functions (Spaulding, 1961: 179; Roethlisberger and Dickson, 1939). The informal organization aboard ship includes tradition, custom, ritual, initiation, and myth—all of which play a vital part in the sailors' daily shipboard lives. These aspects of the informal organization, though not explicitly sanctioned by the formal organization, are tacitly understood and accepted by it, because they serve to enhance, preserve, and implement the formal goals. They represent what Williams (1960: 379) calls "patterned evasions"—regularized ways of getting around the demands of the formal organization, usually with the result of accomplishing the expectations in a quicker and more efficient way. One group of observers, reporting on the informal organization in an Air Force enlisted training program, concluded that the Air Force expected its trainees to indulge in patterned evasions (Sullivan et al., 1958: 663). Another writer observes that in the Army "a large part of the customs of the informal group supplemented or implemented the official regulations and relationships" (Anonymous, 1946a: 369).

I will discuss just those role expectations in the informal organization that are tacitly endorsed by the formal organization. Sailors' enactments of those informal roles can still be considered primary adjustments. Role behaviors that are not sanctioned by the formal organization, that interfere with its goals, and that seem to be self-defensive will be discussed later as "secondary adjustments" (Goffman, 1961a: 188-189).

The following are some examples of the informal organization aboard ship that contribute to the effectiveness of the formal structure and purposes:

- *Modified chain of command:* Communication will be established between staff A and staff B, rather than from staff A to his or her officer in charge, to the officer in charge of staff B, and then to staff B. This facilitates operations that might be aborted or delayed by unnecessary bureaucracy.
- *"Scuttlebutt" (rumor):* Mouth-to-ear advance information about ship movement, new assignments, promotions, and so on. This tenses the crew or the individual, providing a preparatory set that increases efficiency when the order is officially given.
- *"Jerry-rigs":* Using unofficial, pirated, or homemade parts to maintain equipment in full operation.

With its myths, traditions, rituals, customs, and initiations, the informal organization makes available to the new crew members the expectations for the "seagoing" sailor. In return for their enactment of this role, they are granted membership in the informal organization, which in the military is crucial. One investigator emphasizes this point, observing that "the offending member of a street corner gang may find refuge in a rival gang. The offending machine politician may sell out to the rival machine or an entirely different social world. . . . The member of a military group rarely has such an alternative. He belongs to the informal social group or he is isolated" (Anonymous, 1946a: 369).

Enactment of the formal role (adherence to rules, regulations, and adequate performance of duties) is sufficient to link sailors to the Navy as a whole. Only membership in the informal organization (achieved through compliance with on-board traditions) can blend them into the shipboard society.

LEARNING THE INFORMAL ROLE

As has been mentioned, the ship is a total institution, justified on the grounds of an instrumental purpose. For the informal organization, the guiding purpose is to bring the ship safely to its destination or task completion. If the vessel is not at sea, it would seem that the informal organization, devoid of purpose, would become dysfunctional unless in an unfamiliar or hostile port. If the informal organization did, in fact, break down, then it might be expected that the formal organization would lose a powerful source of control over the sailors. However, the informal organization does not break down when the ship is not at sea. It extends itself ashore by the expedient of including in its expectations the informal role of "liberty hound"—the sailor always goes ashore when the ship is in port.

Putting to Sea

To get a closer look at the informal organization, it might be fruitful to follow some sailors, just graduated from boot camp, up the gangway and aboard their first ship. This ship, a vessel usually much at sea, has been tied up at the dock for about three weeks, being repaired and refitted. The sailors report to the officer of the deck, and as their papers are being recorded in the log (thus making them members of the formal organization), they look around. What they see is rather a disappointment. The ship that they have heard so much about in boot camp, the supposedly living, breathing ship that the instructors spoke of with a faraway look in their eyes is little more than a huge hulk of dirty gray machinery.Rusty wire curls snakelike across an oil-splotched deck. Tools, metal chips, stumps of welding rods, and buckets of odd parts are strewn about. Raw splashes of red lead paint cut and gash across the gray bulkheads and hatches. This certainly is not like the *U.S.S. Recruit*, the neat, clean, and organized mock ship at boot camp! It is not like the ships in the recruiting and training films.

Berkman (1946: 380) describes an armed guard merchant ship as being "no ship at all" when in port. The vessel is disorganized, unkempt, and seemingly without order or purpose. To new sailors reporting aboard, this is certainly not what they have learned to associate with "shipshape." This is not a "taut ship." There is no evidence of a social unit at all. Social interaction among the few people on board seems to go no farther than "I have the watch, sir" and "I have been properly relieved, sir." The new sailors are shown briefly around their living quarters, given liberty cards (passes), and told that they might as well go ashore.

Let us assume that these new additions to the ship's roster report back as preparations are being made to put to sea. Behold! A transformation! Sailors are bustling around, laughing and jabbering, performing tasks sharply and efficiently. Everyone seems to be making the right moves, to know what to expect. There is a vibrancy all about. Each sailor is "a member of a unified group whose boundaries are distinctly defined" (Berkman, 1946: 382). As the ship steams away from port the communication system snaps on and "This is the captain speaking!" reminds all hands that the formal authority is in full force. The ship, now at sea, has again become a total institution.

Berkman (1946: 384) sums up this transformation when he observes that "social stability and unity reappear with the re-establishment of routine that is meaningful in the light of the ship's operations." The crew seems glad to be back at sea, and expresses this feeling verbally as they settle down for the voyage. The informal organization had fully reinstated its purpose.

As the ship cruises out of sight of land, the sailors go below and shift into their "steaming uniforms" (a "steaming hat"—snow white, but frayed with age and use; "steaming dungarees"—clean and pressed, but the blue chambray shirt and denim pants are faded by repeated scrubbings, and are neatly patched in several places). The metamorphosis is completed.

In the midst of this activity stand the new sailors. Everyone seems to know what they are doing but them. The passageways are like mazes, the noises are frightening. They cautiously climb down ladders that others bound down. They have a hard time walking on the pitching, rolling deck. They feel alone and conspicuous. The ship heads into rougher water. The new sailors are about to become part of the shipboard society. Their initiation into the informal organization is about to begin.

According to Berkman (1946: 380), some of the events that "sailorize" the new crew members are rough weather and development of "sea legs," a shipboard initiatory ritual, standing watches, general quarters (battle stations), and shipboard discourse. These elements of life at sea are instrumental for clarifying the role expectations of the informal organization and for providing a wider understanding of the total sailor role.

Getting Seasick and Other Initiations

Sailors often joke among themselves that the onset of rough seas is bound to bring the greasiest possible meals to the chow table. As the cooking odor of spareribs and sauerkraut wafts throughout the rolling, pitching ship, all eyes are on the new sailors. When they walk by, little discussion groups stage whisper, "This will probably go on for days!" "I knew sailors turned so green they used them for starboard running lights!" If the new sailors ask for advice about the seasickness they fear is seizing them, they will be told something resembling the following contradictory suggestions:

- Chew gum; chew crackers; drink tea; drink saltwater; stay in bed; keep walking around; eat a lot; eat a little; don't look up; don't look down.
- Next time you come aboard, come aboard drunk. Then, by the time you sober up, your sea legs will have grown to the deck.

If the new sailors become visibly ill, they get considerable sympathy from the older hands. They take their watches and answer to muster for them. The new crew members are becoming part of the informal organization through a rite of initiation.

Subsequently, the new sailors are subjected to several lesser, but firmly established, initiations. The following are some examples:

- You've got the mail buoy watch, sailor. (There are, the new crew members are told, "mail buoys" scattered about the ocean that contain mail for the personnel aboard. The victims are given a boat hook and stand watch,

scanning the horizon for the appearance of such a buoy, which does not exist.)
- Run down to the post office and get me half a dollar's worth of sea-stamps. (Sea-stamps are said to be necessary for letters mailed from ship to shore. They do not exist.)
- Go down to the paint locker and get some striped paint (or white lamp-black, number paint, red oil for the port running light, a bucket of steam; none of those items exists).
- Congratulations! You've earned fourth-class liberty. ("Fourth-class liberty" means putting on a dress blue uniform, standing on the ship's forecastle, and staring at the shore through binoculars.)
- The following is heard over the loudspeaker system: "Now hear this! A sea-bat has been captured and caged on the fantail. All hands interested in seeing it, lay aft." (The nonexistent "sea-bat" is housed in a low box, with a small open door in the front. As the victims bend over to peer into the cage, they are smartly bashed on the rear with a broom.)

In observing some of the traditional shipboard initiations, Berkman (1946: 385) comments that "the very fact of this ribbing indicates a measure of acceptance. Furthermore, it represents an addition to the nautical experience and lore that the new sailor is acquiring" and distinguishes him or her from civilians or from any new persons who may subsequently report aboard.

Initiations are also held every time sailors are promoted. Only those who hold a rating equal to or above the promotees can serve in the initiation, which usually consists of a chase, a capture, and a dunking. The promotees' new insignia are "pinned on" their shoulders by several fists. In return for this recognition, they must give cigars to all their peers and superiors. The promotion initiation for chief petty officers is far richer, calling for the initiate's wearing of some clownish costume for 24 hours, standing absurd watches (such as guarding the ship's fog whistle), and finally, the reading, with all hands at quarters for muster, of a document that petitions for the older chiefs' acceptance of this lowly initiate into their ranks.

Crossing the Line

The most impressive and most elaborate initiation ceremony of all is the extensive program involved in *crossing the line*. The night before the ship is scheduled to cross the equator, a colorfully costumed "Davy Jones" crawls, amid a glare of spotlights and great fanfare, out of a hawse pipe (where the anchor hangs), and demands to see the officer of the deck. Davy Jones quizzes that officer about the name of the ship and its destination, then demands to see the captain. When the captain comes to the bridge, Davy Jones reads a summons from Neptunus Rex, the King of the Sea, ordering the captain to prepare for a visit from the Royal Highness on the following morning. Davy Jones then takes leave.

On the following morning, Davy Jones reappears and announces that Neptunus Rex is about to make his entry. The flag of Neptunus Rex is run up, the ship is stopped dead in the water, and all hands are ordered to fall in at quarters for muster. Neptune (usually played by a senior chief) makes a grand entry with a retinue (played by other enlisted sailors): Amphitrite, the royal baby, the royal chaplain, the royal navigator, Neptune's officer of the day, judges, attorneys, barbers, doctors, bears, and police. After informing the captain that the royal navigator will take over the ship, Neptune ascends a throne and commands that the initiation of "pollywogs" begin. (All personnel who have crossed the equator, and can prove it by showing certificates, are "shellbacks" and are members of the retinue. Those who have not crossed the equator are called "pollywogs," and are about to undergo a hazing that will make them fit subjects for Neptune's kingdom.) Summonses usually have been issued the night before, ordering the pollywogs to appear before the court and answer charges made against them (often dealing with physical characteristics or personal idiosyncrasies of the victims). The pollywogs are always found guilty as charged, and sentenced to such things as dunking into a tub filled with saltwater and garbage, hair clippings, kissing the royal baby's belly (always the fattest shellback on board). Officer pollywogs are also sentenced, but usually to more sophisticated punishments—such as polishing brass in the chief's quarters.

After the ceremony is completed, usually by noon of the same day, all hands are shellbacks, and the initiates are given their certificates of membership. A spirit of unity abounds. This event will be talked about and relived many times in the future, and each time it will reinforce the cohesion of the crew. So important is this occasion for the sailor that squadrons of ships have been known to sail for days just north of the equator, waiting for favorable weather before crossing (Lovette, 1939: 273).

The "crossing the line" initiation is an operation of the informal organization that is wide enough in scope to encompass the entire vessel, and seemingly to usurp the power of the captain. However, the ceremony is given full cooperation by the formal organization—a "we feeling" crew better carries out the formal goals of the ship. One ship's captain, writing of the tradition aboard a U.S. Navy vessel over a hundred years ago, said of the ceremony:

> Its evil is transient, if an evil there be; while it certainly affords Jack a topic for a month beforehand and a fortnight afterwards; and if so ordered as to keep its monstrosities within the limits of strict discipline, which is easy enough, it may even add to the authority of the officers, instead of weakening their influence [Lovette, 1939: 238].

Such role reversals, which allow subordinates to play an imitative superior role, help to clarify mutual expectations. Dornbusch (1955: 319) reports a similar phenomenon in the Coast Guard Academy on their traditional "Gizmo Day," during which the lower classmen were allowed to haze the upper classmen. The result of this turnabout was a greater realization of role expectations.

Standing Watches, Speaking the Language, and Telling Sea Stories

Standing watch "sailorizes" new crew members by virtue of the responsibility they are given and the communication network into which they are linked. When they are on lookout, they are aware that the sleeping crew members are depending on them for safety. The watch standers wear a set of headphones, and are connected with the bridge and all other people, above and below deck, who are on watch. The sailors routinely reporting, the officer of the deck giving engine speed and direction changes, the background noises of a ship alive remind them that this is a team of which they are part. As Berkman (1946: 386) observes, sailors on watch do not, cannot feel alone. This is accentuated during general quarters, when all hands are assigned to specific battle stations for real or mock combat.

Although facility with shipboard argot was begun by the sailors when they were in the Naval recruit training center, communication with the "old salts" aboard ship initially is still a challenge. In boot camp, there was some tolerance for the slip of a civilian term. On board ship, such mistakes are met with chagrin or disgust. Sailors do not get up and make their beds. They "heave out and trice up." They do not ask if they can smoke, but if the "smoking lamp is lit." Sailors who are assigned to the engine room are "snipes"; those who work on deck are "deck apes." Electronic technicians are "twidgets." "BU-PERS" is not a disease, but the official abbreviation for the Bureau of

Naval Personnel, which office accounts for the sailors' existence. And so on—for several thousand words.

Tall tales, or "sea stories," are an omnipresent part of shipboard discourse. The majority of them deal with feats of daring or comedy while at sea and with feats of alcoholic or sexual excess while ashore. The sailor role expectations of the informal organization include that of the "jolly tar" and the "liberty hound." Civilians also seem to expect and reinforce this kind of sailor behavior, as demonstrated in the following civilian expressions: "drunk as a sailor"; "sailor bait"; "wild as a sailor on shore leave"; "sailor: a wolf in ship's clothing." Furthermore, sailors have been convinced in Naval training that they are "in the Navy now," and divorced from most of the demands and role expectations of civilian society. As a senior petty officer put it:

> One thing I know, mate. No matter what I do on the beach, no matter how fouled up I get or how broke I get, I've always got my chow and my rack [bed] aboard ship.

Hitting the Beach

As the ship approaches port, the anticipation of liberty electrifies the crew. Sailors off duty are shining shoes, brushing uniforms, showering, and getting ready for liberty (shore leave). The ship is tied up to the dock, the gangway is affixed, liberty call is sounded, and the sailors "hit the beach," scattering in all directions. The shipboard society for the most part evaporates. The purpose of the informal organization, safely to sail our ship, has been temporarily lost. It is the task of the "liberty hound" role expectations to sustain the power of the informal organization over the sailors ashore.

The "Bitching" Sailor

Many of the traditions and customs of the ship's informal organization are accepted by the formal organization because of the ultimately positive results. It is not unreasonable to assume that these behaviors originated as a way of maintaining some individuality in or element of control over the formal organization. But they have in practice been assimilated by the formal organization. At one time, to cite another example, sailors might have defended themselves against the demands of the military by complaining bitterly about their fate, and by expressing hope for the day when they could "get the heck out of this canoe club." Now, however, the "griping sailor" role is expected and sanctioned by the formal authority. That "sailors aren't happy unless they are complaining" is clearly understood by all concerned.

SECONDARY ADJUSTMENTS

Are there, then, any shipboard sailor behaviors that operate at an informal level and are at odds with the demands of the formal organization? Indeed there are such "secondary adjustments," which Goffman (1961a: 189) defines as the way that the "member employs unauthorized ends or means to get around organizational assumptions." They consist of "those ways in which the individual stands apart from the role and the self that were taken for granted by the institution." Secondary adjustments are similar to what Williams (1960: 381) considers to be the "personal or idiosyncratic interpretation" of social norms.

In his study of the asylum as a total institution, Goffman (1961a: 190) found that the most fertile areas for secondary adjustments were the clinic, the supply center, the kitchen, and the technical shops—all of which provided opportunity for an expression of individuality. The following are some examples of secondary adjustment within these areas as they exist on a Naval vessel. The sailors:

- "work a deal" with the master-at-arms to get a good bunk and locker position for themselves;
- make arrangements to get their clothes pressed neatly by the laundry;
- arrange to get better "mid-rats" (snacks given by the galley crew to sailors standing the midnight watch);
- get the barber to cut their hair less severely than the regulations specify;
- have a yeoman (clerk) in the administration office ensure that their requests for leave, transfer, and other administrative items are processed before others;
- get into the watch section with the most time off.

These arrangements and deals are made possible either through friendship or by a basic barter system of goods and services. They are illegal in terms of the formal organization. The exchange system is to be used, however, as Turner (1947: 346) points out, "personally, not impersonally. The assumption is that the goods acquired are secondary to friendship."

A complex network of interpersonal relationships exists throughout the ship, friend helping friend and group helping group to maintain some control over the living situation at sea. For example, as reported in my field notes:

> We were assigned to a shipboard shop which was fully equipped with electronic equipment and components. As such, we became the radio, T.V., and electrical appliance center for those members of the crew we considered to be our friends. In return for parts for and services to the personal property of the crew members who came to us, we were rendered what goods and services they could supply. One of the cooks gave us fresh ground coffee for the percolator and hot plate one of the electrician's mates had given us. A yeoman saw to it that our personnel requests were always processed rapidly. One of the storekeepers made certain that our spare parts bin was always full, and not only with components called for in our formal inventory. The medical department, ordered to give us a certain amount of alcohol per month for the cleaning of antennas, had a chief who was the "buddy" of the chief of our shop, and who would never ask questions when we returned for a refill before the end of the month. We, in turn, would treat two of our boatswain mate friends to a little something extra in their coffee, and they, reciprocating, would have their work details take extra care with the maintenance of our work spaces. If an officer whose T.V. we had repaired was the inspecting officer for the week, we could expect an "excellent" inspection rating.

Turner (1947: 346) observed that the officer whose duty it was to assign the staterooms found it easy to get extra food in the wardroom. Similarly, the ship's photographer who provided the ship's service officer with personal pictures was allowed to have first choice of new items arriving in the ship's store.

The widespread "appropriating" of various types of Navy property and making it one's personal possession is an interesting phenomenon. Sailors do not consider it stealing to smuggle parts or tools off the ship for their cars or hobbies. In fact, the informal organization has a legitimized euphemism for that acquisition—"to cumshaw" (a Chinese word, meaning a gratuity or tip; a phrase of thanks used by a beggar). It connotes a "by gosh, I deserve it because I have certainly done enough for them" attitude. It is understood that one does not turn in shipmates to the authorities for such conduct. Similarly, the informal organization encourages "gundecking," the falsifying of inspection reports, which are assessed by sailors to be bureaucratic formalisms and not pertinent to the survival of the ship and its crew (Altheide and Johnson, 1980: 179-227).

Modifications to regulation uniforms are another example of secondary adjustment. Although outwardly appearing to be dressed "by the book," many sailors have had elaborate designs (called "dragons") embroidered on the inside of the cuffs, under the collar, and on the flap of the thirteen-button pants of their dress blue uniforms. "Tailor-made" uniforms can be purchased at civilian stores, and are made of smoother material, fit tighter, have additional pockets inside the jumper, and have very wide bells on the bottom of the trousers. Anyone whose alterations attract the attention of officials in the formal organization is subject to punishment. It is interesting to note that most of these modifications are performed by new sailors. Those who had but a short time of Naval service would still be close to the civilian days when they could choose to wear what they wished. The "old salts" usually look askance at sailors who alter their uniforms in nonregulation manner, commenting that such individuals need to be "squared away."

Tattoos are strongly advised against by the formal organization, and yet a great number of sailors are thus adorned. Most tattoos are not reproductions of the *Constitution* or emblems of the U.S. Navy, but are memorials to primary group relationships: "Mother"; "Mabel"; "The Three Musketeers." Thus they might be considered testimonials to the importance of affectional relationships the sailor has had outside the formal organization.

Beards and mustaches, if trimmed by male sailors to their own specifications, can be a means of secondary adjustment. On one ship with which I am familiar, the commanding officer permitted all hands to grow beards, so long as they were kept clean and neat. Approximately 200 of the 500-man crew sported some variety of growth: full beards, goatees, handlebar mustaches, side burns. Later, a new captain took over the ship, and ordered that no sailors could grow beards unless they submitted and had approved a special request to do so. Furthermore, if given permission, the sailors would not be allowed to trim their beards—just let them grow. Similarly, they would not be able to shave until after the voyage had been completed. Only 9 of the 500 now sported beards. The individuality had been removed from their behavior.

Some kinds of fads are forms of secondary adjustment aboard ship. There are times when all that seems to matter is who is the leading acey-deucy (backgammon) player, or the best pinochle, pedro, or bridge team. There are verbal puzzle crazes, crossword puzzle crazes, and now, in the modern Navy, stereophonic radio crazes. These activities often take place during working hours, and are thus disapproved by the formal organization. Some sailors escape detection by acquiring, through a friend in the engineering division, an empty compartment or space for their recreational use.

CONCLUSION

When they went aboard their first ship, new crew members discovered that their sailor role socialization had by no means been completed in the Naval recruit training center. The ship's formal and informal organizations included additional role-taking demands, sometimes similar to, sometimes different from, but always more extensive than the behavioral expectations in boot camp. Furthermore, whereas they recently had been the senior advanced recruits in boot camp, they now were the most junior sailors aboard ship, in both the formal and the informal organizations. The greater the disparity between the expectations they learned in boot camp and the expectations they met aboard ship, the more the new sailors experienced "reality shock" (Dornbusch, 1955: 321). That phenomenon is not unique to sailors and ships, but can be found in almost any setting where individuals are socialized for some role, graduate from that socialization process, and then attempt to enact the role in the "real world." They are again faced with feelings of isolation and uncertainty, and are offered belongingness and predictability if they are willing to conform to the new role expectations.

The new sailors entered the ship's formal organization through official assignment and were taught the formal behavioral expectations by supervisors appointed over them. They learned those expectations "according to the book." The new sailors entered the informal organization through a series of time-honored, historical initiations. They were taught its expectations by informal leaders and interactions with the more experienced crew members. The initiations were intended to be humorous but purposeful, and involved such rites of passage as seasickness, phony job tasks, and crossing the line. It is not uncommon in many occupations, especially blue-collar jobs, for senior workers to tease novice employees and play practical jokes on them (Roy, 1959-1960). Those initiations effectively teach the new employees about the informal leaders, the cohesion of the work group, and the relative power of the informal organization as compared with the formal organization. Once initiated, novices are elevated in status and can participate in the initiations of the beginners who follow them into the work setting.

Sailors' accommodation of formal role expectations and of those informal expectations that are encouraged or tolerated by the formal organization can be called primary adjustments (Goffman, 1961a: 206). Accommodation of informal role expectations that are not sanctioned by the formal organization can be called secondary adjustments (Goffman, 1961a: 188-189).

The new crew members quickly learned that there was greater opportunity for role making in the ship than there was in boot camp. In their formal role as crew members, they could acquire permission from higher authority to perform their duties with whatever innovation was judged to contribute to the goals of the formal organization. As members of the shipboard informal organization, they could make roles, so long as their behavior found acceptance among some of the shipmates with whom they interacted. Opportunities for autonomy existed in both primary and secondary adjustments, although there was more latitude for creativity in secondary adjustments.

It is not unusual for innovative roles made by individuals in the informal organization to be coopted by the formal organization if they somehow advance its purpose. When that happens, the informal roles become formalized; they become roles to be taken rather than roles that are made. The creativity in them can be diminished. For example, initiating new crew members aboard ship would have lost much of its spontaneity if it became a rigid role requirement of the formal organization. The result would have been the same if a role became rigid and forced in the informal organization. When roles involving considerable autonomy lose that quality, people will attempt to make new roles to suit the purposes.

The informal organization of the ship, like informal groups in any total institution, bureaucracy, or other work setting, can provide members with alternatives for creativity, autonomy, and self-expression. Aboard ship, it consisted of a network of roles made by sailors for sailors. More importantly, it constituted a social setting in which new roles could be made.

4

STAGING EMOTIONAL ROLE BEHAVIOR
Fans and Players
in a College Football Game

Virtually all theories of emotion assume that people's feelings are rooted in their physiology. But there is considerable debate about the degree to which physiology determines emotional responses (Schachter and Singer, 1962). The symbolic interactionist perspective on emotions, as summarized by Shott (1979: 1323), assumes that

> within the limits set by social norms and internal stimuli, individuals construct their emotions; and their definitions and interpretations are critical to this often emergent process. Internal states and cues, necessary as they are for affective experience, do not in themselves establish feeling, for it is the actor's definitions and interpretations that give physiological states their emotional significance or non-significance. . . . Symbolic interactionism is well suited for bringing out the interplay of impulse, definition, and socialization that is central to the construction of feeling.

The roles people enact in everyday life include behaviors that correspond to several discretely labeled emotions. The labeling is provided

This chapter is a modification of my earlier published paper, "The Staging of Emotion: A Dramaturgical Analysis," *Symbolic Interaction* 5 (Spring 1982): 1-19. Used by permission.

by others with whom the individuals interact and by the individuals themselves, consistent with their self-concepts and with their accustomed modes of self-expression (Cooley, 1902; Riezler, 1943; Goffman, 1967; Gross and Stone, 1964; Clanton and Smith, 1977; Glaser and Strauss, 1966; Kemper, 1978a, 1978b; Hochschild, 1975, 1979; Clanton, 1978; Scheff, 1979). Emotions are not in themselves roles; they are part of the behavioral expectations associated with the roles people enact. We expect parents to display love—not hatred—for their children, social workers compassion—not disgust—for their clients, and clergy empathy for—not envy of—their penitents.

An individual enacting a particular role or involved in a particular event does not usually express or feel more than one emotion at a time. However, some social situations call for a series of emotional presentations, often in a programmed order. For most people, that can be an interesting if not enjoyable experience, at least after the event is over. For example, at the wedding of a close friend, a person might in some sequence or another display sadness, jealousy, happiness, loneliness, anger, love, and sorrow. A specific social situation, depending on how people perceive their roles in it, can evoke a remarkable diversity of emotional performances.

Guided by the symbolic interactionist perspective, and also by Berger and Luckman's (1967) observation that reality (including emotional reality) is socially constructed, I will report the conditions that influenced the emotional responses I both observed and experienced in an elaborate social situation—a college football game.

My use of such dramatistic metaphors as "staged," "actors," "performance," and "scripted" does not imply that the emotions I will describe were faked (Brissett and Edgley, 1975). Some of the players and fans no doubt felt the emotions more deeply than others, but the expressions of emotion overall were quite real and were socially acknowledged as being so. That individuals are versatile in expressing emotions does not deny the genuineness of emotional experience. The use of theatrical language highlights the elaborateness of the interactive process by which emotional role behaviors are constructed to specific social settings. It also underscores the flexibility and creativity with which individuals can take or make roles and the emotional behaviors associated with them.

I will not address the physiological bases of the emotions I describe, but will assume that a social consideration of emotions can be abstracted from physiology.

Several researchers interested in sport as a topic for study have discussed the functions of emotions in that context. The expression of

emotions by players (especially amateurs) or spectators has been interpreted as: a form of catharsis for personal frustrations or social strains
(Ferguson, 1980; Elias and Dunning, 1970); an element in social control (McIntosh, 1971; Snyder and Spreitzer, 1975); a manifestation of
important social symbolisms (Keenan, 1966; Lahr, 1976; Zurcher and
Meadow, 1967); an affirmation of societal values (Luschen, 1967;
Krawczyk, 1973; Wohl, 1970; Deegan and Stein, 1978); and an aspect
of the quest for new experience and role enhancement (Sloan, 1979;
Bernstein, 1975; Steele and Zurcher, 1973; Hilliard and Zurcher, 1978).
Those interpretations speak to the institutionalized nature of sport
roles and the emotions associated with them. Furthermore, such formalized sports as college football are conducted in large part to serve
organizations: to make money, to train players to be professionals, to
encourage alumni donations, to attract students, and to enhance
organizational prestige. The staging of emotional role behavior, resulting in participants and spectators having a good time with their enactments, is beneficial to the sponsoring organization.

The football game I will describe in this chapter was a scheduled
conference contest between Alpha University and Beta University.
Alpha and Beta obviously are pseudonyms. I do not use them to
disguise, respectively, the University of Texas at Austin and the University of Arkansas. The pseudonyms are shorter, save space, and
make it easier to consider how the findings might apply to other social
settings.

The Alpha-Beta game, always representing a major rivalry, was the
last of the season for both teams, each of which had about as many
losses as wins for the season. It was rumored to be the final game for
the Alpha and Beta head coaches. After having managed their teams
for twenty years, they were going to retire. Consequently, the setting
provided a major and a minor theme for the analysis of emotional role
behavior. The major theme was the game and the events associated
with it. The minor theme was the special circumstance of a head
coach's retirement.

Alpha University has a "visiting coach" program in which three
different faculty members are for each home game invited to be "on the
inside" during all pertinent activities before, during, and after the
game. As the Alpha head coach put it, "the visiting coaches become
members of the family for a day." In this case, that "day" lasted about
eight hours. The visiting coaches first were given a tour of the football-
related facilities and business offices. They met the coaches, trainers,
players, and support staff. They attended the player-coach meetings
before the game, ate the pregame meal with the team, and were privy to

the players' preparations in the locker room, such as taping, donning uniforms, getting "psyched up" for the game. The visiting coaches accompanied the team throughout all the game activities. They were given both "press" and "bench" passes, and thus had opportunity intimately to observe the action of the game "right down in the trenches." The visiting coaches were also with the team in the locker room during halftime and after the game.

The coordinator of the visiting coaches' day with the team was the "brain coach" or scholastic counselor. He guided the visitors through the activities, was available for any questions, and made the appropriate introductions. He did not, however, unduly structure the visitors' game observations. They were free to explore as they saw fit.

I was invited to be a visiting coach at the Alpha-Beta game by the Alpha head coach and quickly accepted. The visiting coach role provided a unique opportunity for informative participant observation. Throughout the day, I took notes on what I observed and informally interviewed several coaches, players, fans, and other involved individuals. However, my description of what occurred is based not only on what I observed and what I learned from the interviews, but also on what I myself felt as a person enacting a role in the setting.

College football games are staged events in which the roles of players and spectators are well structured. Their roles, and the expression of emotion associated with the roles, are orchestrated in the game setting. People are expected to take the roles and display the relevant emotions as directed. In order to do so they look to individuals with whom they are interacting for cues about how to act and to feel. But they interpret those cues, and enact the roles according to that interpretation. Consequently, they vary in the extent to which they "get into" the action of the game. Some of them allow the roles to engulf their self-concepts, at least temporarily. Others merely "go through the motions" expected of them by others. People have and use autonomy and choice in those settings that stage emotional role behavior.

I will present examples of the staging of emotional role behavior under three main headings, as they occurred chronologically during my day as a visiting coach: pregame activities; the game; and postgame activities. The examples will illustrate how emotional role expectations can be established elements within institutionalized social structures and how they can emerge from people's interactions in specific social settings. The examples also will show some of the ways that individuals conform to or create emotional role behavior.

PREGAME ACTIVITIES

The Stadium: Social Construction
of the Stage

Five hours before the kickoff (scheduled for 8:30 p.m.), the football stadium already was alive with activity. Groundskeepers, maintenance personnel, and security staff scurried to complete final inspections of the facilities and the field. Concessionaires checked their stockpiles of junk food, banners, badges, programs, and seat backs, and assembled the army of young hawkers they later would release among the fans. The Alpha and the Beta University bands rehearsed their marching programs. Television technicians and commentators coordinated equipment and cues so that the national network of viewers could share the game spectacle. Radio broadcasters reviewed their charts and player rosters, and prepared to bring the game to those without access to television. Newspaper reporters already were typing lead-ins to their stories for tomorrow's sports pages. Near the entrance to the press box, an elderly man wearing a Beta sweater cautiously "howdy'ed" a younger Alpha alumnus, who peered back at him from under an Alpha emblazoned hat and replied, softly and with an expectant smile, "We're going to whip your ass tonight."

As we looked down on the rest of the stadium from our vantage point in the press box, the brain coach commented:

> I almost think I like this part of the game day best. The stands are empty, but you know they soon will be full of cheering people, and the field will be occupied by fired-up athletes. Even now, you can feel the excitement to come. There is electricity in the air. Can you feel it?

Indeed we could feel it. That is, the three of us who were enacting the visiting coach role said we did. More importantly, the brain coach, as one of the many stage setters and role models now on the scene, had instructed us that we should feel it.

What exactly was it that we were supposed to be experiencing? What was the substance of the "electricity"? We were being called upon to declare a shared state of diffuse emotion. Nothing really specific yet; more of a generalized arousal that, as we had been advised, would be sharpened and directed later, when the game began. From the cues being provided by the stage setters, and from our own previous experience in similar settings, we and other spectators could expect to enact a range of emotions throughout the game. We were to be ready to enact, at different times during the game, affection for other fans and hostility or even hatred for the opponents. We might be called upon to show compassion for the injured. If the game went well for the team, we would be expected to show pride, joy, and perhaps ecstasy. If the game went badly, it would be appropriate for us to display anger, disappointment, disgust, and perhaps even shame. The pregame shaping of emotional role expectations by stage setters is typical of contrived competitive games and probably of all staged emotional events. The interactive process of giving and accepting expectations usually is not abstractly examined by individuals during the act. The exchange of expectancy cues becomes routinized, part of the background, yet profoundly operates.

The Fans: Social Construction of Expectations

The expectation for an emotional experience, the preparatory mental set for that experience, was being structured for fans throughout the campus and in areas around the campus. The night before, a massive pep rally had promised students that they were certain to share dislike (for the opponents), love (for the team and fellow rooters), and joy (for the victory). Fraternity and sorority parties reinforced the notion that all were to experience an exciting range of emotions at the game. In several settings, such as bars, private homes, and university facilities, graduates of Alpha and Beta universities informed each other about the emotional role expectations they had for the game. It was to be a time for "going wild," and for "letting your hair down." Caravans of automobiles paraded the streets around the campus, the drivers honking horns and the occupants loudly cajoling pedestrians to share the "spirit" (Snow et al., 1981). The term "spirit" is a good example of a general label assigned to a diffuse heightening of emotion that can through further social interaction develop into specific emotional role enactments.

The pregame interactions among the fans heightened shared expectations for an emotional experience, and defined what the components of the experience were to be. By this time, there was a mutual expectation that loyal Alpha and Beta fans should feel a generalized excitement and should manifest that feeling to each other. Instructions concerning what was to be felt came not only from interactions with other potential game spectators, but from the pregame media blitz, itself a symbolic phenomenon. Those who had some difficulty getting spirit for the game could be helped by readily available alcohol or marijuana. Social drugs would ease inhibitions and could contribute to the anticipation for emotional experiences. All of these factors worked together essentially to "spiral" the readiness of fans for a proper set of emotional responses to the game (Heirich, 1971).

Not all fans experience, share, or want the same level of emotional readiness for the game (or for any other situation in which emotional role behavior is scripted). The scenario for general excitement and for specific types of emotional response is widely disseminated and understood. However, individuals vary in the degree to which they accept the scenario, enact the role of fan, and display the expected emotions. Some people and some situations demand more "time out" behavior from the roles they usually enact (Goffman, 1959, 1967). Enacting the role of fan, including the associated emotions, can be a "time out" or a distraction from other routine roles. Furthermore, the nature of the social interactions in which fans find themselves before a game vary, some more and some less evocative of emotional performance. Finally, people attending the game vary in the degree to which they have had previous experience with staged emotional settings. They thereby differ in the degree to which they are influenced by internalized expectations for emotional display.

The Team: Social Construction of Mood

The term "mood" suggests an interactionally derived, though rather privatized, diffuse emotional state which, if appropriately cued, can be channeled by the individual into very intense role behavior. A depressed mood, for example, can be cued into acts of self-harm. A hostile mood can be cued into acts of harm to others.

Individuals enacting the role of fan are influenced by others to get into the appropriate spirit for the game, that being a comparatively lighthearted state of diffuse emotional readiness. Individuals enacting the role of player are influenced by others (especially by coaches and trainers) to get into the appropriate *mood* for the game, that being a comparatively serious state of diffuse emotional readiness. They are instructed to concentrate on the forthcoming game, and to get "psyched up" for it.

How do players achieve the proper mood for the game? They do so by engaging in what Hochschild (1979) has called "emotion-work." They labor, in a manner consistent with cues from others with whom they interact, to anticipate emotions appropriate for the situation.

The Pregame Meal. The first episode of emotion-work I observed was during the pregame meal, which began at 3:00 p.m. and ended at 3:45 p.m. Clearly this was in effect a time for something more than ingesting nutritious food. The players ate together in clusters of from two to six persons around small tables. Some of them sat alone, apart from the others. The conversation, what there was of it, was surprisingly hushed. No one spoke loudly or at length. The three of us who were visiting coaches at first were more animated and vocal than the others present. But we quickly accommodated the prevailing tone, specifically following the role example of the brain coach. I found myself speaking barely above a whisper, and by that act being influenced to feel that this, apparently only a meal, was really a prebattle ritual, deserving of somewhat reverent conformity. I searched the faces of the others for further cues as to how I should be behaving in this setting, but then realized I was already responding as expected—with awe.

Was the hushed tone and limited conversation typical of pregame meals? The brain coach responded:

> Absolutely. The players are supposed to be concentrating on the game, on what it means to them, and what their job is in it. They should be in the proper frame of mind. It is a serious business. They are about to take a tough examination in front of a whole bunch of people. Right now they should be dealing with the fear of getting hurt, with what it means if they win or lose, and with respect for the other team. This is no time for idle chatter.

All the players gave the appearance that they had read and accepted the social script summarized by the brain coach. Whatever they might actually have been feeling, the players unanimously gave the impression of thoughtfully dealing with anxiety and responsibility. They reflected the proper mood, one of emotional control and single-minded intent.

I commented to one of the team cocaptains that I was surprised by the hushed demeanor of the players. He sharply replied:

What did you expect? Did you think we would be running around and grabbing cheerleaders' asses? The "rah, rah" stuff is OK for the fans. They can afford it. We need it from them, but now's not the time for us.

The players' serious mood was facilitated not only by interactions among the coaches, trainers, and players during the pregame meal, but by a unique feature of the dining room setting. In one corner of the room, on two long tables, the trainers throughout the meal applied tape, braces, padding, and other extra protective devices to players who needed them. Silently and sternly, those players who were to be thusly girded would, after finishing their meal, remove whatever civilian clothing necessary and take a place on one of the tables. In the presence of all, as it were on a special stage, they would have their injuries, special weaknesses, or preferred armor catered to. "We do it here to save time, before the players put on their uniforms," commented one of the trainers. "But it also sort of reminds them that this is not one of your run-of-the-mill meals with the boys."

Throughout the pregame meal, the mandates for proper display of mood were impressive and effective. The players should, as revealed by thoughtful "faces" and performances, be anxious but controlled, worried but confident, proud but "cool" about it, and by all means serious. They could be fearful, but not disablingly so. They should be certain of victory, but should respect the foe. The verbal and nonverbal cues for the display of this shaped and mixed mood steadily manifested "shoulds," "oughts," and "supposed to be's." The stage was set for feeling of the *right* mood. If you did not actually feel it, you had better at least give the appearance of doing so.

At what point would the preparatory mood be converted first to a more flamboyant expression of emotion and then to physical action? The transformation of the emotional role behaviors would be staged through several settings, beginning with the team meeting.

As the pregame meal concluded, the visiting coaches received a special message about the emotional potential for this particular game. One of the assistant coaches approached us and said, smilingly but sadly, "After this game you might be the only coaches left on the team." The brain coach, seated with us, somberly nodded assent. We were to be present during the Alpha head coach's retirement. How should we feel? How should we act? The instructions would not be ambiguous. Sadness would also be part of the emotional behavioral expectations.

The Team Meeting. After they had finished the pregame meal and whatever special taping they needed, the players returned to their rooms in the athletic dormitory. "They can be alone for a little while if they want to, and get the butterflies in formation," advised an assistant coach. Getting "the butterflies in formation" seemed an apt way to summarize the expectation that a generalized mood was to be converted to more specific emotional role behavior.

At 4:00 p.m. all of the players and coaches gathered in a small auditorium for the team meeting, a routine part of the game-day schedule. As soon as everyone was seated, the chief assistant coach took the podium. Without any introductory comments, he crisply ordered, "Let's review the slides." The lights were dimmed, and a series of Beta University play formations were flashed on the screen. The offensive and defensive coaches took turns highlighting aspects of each slide, and briskly asked individual Alpha players what they were supposed to do in that play situation. The players responded to the questions briefly and precisely, usually punctuating their answers with a "sir." Their tone was businesslike; still no "rah rah" displays. But the players' voices, keyed by the coaches' intense questioning, became noticeably louder. Several of the players leaned forward in their seats, pressing toward the screen. There was more body movement among them, and more sidelong verbal and nonverbal interaction with fellow players. The diffuse and privatized pregame mood that had been constructed among the players was beginning to be transformed, by the direction of the coaches and the presentation of targets for action, into more specific and overt emotional role enactments. The transformation was carefully paced and timed.

After the general review of the slides, the offensive and defensive players divided into two groups for detailed instructions from the coaches. Then the offense and defense each split again into smaller sections, by position groups and special assignments, for individualized review. The level of player animation continued as it had been at the end of the collected team meeting. It did not increase. There still was no cheering, shouting, or exhortations about ultimate victory. I asked one of the senior halfbacks what would happen if, during the team meeting, a player would jump up and yell something like "We're Number One!" The halfback smiled, shook his head, and replied:

> We all know better than to do a dumb thing like that. The team meeting
> is not the place for that. It's a time to be cool, man. You know, to be
> getting it up, but not getting carried away.

The brain coach guided the two other visiting coaches and me out of the auditorium and toward the athletic dining room, where we were to have pregame coffee. A few of the players had returned for additional taping by trainers. The Alpha head coach sat at a table with the chief trainer. The brain coach introduced us. We talked briefly about the upcoming game. The head coach spoke softly and matter-of-factly. I commented that I was impressed by the complexity of the football business. He observed:

> Yes, football has become increasingly complex, on and off the field. For example, now we have a very complicated rule, it takes about three pages in the rule book, concerning what the linebackers can say, and how they can say it, so that they won't be deliberately drawing the offensive line offsides. Hell, [the Beta coach] and I solved that problem between us, long before the rules were laid down. It was getting to be a problem, throughout the league. Linebackers were making noises like offensive signals, in order to pull the offensive line offsides. Something had to be done about it. So he and I just sat down one day and said that our linebackers, at least when our teams were playing each other, would not do that. And we never did. It was a gentleman's agreement.

I was saddened by his comment. Why? Retirement can be a depressing event, but the Alpha head coach would remain a tenured full professor and director of athletics, hardly a demeaning job. Furthermore, nothing in his own role behavior called for the response of sorrow. Under other circumstances I would have interpreted this comment abstractly, as an interesting observation on the bureaucratization of college football. The brain coach sat next to me, head down, staring at his coffee. The chief trainer concentrated on aimlessly unwinding and rewinding a roll of gauze. Both were unsmiling and somber. The other two visiting coaches listened silently. Again it seemed clear that this was to be an event that would include sadness as part of the emotional role expectations. These were the cues I saw, and that was the emotional response I felt and enacted.

The head coach abruptly stood, shook our hands, and announced it was time for him to go back to work. He left the dining room. The brain coach took the three of us visitors to the stadium and the Alpha locker room.

The Locker Room. Shortly after 6:00 p.m. the football team and coaches had as a group walked from the athletic dormitory to the stadium. Once in the locker room, the players quickly attended to the task of donning their pads and uniforms. They were animated, but businesslike. Interaction among them for the most part was limited to requests for help with fastening or centering padding. There was no cheering or other kind of exhortation. The players obviously were tense; several seemed nervous and fidgety. But there was no other overt display of emotion. The brain coach informed us that this was typical of the pregame locker room: "The tension is highest now for the players. This is the hardest time. All that energy building up, but they have to wait. They can't do anything with it."

In fact, the players were not supposed to do anything with the tension and energy. That is, they were not supposed to display premature or undue emotion. Dozens of hand-lettered signs were taped to the players' lockers, the walls, and even to the light fixtures. "Kill the Betas!" "Smash 'em, Alphas!" "Go, Alphas!" The signs had been put in the locker room by sorority members. The players did not seem to notice the signs. The cues for their emotional role enactments were being directed by the several assistant coaches, trainers, and physicians who moved among the players, softly speaking to them individually or simply patting them. "They're uptight now," commented an assistant coach. "We want to make sure that uptightness is turned outward when the right time comes." The right time, of course, was the game itself. The staff were guiding the players in their emotion-work.

The Warm-Up. At 7:25 p.m., the chief assistant coach announced that it was time for the players to "take the field" for the pregame warm-up. The team cocaptains, who moments before had as the other players appeared tense but cool, on cue suddenly exploded with exhortations. "This is *it*, men, let's *do* it!" "Let's get out there and show those Betas!" "All right, all right, let's *go!*" Some of the players responded with "right on!" "yeah, let's *do* it!" and other exclamations of agreement. Most of them, however, moved silently and quickly out of the locker room, their faces still displaying a studied intensity.

The visiting coaches went out with the team. Exiting from the locker room, passing through the underside of the stadium, and then entering the playing field was a remarkable and profoundly staged emotional event. The locker room door was thrown open by an assistant coach, revealing a small crowd of well-wishers who had been formed into two parallel lines leading to the field entrance. Many of the well-wishers were players' parents, girlfriends, or other close associates. Some were autograph seekers, particularly ardent fans, or people curious about the pregame scene. The players jogged between the parallel lines of people, heads down, silently, with an occasional nod to someone they knew. The crowd was noisy, its members shouting encouragement to individual players and to the team in general. The physical proximity of the small crowd, and the manner in which their shouts were amplified in the enclosed, cemented underside of the stadium, was an impressive manifestation of the emotional urgency of this event. I restrained the inclination to shout with the well-wishers and, like the players, jogged head down and silently through the parallel lines. I felt nervous, even anxious, and yet remarkably energized. I wanted to shout, but did not—because it would not have been consistent with how I perceived my role. The effort at containment seemed to make the feeling of excitement more intense. I was at the end of the line of jogging players. Some of the spectators closed in behind the players, blocking my path. I felt resentful. I had adopted the players' emotional role behavior, was enjoying that interaction, and did not want to be isolated from the setting. Being isolated from it made my enacted role seem foolish, patently out of context. I checked to make certain that the symbols validating my behavior, the bench pass and press box tags hanging from my coat buttons, were clearly visible. I then shouldered my way through the well-wishers and caught up with the team.

Entering the field from the underside of the stadium was a powerful experience. Suddenly I was on the tartan track surrounding the field; then I was on the astroturf. I was standing on the major stage of the event. The players were milling around, now openly showing their excitement, loudly and exuberantly. They slapped each other, pounded each other's helmets and shoulder pads, and screamed encouragements to each other. The coolness and the containment of emotions were gone. "*Now* is the time for them to show how fired-up they are," advised an assistant coach. "The other team is watching, the fans are watching. This is it." The assistant coaches facilitated the change in the players' emotional role behavior by moving among them, shouting with them, patting them, and in general "firing them up." The situation demanded an overt representation of excitement. The diffuse emotions experienced by the players up to this point had been, as a result of the interactive process of emotion-work, focused in a specific display of impassioned courage for victory.

The noise level on the field was incredible. The collective roars of over 50,000 people, the cheering sections, the bands, the assortment of bells, whistles, and sirens, the thunderous public address system, and the shouts of the coaches and players combined to be nearly deafening. The complexity of interactions on the field, even during the warm-up period, was similarly striking. Coaches, cheerleaders, police, players, media people, and others rushed about conveying instructions. People kept bumping into each other as they hurried to issue an order, take a photograph, restrain a fan, conduct an interview, lead a cheer, or rehearse a play. Their interactions combined to elevate the level of emotional display on the field. The players clearly responded to and were part of those interactions.

I turned for a moment to look up at the stands—tens of thousands of people seemed to stare back. I felt strangely embarrassed and self-conscious. A few seconds before I had been committed to and involved in the interactions on the field. The crowd had been part of that interaction, but now in my perception was separate from it. I shoved my hands in my pockets and walked nearer to the bench, getting closer to the coaches and players, entering the scene more deeply so that my role would be revalidated in context. The crowd again became a background component of the setting, and I again felt comfortable with and fully enacted the role of a visiting coach and a partisan participant. In retrospect, Goffman's (1961b, 1963, 1967) and Stone's (1962) observations on the structural processes of embarrassment and alienation from interaction were supported by what I experienced in the warm-up setting. To the degree that I was structurally distanced from my role as visiting coach, I felt uncomfortable with displaying the expected emotional demeanor.

The Last Pregame Cue: The Coach's Speech. The warm-up period was quickly over, and the players returned to the locker room. They were quite animated now. The locker room reverberated with their shouts as they adjusted their equipment, made minor repairs, and urged each other toward maximum performance. "Get 'em, Jones!" "Smash 'em, Smith!" "Make 'em eat your dust, Brown!" "We're Number One! We're Number One!" Two of the players faced each other, their noses only an inch apart, and screamed at each other "Hit 'em! Hit 'em! Hit 'em!" I asked an assistant coach about the increase in emotional display, and the contrast of that expressiveness with the player constraint prior to the warm-up period. He replied: "Look at them. They're all sweating now, and breathing hard. You can't be really psyched up without sweat. They're ready now! They're ready!"

The players indeed were perspiring heavily; several of them were gulping air, almost as if they were deliberately hyperventilating. The diffuse emotions that had been "worked" before the warm-up were being linked with physical effort and, more importantly, with specific action. The coaches had, in the structured setting of the warm-up drill, cued the players to focus their "psyched up" state on physical acts that might provide victory over the opponent team. It was now appropriate to be more emotionally flamboyant, so long as the feelings were physically purposive. This particular warm-up drill or this particular set of coaches' cues did not alone influence the players to link emotion-work with overt emotional display and physical action. The structural phasing and the coaches' cues served a gatekeeper function for the players' role enactments. But the players had been involved, during their football careers, in dozens of games. They had a history of previous socialization concerning game behavior and a familiarity with how and when they were to focus emotional display. The enactment of player-related emotional behavior was part of their self-concepts. Those experiences validated and legitimized the cues provided in the current setting and by the current coaches.

The chief assistant coach instructed the players to take seats in the "skull session" section of the locker room, an alcove containing chairs and a blackboard. As the players did so, they again fell silent. The scene had changed, and the cues once again dictated a shift in emotional role expectations. All 55 players, still sweating, their faces flushed, their bodies tensed, took seats in the chairs or knelt on the floor. Most of them stared straight ahead, some looked at their knees, a few fidgeted with shoelaces, helmets, or their taped hands. It was so quiet in the locker room that the sounds of the crowd in the stadium outside could be heard clearly. One of the players rose, on cue from an assistant coach, and delivered a short but incoherent speech about this being the seniors' last game. A few of the players applauded; most remained silent.

The Alpha head coach entered the skull session room, and strode to the front of it. He paced nervously before the blackboard. The players watched him intently. He looked at his watch, stopped pacing, and stared at the players. Then he spoke, urgently, but in a businesslike manner:

> The longer I have been in this game of football, the more I've come to believe that it's psychology that wins games. It's the people who want to win the games, and show it, that win. I'm convinced this is the answer. If you really want to win a game, you don't feel the pain. In fact, you like the pain. When somebody hits you, you feel a challenge, you don't feel the hurt. It's a test of courage and pride in order to overcome the pain, in order to win the game. Our football team has a lot of injuries. We have been hurt a lot this season. But *they* are the same way. They have a lot of injuries. They're almost exactly the same as us now. They have almost got the same record, the same injuries, the same need to win. It's going to be a question of who wants to win the most. This is a great chance to give the team a sense of pride. If you want to, you can do it.

The Alpha coach paused for about five seconds, stared at the team again, and firmly said, "Don't be the only Alpha team to have a losing season in twenty years." He then snapped, "Cocaptains!" It was a mandate. The cocaptains bowed their heads and led the team, all of whom also bowed their heads, in the Lord's Prayer.

The players had again been directed to convert diffuse emotion into a display of specific emotions. "Winners'" emotional role expectations involved their being able to transform their "psyched up" condition into overt courage and pride. They should not show fear of pain. They should mobilize courage and pride into victorious action against the opposing team. If the team loses, then the players should be prepared to have shame as the focus of their emotional role behavior.

The players moved out of the skull session room and toward the locker room door. Several of them began to shout "Get the Betas!" "Bring on the Betas!" "Go Alphas!"

The team left the locker room for the field, again jogging between the lines of well-wishers, whose number had quadrupled since the warm-up period. The players ran onto the field, escorted by cheerleaders, mascots, and assorted student spirit groups. Upon reaching the bench, the players burst into unrestrained enthusiasm. All of them were shouting. Many of them jumped up and down, pounded their fellow players, clapped, or shook their fists in the air. They clustered together for a final word from the head coach, merged hands, and the starters took their positions on the field. The head coach had called for an open show of courage and pride. The players enthusiastically complied, loudly supported by the crowd in the stands.

THE GAME

From the kickoff until the end of the game, the players on the sidelines screamed encouragement to their teammates on the field. Most of those encouragements were praise for good performance. Many of them, however, were urgings to sustain the expression of courage and pride. "Suck it up, Smith!" "Shake it off, Jones!" "Hang in there, Brown!" The assistant coaches, trainers, and team managers also directed the players, individually on the sidelines, to maintain the level of performance, both emotional and physical.

The Crowd: The Orchestration of Emotions

Turner (1974) has reported that groups experiencing "liminality" can subsequently experience "communitas." Liminality is characterized by a sense of anonymity, uncertainty, confusion, and anxiety among group members. It can be present in the early stage of a group's development, or can be generated in later stages by some unforeseen catastrophic event. Liminality can be replaced by communitas, which is characterized by a sense of cohesiveness, mutual affection, and coherence of purpose. One of the key elements in the evolution of a group from liminality to communitas is that along the way the interacting members share intense emotional experiences.

Turner's observations were based on fieldwork among tribes of preindustrial people. Deegan and Stein (1978) have argued that the contemporary college football crowd manifests a shift from liminality in the early part of the game to communitas in the later parts. Fans come to the game uncertain about the outcome, subsequently share the uncertainty, overcome it by engaging in game rituals, and enjoy the resulting social bonding that the mutuality generates (Klapp, 1969).

Fans at a football game, in contrast to preindustrial tribal groups, engage in *voluntary* liminality. They even pay to have the experience. Having paid, they expect a satisfying liminal/communitas experience that includes centrally, I suggest, the opportunity to enact a *repertoire of emotions* throughout the game. Each play at the onset presents an uncertain outcome that, as it becomes known, can be responded to consensually. The liminality/communitas cycle is repeated with varying degrees of intensity in each play, ideally evolving the crowd toward mounting levels of camaraderie. The fans need to be coordinated in these role performances. They want to convert the diffuse pregame spirit into specific emotional displays. To do so fully, they expect direction from role models. What emotion should the Alpha fan be showing now? What emotion should the Beta fan be showing now? As have the players, the fans have nearly all had previous experiences with football games. They all have been participants in other staged emotional settings. Those socialization experiences, involving the enactment of emotional role behaviors, have more or less become part of the fans' self-concepts. Their responses to and expectations for football games, including this one, are influenced by their earlier experiences.

Cheerleaders can be key orchestrators of fans' emotional role performances. Essentially, the cheerleaders remind the fans of what Hochschild (1979) has called "feeling rules," and help the fans to implement them. Feeling rules govern what people should experience emotionally, or display emotionally, in particular social settings. The rules are developed in and understood through interaction among people in the setting, much as emergent norms are developed and understood in episodes of collective behavior (Turner and Killian, 1972).

Cheerleaders are not alone in serving the orchestration task. The announcer on the stadium public address system can also coordinate emotional responses. So can radio announcers, if some fans in the stands are listening to transistor radios and in turn are transmitting directives for emotional response. Usually there are, scattered throughout the crowd, several informal cheerleaders (with or without transistor radios) who, themselves fans, evoke coordinated emotional performances among other fans in their proximity. Probably they are persons who have had more experience with emotional cueing at games and have received reinforcement for that quasi-leader role.

The formal cheerleaders, the announcers, and the informal cheerleaders function as do "prompters" in a play. The influence of the prompters on the fans can be seen and heard from the field level. In football games, after each down, there are discernible epicenters from which fan response widens. A person jumps up in excitement and others follow suit, not just behind him or her (where vision might be blocked), but in front as well. A person cheers or moans, and there begins around him or her a ripple of similar responses. Such individuals are similar to the "keynoters" whose comments mobilize others' collective action in protest crowds (Turner and Killian, 1972).

Not all emotional prompters are attended to equally, nor are there necessarily only a few prompters. After a spectacular success or failure by a team, or during a particularly important series of plays, fans can seem to respond as one. Actually they do not. Viewing them from the field, it is apparent that the fans, even when seeming to emote simultaneously, are reacting in waves. People cue each other interactively with greater or lesser effectiveness and with faster or slower timing, depending on what happened in the down. At some points there are thousands of people enacting roles as prompters.

Halftime

When the gun sounded to indicate the end of the first half of the game, the teams quickly left the field for their locker rooms. The Alphas were ahead 10 to 0, and were shouting praises to each other as they entered the locker room. One of the assistant coaches yelled, "Don't celebrate too much yet. We still have thirty minutes of football left to play!" The coach was instructing the players that it was acceptable to express celebration emotions at this time, but not to overdo it.

After a few minutes for toweling off and replacing damaged equipment, the players were directed into the skull session room for the usual halftime speech. The Alpha head coach immediately went to the front of the room; the players fell silent. "Men, you're playing a hell of a game, and I'm proud of you," he said emphatically. Then, in a very businesslike manner, he reviewed adjustments in the offense and defense to be made in the second half of the game. He addressed some of the players by name, advising them of strategies by which to overcome some problem or to capitalize on some opponent weakness.

There was no "Rockne" speech, no impassioned plea for more effort. I asked the brain coach if this was typical. He responded:

> Yes, if the team is ahead, playing well, and is already fired up. A good coach doesn't get in the way of momentum by trying to whip it up when it's already there. He's got the flow going, so he just guides it. If the team is losing and is down, then he goes to work on them to get it up. He lets them know they're looking like a beaten team and they'd better shake off that look. They've got to believe in themselves and show that to the other team.

The brain coach was citing the head coach's influence not only in the technical aspects of the game but in managing the player role and in maintaining the team's momentum (Adler, 1981; Adler and Adler, 1978). If the players were enacting the appropriate emotional role behavior, he did not interfere. If the enactment was inappropriate, he intervened accordingly.

During halftime, many of the fans had left their seats in order to get refreshments, stretch, and use the lavatories. Most of them reverted to closer interactions with friends and acquaintances. The bands and marching groups paraded on the field for the halftime show, and the student cheering section conducted its usual card tricks. These events were not responded to by the fans in as concerted a manner as the game events. They were, however, continuing reminders for fans to keep up their spirit even during this intermission.

In the locker room, the players had spent a few minutes with their respective specialty coaches. The head coach interrupted, "Okay, let's play football!" We left for the field. This time the noise level among the players was so high that the shouts of the well-wishing fans were barely noticeable.

The End of the Game

When the final gun sounded, Alpha had defeated Beta by a score of 29 to 12. About one minute before game time elapsed, the public address system announcer asked the fans to give the head coaches of Alpha and Beta universities a standing ovation. It was an unusual request, with which all of the more than 50,000 spectators enthusiastically complied. The message was clear. Both head coaches were retiring.

At the end of the game, the Alpha head coach had taken off an old warm-up jacket he had put on shortly after the game began. It was frayed, and seemed a bit too tight on him. He replaced it with a newer jacket. The rumor along the sidelines was that the jacket was the first he had worn as Alpha head coach, and he wanted it to be the last. Whether the rumor was correct or not, it further signaled sadness as one of the emotional modes that later would be expected and enacted.

The players carried the Alpha head coach on their shoulders to the center of the field. The Alpha band played the alma mater. Fans and players joined in the singing. The emotions expected for the moment were pride and joy, and all present seemed to be performing accordingly.

For about fifteen minutes, the field was filled with players, fans, and media people. Then the Alpha head coach abruptly jogged toward the locker room. The players and coaches followed him. Most of the fans now were moving out of the stadium. The game was over. Technicians began to disassemble their gear. Clean-up crews went to work on the stands. Concessionaires closed their booths. The major stage was being unset.

POSTGAME ACTIVITIES

The Alpha locker room was tumultuous. Players and coaches were shaking and slapping hands, hugging each other, applauding team-mates, and shouting "We're Number One! We're Number One!" even though they had won only six of eleven games during the season and were number one in no rankings. The expected emotion had become unmitigated joy. "Now they can let it all hang out," commented an assistant coach in response to my inquiry. "This is your typical win-ning locker room. If we had lost, anyone yelling about being number one, and looking happy, would be out of line. Now they can do or say almost anything, and it's okay. They're winners."

Though they were loudly celebrating the victory, the players quickly removed their equipment, took showers, and donned street clothes. The floor was covered with twisted tape, bits and pieces of plastic protective foam, and dirty strips of gauze. One of the assistant coaches announced that the head coach wanted to speak with the team soon, but since he was not present, the joyful noise continued. When he did arrive a few minutes later, he slipped quietly into a small coaches' room in the corner of the locker room. All of the assistant coaches followed. Two of the player cocaptains noticed the conver-gence of coaches. "Here it comes," one said to the other. Neither of those cocaptains continued in the celebration. They both sat down quietly and somberly. One put his face in his hands. A few of the players near them saw their reaction. They too fell silent.

Three or four minutes later, the head coach and the assistant coaches came out of the coaches' room. All of them appeared saddened; three of the assistant coaches were red-eyed; one had tears on his cheeks. Seeing this, more of the players became quiet. The cues were changing from joy to sadness. One of the cocaptains shouted, "It's the head coach! Listen up!" The locker room became hushed. The head coach climbed atop a bench, and began:

> You have been . . . I know you have been . . . you've been . . . there have been several . . . I know you have heard rumors about what might happen tonight. I want to read to you . . . I want to read to you the statement that I just gave to the press.

He was stammering. His usually level gaze dropped to the floor several times. He haltingly read the prepared statement that announced his retirement as head football coach. He then added, again haltingly:

> I am indebted to you all for being able to finish my coaching career here without a losing season. You all . . . did it. I am . . . indebted to you.

The players, only moments before wildly joyous, now universally appeared crestfallen. I asked a freshman player, standing next to me in the corner of the locker room, how he felt about this. He replied: "I only talked to the man twice in my life, but I feel sad. This is a sad time. Look how those seniors are breaking up." The cues were for sorrow. Even those players who barely knew the head coach (most of the younger players interact primarily with assistant coaches) displayed the emotion of sorrow.

A senior cocaptain took the head coach's place on the bench. He spoke:

> I want to say a few words about the Coach, and what he means to us. I want to speak for the entire team. He has been part of our lives. He has not only taught us how to play football, he has taught us how to be men. He has taught me how to be a man.

Tears streamed down the cocaptain's face. He literally sobbed as he stepped down from the bench. The head coach came over and hugged him, and opened his embrace to include two other players who were standing near. "I love you guys," he said softly. His eyes brimmed with tears. Other players also began weeping, often looking to one another as if to share and validate the emotion. I felt a discernible lump in my throat. The cues for sadness in the setting were overpowering. This was a special moment in which to participate, and the moment called for sorrow.

The Alpha head coach left the locker room. There was silence for about fifteen seconds. The players began to converse, first in whispers, then in louder voices. No more than two minutes after the head coach's exit, the locker room was again in pandemonium. Led by some of the senior players, the team enthusiastically resumed its celebration. Joy was again the expected emotional role behavior, and shouts of "We're Number One" abounded. The players laughed and cavorted as they left the locker room.

The head coach himself went from the locker room directly to a press conference. There he spoke clearly, coolly, and unhaltingly before the media cameras. There was no demeanor of sadness about him. He was all business.

Within a time lapse of about twenty minutes, the players had in turn displayed joy, then sorrow, and again joy, all appropriate in turn and in context. The head coach too had displayed a dramatic contrast in emotional demeanor, as was expected in the different settings. Players and coaches cued each other throughout the interaction, some serving more as emotional prompters than others.

The emotions displayed and felt were by no means artificial or shallow. Certainly the depth of feeling and the degree of expression varied among the participants. But the emotional display was real and vivid. That it so rapidly shifted does not detract from its personal significance. Rather, it illustrates the power of the interactive setting for shaping emotional role behavior. Furthermore, it exemplifies the capacity of human beings for accommodating and shaping the settings, and for experiencing and displaying a versatile emotional repertoire within a specific role.

Some of the assistant coaches did not, once having been saddened by the confirmation of the head coach's retirement, again adopt the joy of celebration. One of them explained, "You know, I've just lost my job. The cheering is over for me." Head coaches routinely hire their own assistant coaches. Sometimes even in a powerful interactional setting, the expectations for a particular emotional display cannot evoke the contextual performance from a participant. He or she has alternate expectations to meet, outside the setting, which emerge as primary.

CONCLUSION

Emotions are not roles, but are part of the behavioral expectations associated with roles people enact. Though emotions involve physiological reactions, the manner in which people display those reactions is shaped by past socialization experiences and by current interactions with actors in specific social settings. Some emotional role behaviors are institutionalized, for example, grief during a funeral service. Some emerge almost totally from interactions in a unique social setting, for example, panic during a nightclub fire.

People can be involved in situations that call for not only one, but for an array of emotional responses. Indeed, individuals often seek and even pay for participation in staged events where they are directed to display a variety of emotions, such as plays, movies, symphonies, rock concerts, sports competitions, discos, and encounter groups. They enjoy those experiences.

The Alpha-Beta college football game was an example of a staged event. In that event, the orchestration of emotions began with the arousal of expectations for an emotional experience. The expectations generated a diffuse emotional state, which ultimately was directed into a series of discrete and identifiable emotional displays. Among the football fans, the phasing of role behavior first was manifested in their expectations for an exciting game, then in their expression of spirit, and finally in their emotional reactions during the game. Their emotional performances were directed primarily by the media, by formal and informal prompters, and by interactions with other fans. Among the football players, the phasing first was manifested in their expectations for a challenging game, then in their expression of mood, and finally in their emotional reactions during and after the game. They were directed in these performances primarily by coaches, fans, and interactions among the team members.

It is typical for people in staged events to display remarkable shifts in emotional display within a short period of time. Football fans expressed happiness after one down, anger after the next, anxiousness after the next. In the locker room, following the game, the players expressed joy, then sadness, then joy again. The changes in emotional role behavior were specific to the setting, influenced by how people perceived the situation at the moment, and by what they interpreted to be the appropriate emotion.

That emotional role behaviors are manipulated in such staged settings as football games does not imply that people are necessarily passive compliants in those events. Nor does it imply that the personal experience of emotion usually is a shallow facade. There are profound differences in both emotional experiences and emotional displays across individuals and across settings. Some people feel emotional responses more deeply than others. Some are more independent than others from cues in the social setting. Those variations are in large part the result of previous socialization and reflect differences in self-concept.

In the normal course of everyday life, individuals become involved in situations where they effect a pattern consisting of the kind of emotional behavior a role or setting calls for, the feelings they actually are experiencing, and the kind of emotion they actually display. In a protest crowd, for example, a person feels and displays the anger expected in that setting. Another, however, though shouting angry slogans and in general conforming with the angry behavior expected, actually feels sad because crowd protest has become the only recourse after other attempts to right a wrong have failed. At a graduation ceremony, a person feels and displays the joy expected in the setting. Another joins in the celebration, loudly sings the alma mater with others, but actually feels anger because he or she did not receive anticipated graduation honors.

People also effect a pattern consisting of the intensity of emotional behavior a role or setting calls for, the intensity of the feelings they actually are experiencing, and the intensity of the emotion they actually display. In an encounter group, for example, a person very intensely feels and demonstrates unconditional love for the other participants, as expected in that setting. Another feels some affection but not intense love for the others; nonetheless he or she does and says the things that are perceived to represent that intensity. At a banquet honoring the job promotion of a coworker, a person feels the intense happiness expected in the event, but chooses to be restrained in demonstrating that happiness because that seems more dignified. Another actually is only mildly happy about the coworker's promotion, but displays unbounded happiness because it seems appropriate.

Even in powerfully staged settings that reflect widely accepted cultural values and historical traditions, people reveal considerable autonomy when enacting roles and associated emotional behavior. Staged events usually are voluntary. People take a participant role in them because they want to. They choose to conform more or less to the directions for emotional display. If they desire, they can make emotional roles for themselves by becoming prompters in the setting. As in most social situations, people participating in staged events can think about the roles they are expected to enact, and assess them in terms of how the enactments fit with their own expectations and self-concepts. If they do not like the fit, they can remain at the event but not perform as directed, or they can leave before the event is finished.

This chapter presents the example of sorority hashers, male college students who were employed as part-time kitchen help in sorority houses. In return for their work, the hashers were given meals and, in some cases when they had additional responsibilities, a few dollars per month. The job consisted of setting tables, washing and drying dishes, cleaning the kitchen, mopping floors, disposing of garbage, general handy work, and such occasional tasks as carrying luggage for the sorority women.

The hashers found themselves in a work situation where they experienced intense conflict not only between two roles they were expected to enact (hasher and college student), but between one of the roles (hasher) and their self-perceptions. They eased the strain mostly by role distancing and by creating new roles in the setting. The new roles became part of the informal work organization, just as the "secondary adjustments" of sailors aboard ship were part of the informal organization (see Chapter 3).

The observations reported in this chapter were conducted, over a period of ten months, by two senior undergraduate students who were employed as hashers in a large, campus-located, nationally affiliated sorority house (85 women, 10 hashers). They had been hashers in a total of five sororities for a period of three years. Under my supervision, the two students kept daily notes of relevant attitudes, behaviors, and interaction patterns among the hashers and the sorority members. The three of us met several times a week to discuss the data gathered and to focus attention for further observations.

The sorority in which the observers worked was one of the largest on the university campus. At the time of the study, and for several years before, the sorority was not among those considered by students to be the most popular. It was generally considered to be a "loser" sorority. We anticipated, following Allport (1954), that the members of a sorority assessed by others to be nearer the bottom of the popularity hierarchy would be particularly concerned about maintaining social distance from their hashers.

In addition to extensive observation in the subject sorority, the two students and I interviewed the hashers, staff, and members of seven other sororities on campus. The seven houses varied in size and popularity and were taken to be representative of the thirteen sororities at the university.

In all of the sorority houses we studied, hashers were expected to accept the assignments given to them by the cooks and head hashers. They were expected to be neat, quietly efficient, and at all times polite to sorority members. In the sorority house we directly observed, hashers were expected not to speak to the members when they were serving them, unless asked a direct question. Dating between the hashers and the sorority women was strictly forbidden.

When the hashers responded to the situation by role distancing and creating new roles they often did so with hostile behavior, as this chapter will show. That behavior was so effective in addressing the role conflict that it was institutionalized as part of the informal work organization. Hostility is by no means the most productive way of dealing with role conflict, but despite its negative aspects it is not an unusual human reaction. Nor is it unusual for hostile responses to be institutionalized as part of a social arrangement. When people perceive that their prestige is being threatened, they often elect a solution that demeans those they see as representing the status threat (Allport, 1954; Gusfield, 1963; Zurcher and Kirkpatrick, 1976).

THE PRESTIGE OF HASHERS

The job of hasher is a service occupation. Those occupations have been characterized by Becker (1951: 136) as including: workers who come into personal contact with the clients for whom they labor; clients who can direct workers in their tasks and apply evaluative sanctions; strong feelings among workers that the clients cannot or do not accurately judge the appropriate worth of their services; workers' resentment of client attempts to control their work; and workers' preoccupation, as they conduct their tasks, with defending against client interference.

Hashers occupy the lowest level in the status hierarchy of the sorority house kitchen. Cooks are at the top of the hierarchy (in order of longevity on the job), followed by the head hasher and then the hashers themselves (in order of longevity on the job). Whyte (1948) noted the rigidity of restaurant kitchen hierarchies, including such detailed criteria as who worked with what kind of food preparation. Orwell (1933: 70) concludes that restaurant personnel "had their prestige graded as accurately as that of soldiers, and a cook or waiter was as much above a kitchen helper as a captain above a private." When we asked nearly 300 university students to rank the prestige of 10 different student part-time jobs, hasher was reported to be at the bottom of the list.

In past years, males becoming undergraduates generally had accepted a stereotype of what it was to be a "college man" (Hartshorne, 1943; Krech et al., 1962). The characteristics and role expectations associated with the stereotype included: (1) a young man who deserves a white-collar or "clean" occupation having considerable prestige; (2) a sophisticate, above average in intelligence, taste, and savoir-faire; (3) a "lover," a "man of the world," who is able to dominate and manipulate coeds; (4) a "hale fellow well met" who can at any time spontaneously join an impromptu frolicsome venture. More recently, primarily because of the instructive impact of women's liberation movements and because males have begun to realize the ludicrousness of those characteristics, the stereotype has begun to lose its effect as a role model, although it still operates (Spence and Helmreich, 1978; Heilbrun, 1981). In the time and setting of this study, the stereotype was still fully effective and the resultant role conflict was significant.

The hashers we studied were part of a generation (the sixties) in which men still were judged by others mostly according to the work they pursued. College students had a middle-class view of work. It should enhance one's prestige, provide for the realization of one's talents, and be satisfying and desirable in itself. That view contrasted with what was reported to be the view of people in the lower socio-economic classes of society, that work is an unpleasant but necessary means of securing food and shelter. It is inherently neither interesting nor desirable (Krech et al., 1962). College students felt that people who had to do lower-class "drudgery" essentially were unintelligent, irresponsible, and inferior (Davidson et al., 1962).

The hashers, themselves college students, were kitchen helpers. Consequently, they were in the situation of having middle-class definitions of and expectations for work but were performing tasks and conforming to expectations that were by their definition lower class. In contrast to what was expected of "college men," the hashers were engaged in menial or "dirty" work that had low prestige and that did not assume "sophistication." Furthermore, they were obligated to be subservient to and socially distant from a group of college coeds.

EXPLAINING THE JOB TO OTHERS

When we asked why they had taken the part-time jobs they did, the hashers gave such qualified explanations as: "It's a means to an end"; "I'm just doing this until I find something more suitable"; and "It's the only job I could get with hours that won't interfere with my class schedule." They stressed the temporary nature of the job, and emphasized their student role. The hashers often indicated that their friends and acquaintances asked them why they did such work, suggesting a violation of what they expected college men to be doing. Some hashers described the job as an opportunity to "get near all those girls" and glossed over the unpleasant realities of being a kitchen helper. A few of the hashers stated that they initially took the job with the hope that they would "get the inside track" to a group of coeds. That hope was never realized in the sorority house we observed. Because dating between hashers and sorority members was prohibited, fraternization had been discouraged to the point where the women and the hashers both felt uncomfortable if they had to interact on a level other than that called for by the job.

The no dating rule in the sorority had been enforced for two years preceding our study. The older hashers spoke of the "good old days a couple of years ago" when the members were "good kids" and "somehow much nicer." The hashers' descriptions of the ideal sorority woman centered on the attribute of "naturalness"—that is, a tendency to "be herself" and not to "look down" on hashers, thus not stressing their subservient work role. A good house to work for was one in which a hasher was "treated like a human being." Good kids and good houses were those that treated the individual less like a hasher and more like a college man. Whyte (1949) observed that a conflict situation resulted among restaurant personnel when persons of high status had their activities initiated by persons perceived by them to be of lower status. Many of the hashers were upperclassmen, yet they had to take orders from and wait on freshmen and sophomore women. Any sorority member who minimized that status threat was appreciated by hashers as a "good kid."

Whyte (1949) also noted that it was not uncommon for female restaurant employees to initiate the action of male employees—for example, waitresses giving orders to male cooks. Since in American society the male sex role generally included the expectation that men were the originators of action between the sexes, that they dominated in heterosexual interpersonal relations, Whyte saw the role reversal in the restaurant as a key source of employee dissatisfaction. He cited a number of occasions where male employees contrived ways to avoid having to receive direct orders from female employees. Similarly, in an analysis of some of the factors contributing to alienation from work, Blauner (1964) observes that "jobs differ in the degree to which they permit the particular 'manly virtues' that in our society are deemed appropriate to a 'real man.'" One of the factors Blauner emphasizes is the degree to which the job allows sexual expression and role dominance with respect to women. The job of hasher included both the sex-role reversal that Whyte views as disruptive of the work situation and the lack of sexual expression and dominance over women that Blauner sees as being a contributing factor to alienation from work.

MUTUAL DENIGRATION:
HASHERS VERSUS THE SORORITY WOMEN

The sorority members generally called the kitchen helpers "hasher" rather than their given names, and were quite free with orders and criticisms. Any praise usually had a condescending tone—"nice hasher," "nice boy," and so on. The women's perception of hashers in the sorority house we observed was indicated by the fact that one of the initiation requirements for a pledge was that she sing a love song to a hasher while he sat on her lap. Similarly, the hashers themselves used that experience as an initiation rite for entrance into their informal work group. The newest hasher was made available to the pledge for the love song, and after he had been so used, he was told by his fellow hashers that he now knew "what working in the sorority is really like."

The hashers routinely referred to the sorority members in derisive terms. Almost always, the labels had animal referents, and the animal was most often the pig—"Here they come, let's slop the troughs"; "Soueee" and "Oink-Oink" grumbled as the hashers walked out of the kitchen to serve the food; "What do the pigs want now?"; "Let's go clean out the feeding pens"; "Mush, you huskies!" Our field notes contained a large number of that kind of statement, as well as many other derogatory comments about the women's manners, breeding, and femininity. It appeared that the hashers were projecting feelings of their own "low-born" work role onto the women. It was as if they were saying, "See, we aren't so bad. Look at those slobs out in the dining room!"

The physical appearance of the sorority members was also called into question by the hashers. "They've all had their faces remolded, and they still can't get dates." "A guy would have to be pretty hard up to take out one of these dogs." "They must have an 'ugly requirement' in order to get into this sorority." The hashers were proclaiming that even if they *could* date one of the women in the sorority, they would not.

THE KITCHEN: THE HASHERS' REFUGE

The kitchen, called "the Inside" by the hashers, was their stronghold. Within it they were in close association with other like-situated individuals. In the dining room, "the Outside," were "them," the sorority members. Interaction through the kitchen's swinging doors could best be described as studied aloofness on the part of the hashers. Orwell (1933: 86) writes of the "double door between us (kitchen help and waiters) and the dining room" and contrasts the spontaneity of emotion, the relative relaxation, and the we feeling of the kitchen with the controlled, tense, and guarded interaction with the customers. "It is an instructive sight," continues Orwell (1933: 86), "to see a waiter going into a hotel dining room. The set of his shoulders alters; all the dirt and hurry and irritation have dropped off in an instant. He glides over the carpet, with a solemn priest-like air." Scott (1963: 38) describes a similar phenomenon in the paddock, the private world of professional jockeys and handlers. When in the paddock with his peers, the jockey or the handler "can no longer fake his behavior. . . . The paddock represents that point where ordinary vigilance in role deception cannot be sustained." Becker's (1951) description of the deliberate isolation of the dance-band musician provides an interesting parallel to the hashers' kitchen stronghold. Becker (1951: 142) observes that

> the musician is, as a rule, spatially isolated from the audience, being placed on a platform barrier that prevents any direct interaction. This isolation is welcomed because the audience, being made up of squares, is felt to be potentially dangerous. . . . Musicians, lacking the usually provided physical barriers, often improvise their own and effectively segregate themselves from their audience.

Hashers were not able to isolate themselves from their "audience" as readily as dance-band musicians or professional waiters. They had to interact with the women in the sorority house, on the campus, and often in the classroom. However, they were not as obligated to restrain themselves from insulting the people they served. Though hashers were expected to be polite to the women "no matter what," and though they were bound by the "gentleman" expectations for college men, they were not subtle in their demonstrations of displeasure with the sorority women.

GETTING THE SORORITY WOMEN'S GOATS

The hashers seemed to get much satisfaction from what they identi- fied as "getting the women's goats." The kitchen often resounded with such gleefully shared exclamations as "Boy, did I get *her* mad!" and "I sure told *her* off!" Spilling food while serving, ignoring an order, sharp answers to criticism, and any other verbal aggression were rewarded with the plaudits of the other hashers—"That'll show them"; "That'll shape her up!" While in the kitchen the hashers deliberately made noises (loud talking, whistling, banging of pots and pans) with the intent of disturbing the women. In the sorority we observed, the hashers saved food scraps from the preparation of the meal, and while the women were eating would overload the garbage disposal unit and convulse with laughter as the mechanism emitted loud and excruciating gurgles, whines, and crunches. "It's hard to tell," reported one chuckling hasher, "which garbage disposal sounds the worst—the ones out in the dining room, or the one in the kitchen."

Orwell described the kitchen personnel's disdain for the customer of the hotel restaurant—a disdain developed as a defense against the "superiority" of the customer. One waiter told Orwell (1933: 113) that, "as a matter of pride, he had sometimes wrung a dirty dishcloth into the customer's soup before taking it in, just to be revenged upon a member of the bourgeoisie." Another waiter scolded Orwell (1933: 114):

> Fool! Why do you wash that plate? Wipe it on your trousers. Who cares about the customers? They don't know what's going on. What is restaurant work? You are carving a chicken and it falls on the floor. You apologize, you bow, you go out; and in five minutes you come back by another door—with the same chicken. *That* is restaurant work.

So also was it hasher revenge. Besides the deliberate casualness toward dropped food and the amused "what they don't know won't hurt them" attitude, on numerous other occasions minor assaults were made on foods to be served to the women—a marble tossed into a gelatin and grape salad mold; a small amount of grass thrown in with cooking spinach ("for those cows"); dinner rolls "thrown around the bases" from one hasher to another before they were placed in the serving basket; a drop or two of blood from the accidentally cut finger of a hasher splashed into a pot of soup ("This ought to make those bloodsuckers happy!"), green food coloring added to the milk; salt shaker tops loosened so they would fall off in the women's plates. The actions themselves were less significant than the glee with which they were shared by the hashers who were "getting to the women."

THE BITS

Inside the kitchen, horseplay was the order of the day, with episodic food throwing and water-splashing bouts, word fads, running "ingroup" jokes, and general zaniness. The sets of activities that the hashers referred to as "bits" were particularly significant. A bit was a relatively organized session of play-acting, originally arising spontaneously, and having a central theme and roles for each of the hashers. During the bit, everything in the work setting—people, actions, and utensils—would be made part of the scene, and the hashers would adopt the argot relevant to the situation enacted. For example, the bit for one work session staged the kitchen and dining room as a hell ship, with the hashers cast as the mutineers, sorority women as "powdered pirates," and the cooks as "Ahab" and "Bligh." Knives became "harpoons," the dinner meat became "salt horse," going out into the dining room was "walking the plank," one buxom sorority sister became the "treasure chest," and so on. In another session the kitchen was part of the Third Reich, with cooks "Goebbels" and "Goering" sending the hasher "Pots and Pans Panzer Corps" out to face the women, who were cast as "storm troopers" and "girdled Gestapo." Serving the food was making a "Blitzkrieg," chicken was a "Luftwaffe Loser," and "bravery under fire" while in the dining room was rewarded with lettuce-leaf medals at an "awards ceremony." Bits, if contagious enough, would go on for more than one work session or even more than one day. Often the same bit would be recurrent, returning for replay every few months and year after year (such as the science fiction or horror movie bit, the gangster bit, and the western hero-villain bit).

The bit served a number of functions for the hashers. It was, not unlike the therapeutic applications of psychodrama, an opportunity for a legitimized expression of hostility. It served also as a distraction from the repetitive drudgery and potential boredom of the hashers' work tasks, allowing them, in effect, to be more creative and expressive while on the job. Furthermore, the bit, affecting the hashers' enactment of an interconnecting and interdependent set of fantasy roles, tightened the cohesion of the informal work group. As one hasher said, not without pride, "When we've got our own laughs going for us, this job is no sweat." Finally, the hashers welcomed the clearly defined and uncomplicated roles of the bit. Even if the play-acting roles were acknowledged as fanciful, they were less ambiguous, less conflict ridden, and less distasteful than their actual work role.

Despite the salutary effect of bits and other behaviors intended to offset role conflict, the hashers rarely went through an entire workweek without stating their intentions to quit the next week. In the sorority we observed, the threats to quit the job totaled about five a day. Furthermore, each new workday brought with it the stated challenge to "finish up faster than yesterday, and get the hell out of here."

On those nights when the sorority members brought male guests to dinner, the hashers were especially belligerent. They venomously commented about the women's dates—"I wonder if she's paying him a flat fee, or by the hour." "God, she must have robbed a grave to get him!" On such occasions, the role conflict of the hashers was exacerbated, since they must wait on college *couples*. Some hashers flatly refused to work on those occasions. Some agreed to work in the kitchen, but refused to wait on tables.

REPRESENTING THE SORORITY

Our interviews and observations indicated that the role conflict experienced by hashers, and their reactions to it, were typical of the hasher-in-sorority situation, though the degree of conflict and defense varied from house to house. Our interviews also revealed that two hasher groups entered intramural athletic contests as representatives of their sororities, but the remaining six groups steadfastly refused to do so. The key variable appeared to be the degree of status differentiation in the house—those with more rigid "class" lines, emphasizing the hasher-college man role conflict, were not represented. The two sorority houses whose hashers participated in intramural sports were more egalitarian in hasher-member interaction.

The social distance between hashers and members was less a function of the size of the house than a function of its relative status on the campus. The "loser" sororities had a greater need to maintain role differentiation within their houses than the "top" sororities. That relation was difficult to assess and is cautiously suggested, considering the techniques used in this study and the fact that the work setting of the hasher was affected by other variables, such as the managerial styles of the house mothers and the cooks. However, in *all* houses we investigated there was evidence of social distance between the hashers and the members, of hasher role conflict, and of the hashers' need to abate that conflict.

CONCLUSION

The sorority hashers experienced intense role conflict. The behavioral expectations associated with being a hasher and with being a male college student were contradictory. Hasher work was perceived to be dirty, demeaning, not very masculine, and decidedly lower class. Furthermore, the job demanded that they maintain considerable social

distance, and take orders, from a group of college women. The hashers'
behavioral expectations as college men were exactly the opposite. They
saw themselves as individuals deserving of clean, prestigeful, masculine, and at least middle-class work. Their sex-role socialization, and
the dictates of the current male stereotype (the sixties) urged that they
not be socially distant or take orders from coeds.

The hashers needed to work in order to pay their way through
college. Part-time employment was hard to get; consequently, students
did not have the luxury of picking and choosing among several available jobs. Being hashers, though unpleasant for them, was better than
no job at all. Furthermore, the hashers' strategies for dealing with the
role conflict not only abated that conflict but in some ways became
fun. Those strategies, like the secondary adjustments aboard the Naval
vessel (Chapter 3), became part of the informal work organization. It is
not uncommon in work and other social settings for creative role
adjustments to become more than defensive reactions. They and the
group cohesion that supports them become sources of personal satisfaction in themselves (Allport, 1961).

The sorority house we directly observed engendered particularly
acute hasher role conflict. The hashers were rigorously "kept in their
place." That house was not among the most popular on campus, but
the members were trying hard to make it so. Social organizations that
are "on the make" to enhance their public prestige generally insist on
rigid internal status hierarchies, thereby increasing the possibility of
role conflict among those individuals at the bottom of the hierarchy.

The hashers dealt with the role conflict in several ways. They readily
supplied excuses or "accounts" (Scott and Lyman, 1968) for continuing in the job. Those accounts usually referred to how being a hasher
actually helped them enact their preferred role of college male. The
hashers effected a vocabulary of motive (Mills, 1940) to explain their
work to others in a way that deemphasized its negative aspects. They
developed a demeaning language with which to describe the sorority
members, usually involving animalistic labeling. When the members
used hashers as initiation objects for pledges, the hashers countered by
using that same event to initiate new hashers into their informal work
organization.

The sorority kitchen was an inner sanctum for the hashers. It was a
backstage (Goffman, 1959) in which the hashers could be themselves
and could create behaviors that offset the role conflict. Inside the
kitchen, the bits were the most elaborate and innovative examples of
hasher autonomy. Bits were imaginative minidramas that included new
and fanciful temporary roles for the hashers. Those invented roles not

only distracted the hashers from the real role conflict they were experiencing, but were enjoyable to enact.

The sorority hashers created new roles for themselves, and distanced (Goffman, 1961b) themselves from the unacceptable aspects of the hasher job. They manifested considerable autonomy in a situation where a rigid work role was expected. In so acting, they ameliorated the conflict between the hasher and college man roles and the conflict between how they perceived themselves and how the sorority women perceived them. Many of their innovative responses were hostile, involving aggressive acts against the sorority members. They replaced feelings of anger and frustration with those of humor and vengeance. Autonomy does not always take a positive turn. Sometimes it is primarily cathartic, allowing little more than an expression of frustration associated with role conflict; other times it is purposive, serving instrumentally to restructure the social situation so as to eliminate the role conflict once and for all (Zurcher, 1970). The direction of autonomy, like other human behaviors, is determined by the characteristics of the social setting, by the kinds of interactions that take place in the setting, and by the kinds of socialization experiences the actors bring to the setting.

The hasher example also reveals that role conflict is not only situationally but historically and culturally bound. Much of the hashers' difficulty was caused by how they, as creatures of the United States in the 1960s, defined the role of college male. Today, the unfounded assumption that men should dominate women, in work or otherwise, has been challenged and is melting away. But, as in all episodes of social change, accustomed role expectations die hard. Women and men continue to experience gender-related role conflicts, and respond to those conflicts with both cathartic and purposive autonomy.

6

MODIFYING A ROUTINE ROLE
Passengers in a Commercial Airplane

Contemporary urban society contains a network of "people pipelines"—social and physical channels in which large numbers of human beings are processed through an organization, usually a bureaucracy or a total institution. The Naval recruit training center discussed in Chapter 3 is a good example of a people pipeline. For other examples, consider how clients are processed through the unemployment, welfare, selective service, health, or educational systems. They are directed from station to station in order to register, be treated, be served, or be informed. Managers of those systems, supported by an extensive collection of rules and regulations (Weber, 1968; Blau, 1963; Merton, 1968), make every effort to maintain the efficiency of people pipelines. The clients in the systems are expected to conform to their processee role (Kohn, 1971; Hummel, 1982; Argyris, 1957; Abrahamsson, 1977). If assigned identity numbers, they are to use those rather than their names. If advised to wait patiently in line for processing, even if for several hours, they are expected to do so.

People pipelines often are traversed by "encapsulated groups" of persons. Encapsulated groups are collectivities of individuals who vol-

This chapter is a rewritten and expanded version of my previously published paper, "The Airplane Passenger: Protection of Self in an Encapsulated Group," *Qualitative Sociology* 1 (January 1979): 77-99. Used by permission.

untarily or involuntarily are clustered together in close proximity by ecological constrictions, mechanical boundaries, or equipment design for the purpose of attaining some goal or reaching some destination. Though they share physical closeness, they are not necessarily a socially cohesive group. Passengers in urban transportation systems (Davis and Levine, 1967) constitute encapsulated groups: airplanes; cruise ships; buses (Nash, 1975); trains, subways (Levine et al., 1973); trolleys; car pools (Adler and Adler, 1982); shared limousines and taxicabs (Davis, 1959); and, to a lesser extent, elevators, escalators, and moving sidewalks (Wolff, 1973).

Being a passenger involves specific role expectations. Depending on the mode of transportation and the restrictiveness of the people pipeline, the expectations can be more or less extensive. Passengers on cruise ships are expected to conform to elaborate dress codes, meal schedules, and social programming. Passengers in elevators can accommodate that role by such simple behaviors as facing forward, speaking quietly, not smoking, and not deliberately intruding on the space of others.

Commercial airplane passengers are processed through a tightly controlled people pipeline and, when they are aboard the airplane, are members of a very constricted encapsulated group. The behavioral expectations associated with the passenger role are extensive and restrictive. This chapter will outline those expectations and will describe how people maintain some degree of autonomy by making as well as taking the passenger role.

In each of the past 15 years, I have averaged between 10,000 and 100,000 passenger miles on commercial aircraft. During my enactment of the passenger role, I kept detailed field notes, especially from 1975 until 1978. I also conducted more than 100 informal interviews with airline personnel and experienced airplane passengers.

THE PROCESS OF PASSENGER ROLE ENACTMENT

The airplane passenger role involves much more than flying on the airplane. It consists of several stages, each of which presents specific behavioral expectations. Those stages include making reservations, arriving at the airport, checking in, boarding the plane, taking off, flying and landing, offloading, and departing from the airport. Though passengers are actually in an encapsulated group only when aboard the aircraft, the stages before and after the flight serve to phase the passenger into and out of encapsulation.

Making Reservations

Having decided to travel by air, customers must initiate contact with the airline in order to reserve space on the appropriate plane or planes. The reservation can be made directly by phoning the airline or by going to its ticket counter. It can be made indirectly by enlisting the assistance of a travel agent. A phone call to an airline is likely to be answered by a recording, politely notifying the caller to wait until a reservation clerk is available. A visit to the ticket counter is likely to involve waiting in line, while agents help others work out the details of itinerary and ticketing. Both phoning and personal visits to a ticket counter place customers in a subservient position vis-à-vis the airline, a posture that sometimes, especially during heavy traffic periods, seems like having to petition for the privilege of enacting the passenger role and entering the encapsulated group.

The use of a travel agent puts an arbiter between customers and the airline, eases their entry into the encapsulated group, and postpones the time when they will have to engage the passenger process directly. However, placing themselves in the hands of a travel agent can mean that customers do not make key decisions about aspects of the trip, especially if they do not know enough about air travel to provide the agent with detailed requests. Most potential passengers have little knowledge of air travel. Whether they are directly contacting the airline or using a travel agent, most people know only where they want to go, the date they wish to leave, the class of accommodations they wish, and the approximate times of day they prefer for flights. Those are the only instructions they give the airlines or the travel agent. Though efforts are made to assign customers the most direct and economical itinerary, choices concerning airline, routing, kinds of planes, and where layovers will be are made by the reservations clerk or the travel agent.

The procedure for making a reservation indicates to customers that engaging the passenger role and entering the encapsulated group is no casual process. They give their names, addresses, telephone numbers, and possibly credit card numbers, linking some essentials of identity to the airline. Tickets, if purchased when the reservation is made, may be mailed or given directly to the customers. They are official documents, indicating a mutual pledge that space in the encapsulated group will be made available to the passengers and that they will occupy the space. Reservations, if made well in advance of the flight, are to be confirmed by customers before takeoff. If they do not make the flight, and do not notify the airline of that intention, they are negatively labeled as "no-shows." Customers do not have to make reservations in advance of the flight, but can choose to buy tickets at the airport shortly before takeoff time. If no space is available, they can purchase tickets, agree to be "standbys," and wait around hoping that there will be enough reservation cancellations or "no-shows" to reopen the possibility of entering the encapsulated group.

Unless customers take steps to the contrary, the reservations phase of engaging the passenger process imposes passivity and status degradation upon them (Garfinkle, 1956), thereby diminishing personal autonomy. Preentry procedures into encapsulated groups typically impose such conditions on new members, justified on the grounds of the need for control, safety, or protection.

How do potential airplane passengers protect their autonomy and avoid passivity in the reservation phase? They do so by acquiring as much information about flight alternatives as necessary to allow them to take initiative concerning the specifics of their reservations. Some possess their own copies of the *Official Airline Guide*, which lists all scheduled airline flights, including types of aircraft, connections, times, costs, meal service, stopovers, and extra services. Others have collected the flight schedules from various airlines, each of which contains the same information as the *Official Airline Guide*. Armed with that information, they choose the best among available flights. They instruct the travel agent or airline clerk to reserve a specific airline, class of service, and flight number.

Once the reservations have been made, customers have with greater or lesser deliberation and control begun the process of passenger role enactment that will end in membership within the encapsulated group aboard the airplane.

Arriving at the Airport

Arriving at an airport prior to flight time can be an intimidating and confusing experience, particularly if it is a large and active airport. Scores and even hundreds of taxis, limousines, highway buses, shuttle buses, trucks, odd-shaped specialty vans, police cars, rental cars, private autos, and shuttle trains zip around a giant, circular pattern of overhead and underpass roads. The scene is a people pipeline orgy. Clusters of vehicles gather in front of the passenger unloading and loading zones. An explosion of signs greets potential passengers, demanding careful navigation, lest a missed turn lead them to the wrong terminal building while minutes tick off toward flight time and anxiety rises. Passengers who drive their own cars to the airport and leave them there for the duration of the trip must locate and use a parking area and then get themselves and their luggage to the terminal. People who elect to travel to the airport by rental car, bus, limousine, or taxi must consider which of those alternatives is best from the standpoint of economy, convenience, and speed. Those considerations differ according to the airport construction, location, and size. The use of public transportation to arrive at the airport can involve potential passengers in an earlier encapsulated group that can facilitate transition to the ultimate encapsulated group within the airplane.

Once passengers get to the appropriate terminal entrance, another scene of crowded confusion is encountered. Throngs of people rush in all directions, seemingly purposefully. Travelers mass around a blurring assortment of ticket counters, shops, restaurants, snack stands, information and insurance booths, rental-car counters, luggage conveyors and carousels, bars, amusement centers, shoeshine stands, lockers, restrooms, and telephone booths. Urgency, transiency, and impatience seem to characterize the travelers, and to set the stage for the role behavior of passengers. Within that milieu, they must negotiate a path to the check-in counter of the desired airline. They then take places in line with other potential passengers and wait to be processed (Mann, 1969, 1970; Mann and Taylor, 1969).

It is not unusual for people pipelines, especially at the points of entry, to be sites of hectic activity and pressing urgency. Individuals seeing such places for the first time perceive a strange and chaotic world and, if entering that world, are at a loss concerning "correct" role behavior. Witness, for example, the thronging confusion at train stations, ship piers, bus terminals, and hospital emergency admission rooms.

The entry points into an encapsulated group can cause individuals to suffer what Wallace (1957) has called "mazeway disintegration." The predictable social world, a relatively certain maze of known rewards for known role behaviors, is replaced by a maze of unfamiliar proportions and expectations. Autonomy is suspended by lack of information and the necessity to conform to an unfamiliar pace of activity.

How do potential airplane passengers cope with the pressure of mazeway disintegration associated with their arrival at a busy airport? Most learn by stumbling about an airport a few times, making mistakes that cause them inconvenience, discomfort, and perhaps a missed flight. For example, they choose a parking lot a half mile from their check-in counter, and stagger the distance with their luggage. They

rent a car from an agency that is housed thirty minutes from the
terminal, when they have twenty minutes to catch the plane. They ride
a limousine that makes numerous delaying hotel stops before arriving
at the airport. They scurry frantically from ticket counter to ticket
counter in Terminal A, looking for the Aardvark Airlines check-in
point, when Aardvark has its counter in Terminal C. From experiences
such as these, by strategic questioning of seasoned passengers, and in
some cases by deliberately reconnoitering the airplane terminals, they
learn to protect their autonomy in various ways:

- traveling "light" (taking only a minimum of luggage, preferably a hanging
  bag and an underseat bag, or some other kind of flight bag that does not
  have to be checked and is not awkward to carry hurriedly);
- if extensive luggage is necessary, making maximum use of "red caps" or
  "sky caps" (porters) who will handle and check the gear;
- scheduling arrival at the airport a full hour in advance of flight time, to
  accommodate contingencies;
- learning shortcuts in the check-in procedure in the event of unavoidable last
  minute arrival at the airport (for example, going directly to the flight gate
  for check-in);
- knowing the fastest, most convenient, and/or cheapest mode of transportation to a given airport;
- having alternative methods of getting to a check-in point if a shuttle system
  breaks down;
- knowing which airlines and airports have curbside check-in stations, thus
  avoiding crowds at counters inside the terminal;
- knowing which airlines and airports provide check-in service directly at the
  flight gate, and if that service is available to passengers with luggage to be
  checked or only to those with carry-on luggage.

The passenger informed about these matters will have taken the
most personally comfortable route to the airport, will upon arrival
stride in the most parsimonious manner directly to the appropriate
check-in point, and will knowingly take a place in line with other
fidgeting potential members of the encapsulated group.

Checking In

Unless circumvented, the official check-in procedure is in two
stages: first, the terminal ticket counter; second, the flight gate. At the
terminal counter, passengers exchange tickets for boarding passes,
learn the flight gate number and boarding time, and, if necessary,
check luggage. At the flight gate, they gain entry into a waiting area by

showing the boarding pass to a watchful clerk, and may be given a seat assignment or a general assignment to a smoking or nonsmoking section in the aircraft. Between the terminal counter and the desired flight gate, the passengers probably have to navigate a glut of tunnels, inclines, stairways, concourses, flight gates, and waiting areas—again amid throngs of other arriving and departing passengers. Somewhere in transit from counter to gate, they will be electronically screened for metal objects and, if suspect, be physically searched by security guards. Hand-carried luggage items will be X-rayed and/or inspected for weapons or explosive devices.

The checking-in procedure varies considerably from airport to airport, depending on the size of and traffic in the facility. Sometimes, as mentioned above, curb service enables customers to check luggage, acquire a boarding pass, and go directly through screening to the flight gate. Sometimes boarding passes and seat assignments are made at the terminal counter. Occasionally checking-in procedures are conducted at the flight gate.

Whatever the staging of the checking-in process, the passengers are monitored and examined by a series of uniformed officials, who are mediators (Goffman, 1961a: 136-137) easing people into the encapsulated group. The boarding pass, the document that identifies the individual as an actual passenger, enables passage through layers of human and mechanical protection around the airplane. Such tokens are commonly demanded in order to gain entrance into guarded organizations, for example, identification cards, badges, code words, cardkeys, uniforms, handprints, voiceprints, official orders, permission "chits." From the terminal counter inward toward the airplane and the encapsulated group, the restriction to admit "passengers only" becomes more intense. Only those appropriately designated and cleared can become members of the encapsulated group. Eventually, passengers reach an area where they can communicate, if at all, with nonpassenger "see-ers off" only by waving over barriers or through glass partitions. Prior to that time, their farewells have been similarly exposed to public scrutiny, perhaps limiting the expressing of emotion and most certainly intruding on intimacy (Weitman, 1970; Goffman, 1967; Schwartz, 1968).

The checking-in process can be disconcerting to neophyte passengers. "I felt like I was on a crowded assembly line, being stapled, bent, folded, and mutilated," reflected one bewildered first-timer. "I can't really remember moving my feet, except that they were tired. I just seemed to bounce from one check place to another, and got lost a few times. But then I would show some airline man my pass, and he would direct me, until after about ten miles of walking, I finally got here to this Gate 15 waiting room. It all seems so automatic and impersonal, I feel kind of numb." Passengers can go through the entire checking-in process without exerting any autonomy at all. They simply flow with the lines and the moving crowds. Their luggage is separated from them. They absorb the boarding time and gate number, and are verified with a boarding pass. They accept seat assignments without expressed preference, except perhaps to proclaim themselves smokers or nonsmokers. They take their seats placidly in the waiting room, and remain there until instructed to board the plane, even if the room is jammed and uncomfortable or the plane is delayed. Novices entering an encapsulated group can be numbed into passivity.

Though only a few people object to the security precautions taken in airports, their privacy nonetheless is challenged when security guards closely scrutinize personal belongings—items usually shielded from the public and contained in identity kits such as purses or attache cases. "We used to get things like vibrators, porno books, prophylactics, and bottles of booze in carry-on luggage when the inspection system first began," laughed a security guard. "And stuff like that would make the passenger blush like hell, or try to make off that the bag was somebody else's. It was hard for us to keep a straight face. Now, you don't get many things like that. People are putting the interesting stuff into their big luggage and checking it through at the counter." It is difficult to maintain an accustomed "front" (Goffman, 1959) when some official is going through your dirty underwear looking for a pistol or hand grenade. The situation is ideal for status degradation and conducive to embarrassment (Goffman, 1956; Gross and Stone, 1964).

It is also embarrassing, and a challenge to autonomy, to be visually and electronically surveyed when walking through the metal screening device—especially if the detector alarm is triggered by your presence. "Christ, I felt like a goddamn criminal," protested a transgressor. "The machine was screeching like I had a tommy gun in my armpit, or something! Everybody in the place was eyeballing me, wondering who this bomb-carrying crazy was. All because of my cigarette lighter!" Novice passengers often walk stiffly and nervously through the screening device, feeling even more clumsy and self-conscious when they have to go through again because of having been too close to the previous examinee or having gone through too quickly for the reaction time of the indication meter. If they do trigger the alarm, they are asked to spread their legs and raise their arms, while officials intensely screen them with a handheld metal detector, in full view of other waiting passengers, until the offending piece of metal is found. If the officials are not satisfied, the passenger can be taken to a closed room and asked to disrobe at least partially for search.

Passengers may defend themselves against challenges to autonomy that operate in the process of checking into the encapsulated group in the following ways:

- knowing the fastest check-in route in a given airport, and using it;
- being aware that the shortest line is not always the fastest, even if labeled "express," and being able to read cues that reveal when to change lines (for example, when the clerk reaches for the *Official Airline Guide* or the information phone, when the customer has a list of itinerary items on a piece of paper, when the customer is arranging flights for several persons, when an animal is being ticketed, when a child traveling alone is being ticketed);
- if not able to travel "light," making certain that checked luggage is well identified, and inspecting destination tags to ensure they are correct;
- knowing the general layout of the terminal, including the locations of multiple concourses and gates;
- learning how to read the schedule displays quickly in order to determine and verify gate number, flight time, and possible delays or changes;
- learning how to read unobtrusively behind-the-counter TV monitors that, if available, often give more up-to-date flight information than the public schedule displays;
- having at least a general idea of available alternative flights in the event that the ticketed flight is delayed or cancelled;
- knowing how to use the courtesy phones to get flight information and to notify friends or family of delays or cancellations;
- having an assortment of quarters, dimes, and nickels available for entrance fees to terminal shuttles and toilets, and for phone calls (sometimes the passenger can contact the ticket desk for a change in reservations or for updated flight information faster by phone than by direct approach);
- avoiding carrying metal objects large enough to trigger the metal detectors, and pacing progress through the device smoothly and properly spaced from other passengers;
- knowing the general seating configuration of the various aircraft in order to make an informed, preferential seat assignment (for example, if a non-smoker, getting a seat the farthest distance from smoking sections; getting an aisle, window, or bulkhead seat, or one near an emergency exit or over a wing; getting a seat in the best position for the movie, or near the galley where service would be more immediate; getting a seat on the shady side of the airplane, or on the view side, for a particular flight; ordering the preferred seat by actual number whenever possible);

- if no seat assignment, watching for cues that indicate imminent boarding, and moving toward the boarding exit in order to get on the plane among the first passengers, thus enhancing the possibility of getting a preferred seat (cues include departure of the food service and luggage vehicles from the plane, check-in clerks sorting through the standby tickets, and check-in clerks taking the passenger manifest to the senior flight attendant for review);
- avoiding the crowd in the waiting room by finding a nearby vacant gate and settling in until flight time and all others have boarded (if assigned a seat) or shortly before flight time (if open seating);
- taking goodbyes from persons without public scrutiny by using empty, uncompleted passageways (almost all large airports have new construction under way), or by taking such leave outside the terminal and entering the passenger process solo.

One certain way of ensuring relative privacy while waiting for a flight is to pay the yearly fee for admission to the "members only" room that some airlines have in larger airports. Flying first class generally widens the chances for acquiring a preferred seat in the aircraft, since that section is usually less crowded. A passenger may gamble on being assigned to the first-class section when possessing a coach boarding pass by stalling until all others on a crowded flight have been assigned seating or have boarded the aircraft, and rushing to the check-in desk before the standbys are assigned seats or have boarded. The result of this gamble can be, however, arbitrary assignment to something like the middle seat in the coach smoking section, when a nonsmoker.

Passengers sometimes attempt to flaunt social standing in the status-degrading process of checking in and waiting. They conspicuously display their first-class boarding passes even when no official is checking them, sport studiously casual travel clothing, and prominently display expensive or "in" hand-carried luggage (such as lizard-skin attache cases, leather and canvas flight bags, crushproof underseat cases with tiny, fold-out wheels and a pull strap for transport, hanging garment bags with monograms, club insignia, and travel stickers).

All of these actions and bits of knowledge help passengers "work the system" (Goffman, 1961a: 212) to some personal advantage in the process of entrance into the airplane and encapsulated group.

Boarding

By the time passengers have reached the waiting room, they have passed successfully through a consecutively tightening series of peripheral areas and staging procedures preliminary to entering the encapsulated group within the airplane itself. They are ready, if not impatient, to get on with the processing and to enter the encapsulated group. When called to board the plane, passengers will walk in orderly single file across or up a ramp or stairway and will officially be "on board." Their passes will have been rechecked by clerks or flight attendants at both ends of the boarding entrance, and then become obsolete except in the case of contested or duplicated assigned seating or when departing and reboarding the plane at stopover points. Physical presence in the encapsulated group now identifies the person as a passenger.

If seating has been assigned, knowledgeable passengers have already taken whatever steps possible to acquire a preferred seat among the encapsulated group members. But if the seating is "open," passengers must engage in a competitive exercise to find and occupy a preferred seat. Within the confines of narrow aisles and low ceilings, passengers hurriedly maneuver around luggage, packages, airline personnel, open overhead racks, and fellow passengers who have already staked their claims and are partially blocking aisles while removing coats, stowing gear, and settling in. As the plane fills with people, the problem of seat choice for the "have nots" becomes more intense. It is then not so much the case of where, but next to whom does the individual want to sit. Conversely, the "haves," those who are settled and have vacant seats next to them, become vulnerable to being joined in close contact by another person who will invade their personal space. The few minutes during which appraisals and cues are generated, exchanged, or avoided between the seated and the seat seekers represent a concentrated period of symbolic interaction. Novice seat seekers quickly disengage from the interaction and seize the nearest of the increasingly few remaining seats. They consequently may find themselves enduring a four-hour flight unhappily bathed in the juicy attention of a rambunctious two-year-old, unwillingly regaled by the incoherent monologue of a gregarious drunk, or uncomfortably breathing the pollutants generated by a chain cigarette smoker who has not made the mistake of sitting in the wrong section.

The novice seated passengers may inadvertently invite seat seekers to occupy the vacancies next to them by radiating unintended invitational cues, and thereby sacrificing comfort and privacy. Or they may structurally create a positional situation that actually facilitates a seat seeker's moving into their turf.

The defense of privacy (Schwartz, 1968) and maintenance of some control over immediate environment are two of the keenest, earliest, and most persistent tasks facing incoming members of an encapsulated group. Personal space, such as there is of it, is carefully and sometimes harshly protected (Sommer, 1969; Dorsey and Meisels, 1969). Knowledgeable and experienced passengers attempt to discourage seat-seekers, and thus protect privacy, through various defensive acts:

• Taking the aisle seat and making themselves (legs, arms, and other sprawlable parts), their possessions, and lowered tray tables (covered with papers, reading materials, etc.) a bulwark that seat seekers would have to negotiate in order to take the inside seats;
• taking the middle seat in a bank of three, and sitting there stolidly, with apparent resolution not to move to the aisle or window seat;
• placing garments, briefcases, reading materials, and/or packages on the adjoining seats or in the floor space in front of the adjoining seats;
• pulling up arm rests to confuse the seat demarcations; pulling down the middle seat back, thus converting the three-bank to two-bank seats;
• placing an "occupied" sign on the adjoining seats, or responding "yes" or "I'm holding it for a [imaginary] friend," to "Is someone sitting here?"
• staring blankly at the eyes of seat seekers or avoiding eye contact altogether as they approach the immediate area (look-away glances seem to be the most conducive to invasion behavior);
• after the aircraft door is closed, assessing the distribution of seating and if necessary moving to a new, more desirable location;
• taking a place in the nonsmoking section even if a smoker on the assumption that nonsmokers are less obtrusive to personal space.

These protective behaviors are serviceable either in first-class or coach sections, although the need to defend personal space is less in first class.

Occasionally, a passenger will elect dramatic behaviors in order to maintain optimum seating privacy within the encapsulated group:

• looking suggestively at each passenger (regardless of sex) who approaches the immediate area, with the expectation that such effrontery will be discouraging;
• lying to a check-in clerk or flight attendant about having a "lung ailment" or other physical malady that necessitates preferential seating;
• holding an opened airsickness bag plainly in view, effecting an expression of nausea, and attempting to give the impression of potentially violent and visible wretching.

There are times when passengers will want some other specific person to sit by them, in order to get to know him or her. Or they may enjoy talking with others during the flight. In such instances, and in situations where passengers simply do not care one way or the other, defenses will not be established. If two or more persons are traveling together, then the defense of seating area, and the whole passenger enactment process and entry into the encapsulated group, can become a shared effort (Goffman, 1959).

After the passengers are in their seats, and the sealed plane begins to taxi to the runway, those who have successfully defended their personal space from seat seekers can be seen to remove the protective barriers and to "set up house." They are, as are the other passengers, ready to take off.

Taking Off, Flying, and Landing

When the door to the plane has been closed and locked and the move to the runway has begun, the passengers are fully committed to membership in the encapsulated group. Unless there is an emergency reason to return to the gate, the encapsulated group will remain intact until the termination of the journey.

As the aircraft taxis, the flight attendants use the loudspeaker system to socialize the passengers concerning the rules for seat belts and backs, tray tables, gear stowage, smoking, safety and emergency procedures, and personal movement around the cabin. They also announce the schedule of in-flight activities (meals, movies, music, and other special events).

The takeoff is a noisy and often bumpy period, during which every person in the encapsulated group is expected to attend to the seriousness of safety and the reality of potential danger. It is a time of maximum passenger restriction and the period during which passengers are most interpersonally quiescent. Most of the passengers sit braced in their seats, either looking straight ahead or watching the ground fall away from them. The thrust of the engines and the inclination of the climb to flight altitude make it difficult to concentrate on matters or behaviors other than those related to the takeoff itself. It is a dramatic demonstration of the fact that the passengers are indeed in an encapsulated group.

When the aircraft has sufficiently cleared the ground, the captain turns off the no-smoking sign, thus affording the smoker passengers an opportunity to elect the first easing of takeoff restrictions. The takeoff phase of the flight is officially ended when the captain turns off the seat belt sign, and a flight attendant announces that passengers are "now *free* to move about the cabin." With that statement, the takeoff restrictions are removed for all passengers. They can drop their tray tables, recline their seats, loosen or unfasten their seat belts, go to the lavatories, and so on. The captain may at this time announce the general flight plan and advise the passengers concerning other in-flight expectations (keeping seat belts loosely fastened, attending to any further instructions from the cockpit, and sitting back and having an enjoyable trip).

The rapid routine of in-flight activities now begins. The longer the flight, the more involved the routine. As members of the encapsulated group, passengers are expected to participate in the routine. The flight attendants structure the environment and socialize the passengers toward that end. The pattern of drinking, eating, watching, listening, and moving is dictated by the flight attendants.

The serving of beverages and meals, especially in a crowded plane, reveals the intensity of scheduling that can exist in the encapsulated group. At its most extreme, as in the case of an evening meal in the first-class compartment during a capacity two-hour flight, passengers are challenged to devour as many as seven courses of food and beverage in rapid succession. From hot towel to finger bowl, not much more than thirty minutes passes. Flight attendants have been known to compete with each other in setting record times for preparing and serving meals to passengers. During that procedure, passengers are expected to be passive and compliant. "I sometimes wish," sighed a flight attendant, "that all the passengers could be tranquilized or hypnotized or something, so they would sit quietly, do what we tell them, and let us serve them without hassle."

Airplanes and passengers fly at all hours of the day and night, and major airports operate actively around the clock. The passenger role in the encapsulated group can demand that the individual remain awake and functioning at times of the day usually reserved for sleeping (Schwartz, 1970). More importantly, flight itineraries can demand that passengers endure long layovers in airports, long periods in lined-up aircraft waiting in turn for takeoff, and long periods in stacked-up aircraft circling in holding patterns while waiting in turn for landing. Travel can be a disheveling experience, even in a relatively rapid mode such as flying. Clothing can be rumpled by hours of cramped seating. Planes are often stuffy and smoky, causing one to feel grubby (Largey and Watson, 1972). Hair is disarrayed in windy airport gates. Beards grow shadowy and scratchy as the trip lengthens. "Faces" become messed. Unaccustomed muscles are strained by hurried runs, with hand luggage, to make flight times or catch connections. Ears are "popped" and sinuses disturbed by altitude changes. Body clocks are disturbed by "jet lag" and time-zone changes. The passenger in the encapsulated group is expected to accommodate such strains on personal appearance and physical senses.

Despite the rigorous routine, the in-flight phase provides passengers with the freest period during membership in the encapsulated group, the time when they have the most opportunity to exercise autonomy. However, the freedom available to all makes the individual passenger vulnerable to intrusions on privacy (Dorsey and Meisels, 1969; Goffmann, 1967; Stebbins, 1972). Friendly neighbors, especially at cocktail or meal times, may want to talk with the individual, or may inadvertently intrude by other behaviors, the style or consequences of which can be disconcerting to the person (Coser, 1961). Or the individual may attempt to initiate interpersonal contact with a neighbor or neighbors, or effect unintentionally offending behaviors, earning an embarrassing rebuff (Sagarin, 1973; Gross and Stone, 1964; Goffman, 1956).

There are several ways by which passengers fend off unwanted attention from neighbors in the encapsulated group. They demonstrate a close interest in working or reading, feign sleep, plug themselves into the stereo system, or emit curt responses to inquiries or statements that cue the neighbor to cease attempts. Passengers enacting rejection behaviors attempt to maintain their "stranger" status (Simmel, 1950; McLemore, 1970; Schutz, 1944; Wood, 1934).

Other passengers might deliberately invite attentions from neighbors by passing gum at takeoff, helping neighbors with assorted "getting settled" behaviors, volunteering or querying about useful flight information, and using cocktail or meal settings as opportunities to initiate contact. If mutual interaction is established, they can effectively sustain either "no-name" social contact or open the relationship to an exchange of names and, perhaps, opportunity for contact outside the encapsulated group in flight.

Passengers manifest that they are not novices and distance themselves (Goffman, 1961b: 45; Levitin, 1965) from expectations that they be passive passengers in the encapsulated group by:

- showing complete familiarity with the aircraft equipment used by passengers (such as air vents, lights, tray tables, sound consoles, seat belts and backs, underseat stowage, closets, overhead racks, lavatories);
- carrying out flight routines and instructions *in advance* of instructions from flight attendants;
- nonchalantly continuing to read or otherwise not paying attention to takeoff safety instructions and illustrations;

- ignoring the members of the cockpit crew who come back to the cabin for perfunctory visits;
- continuing other activities rather than watching the movie (suggesting that they have already seen the film of the month on previous flights);
- casually using techniques to equalize pressure disturbances to their ears;
- refusing drinks or meals or courses until ready for them (within the confines of the service time, the limits of which are shown to be known);
- asking about the content of the meals (and type of wine, if available) before accepting them, and then refusing those items that are not desired;
- unashamedly fixing the cloth meal napkin (if offered) to their chest areas by the small buttonhole in the napkin corner, thus demonstrating knowledge of its purpose and utility;
- prominently displaying their personal copies of the American Passenger Association magazine;
- ignoring travelogue comments announced by the cockpit crew (suggesting they have seen those sights many times before);
- instructing the flight attendants to have the cockpit crew check by radio concerning connections made close by flight delays;
- knowing and utilizing the "free places" (Goffman, 1961a: 230) for informally interacting with flight attendants or for getting more direct service (for example, the galley, or the lounge), and avoiding the "out-of-bounds" places (Goffman, 1961a: 228) for such interaction (such as the cockpit or the aisles);
- knowing how to walk in the aisle during flight, even in turbulence, without appearing physically clumsy.

These activities are enacted effortlessly, unostentatiously, and even inadvertently by experienced passengers in the encapsulated group as they effect the social construction of reality at 37,500 feet (Berger and Luckman, 1966).

Occasionally, passengers are observed to be trying to impress flight attendants and other passengers with their knowledge and experience. They seem to identify with the flight crew and thereby remove themselves from the role of mere passenger (Goffman, 1961a: 226). As "pseudo-pilots" they inform their neighbors, with or without invitation, about flight routine and such events as the noises associated with retracting or extending landing gear, the "smoke" and moisture emitted by the air conditioning vents as a result of condensation, the reason for contrails, and difficult flights they have experienced and survived. They overuse airline argot: "Hey, stew, will you get me the OAG so I can check to see if our ETA into LAX will fit with a ride at about 20 to SAN?" With this burst of jargon, the passenger is asking a female flight attendant to provide the *Official Airline Guide* so that the passenger can determine if the estimated time of arrival of the present flight into Los Angeles International Airport would be soon enough to arrange a connection with a flight that would leave at about twenty minutes past the hour for San Diego International Airport. Such passengers often offer public critiques of the cockpit crew's performance on takeoff and landing and on plotting the plane through turbulent air conditions.

Some passengers in the encapsulated group express autonomy by complaining vociferously about the aircraft accommodations, the food, drinks, service, and virtually all aspects of the flight. They do what they can by harassment and order issuing to reduce the status of the flight attendants to that of menial laborer, and thereby enhance or protect their own prestige. Others engage in such secondary adjustments (see Chapter 4) as conniving to get more than the maximum two alcoholic drinks allowed, smoking cigarettes or marijuana in the lavatories, concentrating on a systematic attempt to "date" a flight attendant, stealing silverware, dishes, or whatever from the plane, deliberately disobeying flight norms and crew instructions, and getting drunk. Secondary adjustments are easier to effect in first class than in coach sections, but are not as demanded by the situation—the greater freedom mitigates the need.

Flying in commercial airplanes involves some risk of death or injury through accident, though statistically less so than other major forms of public transportation and certainly less than personal automobile. Many passengers are nervous while the plane is airborne; some are quite nervous. The anxiety level of passengers generally is highest at takeoff, least high while in flight, unless there is turbulent weather, a known mechanical problem, or delays in a "holding" pattern, and high at approach to landing. Takeoff and landing are the two most dangerous of the routine phases of flying.

Passengers can deal with flight anxieties or boredom by chemical means (alcohol or tranquilizers) or by such other distractions as losing themselves in work, stereo music, card games, conversation, reading, or the movie. Experienced members of the encapsulated group usually bring with them enough material to distract them gainfully for twice the scheduled length of the flight and thus are prepared for delay contingencies. Some passengers face fear of flying head-on, without distraction devices, and experience a "white-knuckle flight." Gallows humor often constitutes part of the preflight conversation among passengers in the encapsulated group who are friends or passengers with see-ers off. The catharsis of expressing anxiety in humorous or even horror stories may be helpful to some passengers, and gives them some sense of confronting and controlling fear.

At some point during the plane's descent toward landing, passengers are ordered back into harness, literally, by the captain. Seats must be taken, seat belts fastened, tray tables locked, seat backs raised, and hand luggage stowed. Headsets, glasses, cups, and other service implements are retrieved. The freedom provided within the encapsulated group in flight is now revoked, and maximum control of passengers returned. Flight attendants inspect for compliance to the instructions.

After the plane has landed, the flight attendants warn all passengers to remain seated and strapped until "the captain brings the aircraft to a complete stop at the gate." Thereby, passengers are given notice that although the plane is on the ground they are still members of the encapsulated group. But thank yous and good-byes are expressed by the attendants, and announcements made concerning the local time, temperature, and offloading procedures, heralding the end of that membership.

Offloading

The aircraft arrives at the gate, and terminating passengers scramble to gather up their gear, put on coats, and jam into the aisles to wait in a jumbled line for offloading. Novice passengers usually conclude it is important to stand in cramped positions and form an aisle crowd in order to hasten their getting off the plane. More experienced passengers remain seated, further exerting control in the encapsulated group. They know that it takes time to attach or extend the offloading apparatus, and prefer to wait in comfort. Furthermore, they know that it is easier to gather up gear and negotiate aisles after the crowd has thinned. The amount of time lost is on balance negligible. If experienced passengers have a close connection to catch, they tell the senior flight attendant, who positions or guides them to the exit in advance of other passengers' opportunity to leave their seats. The more seasoned members of the encapsulated group also are able to determine, or know beforehand, when offloading will be accomplished through more than one door or through a rear door, and time or position themselves accordingly.

Those passengers who are continuing aboard the aircraft for another leg of the flight usually are advised by flight attendants to stay within the encapsulated group. If time permits and they insist on leaving the plane for a while, they must take their boarding passes with them and place an "occupied" sign on their seats. The boarding passes again take on a significant identification function, this time for reentering the encapsulated group. Unless the delay before takeoff is unduly long, or some exigency exists, experienced passengers do not leave the plane. They know that the reboarding process will cast them in with the crowd of new passengers, since all must board together. Reboarders receive no precedence. Furthermore, even though they have placed an "occupied" sign on their seats or on some other seat to which they have decided to move, they realize that those seats might be "jumped" by new passengers who board before them.

As the terminating passengers troop out the door and leave membership in the encapsulated group within the airplane, they are reviewed for the last time by the flight attendants and perhaps by members of the cockpit crew.

Departing the Airport

At the foot of the stairs or the end of the ramp, passengers often are directed by airline agents toward the appropriate route to luggage, ground transportation, or connecting flights. Experienced passengers may know or be able to determine faster alternative routes, through whatever crowds and networks of gates and passageways, and make an autonomous move toward where they want to go. They also know the general procedures for getting cabs, limousines, rental cars, or helicopters—and which is best in this specific airport or city. They know how to find their way quickly off the airport grounds in personally driven automobiles.

In a strange airport of larger size, passengers again are thrust into a melee of hurrying people, but the processing-out procedures usually are faster, less complex, and less confusing than the processing-in procedure. Arrows and signs guide the flow of passengers to common exit areas.

Those passengers with luggage to pick up must wait in the baggage area for the airplane cargo to be unloaded. Then, abruptly, they will begin to scramble for their own pieces appearing on conveyor belts, carousels, or cluttered racks. Experienced passengers avoid the fray by giving their check stub to a porter who will get the baggage forthwith and truck it to a convenient place, by waiting until the anxious crowd thins and it is easier to get the luggage, and by standing close to the point where the luggage first is deposited for retrieval. In many airports, guards inspect check stubs against tagged luggage before allowing passengers to take their gear outside the baggage area. That will be the last credential investigation, unless customs is involved, of the passenger role enactment process and the airplane encapsulated group. After that, the person is no longer a passenger, and leaves the airport. Those passengers who did not have luggage to recover will have shed that role as soon as they left the gate area and entered the terminal proper.

Passenger status can be sustained longer than persons want if their luggage has been lost. Dealing with airlines can continue for several days until the gear is found and returned. This possibility, and the opportunity for greater mobility and alternatives, are the primary reasons that seasoned passengers travel light and if possible avoid checking luggage. But if they do lose luggage, they are aware of the time limitations for recovery beyond which the airline must furnish reimbursement for lost possessions.

Persons who have connecting flights maintain their passenger role, and stay within the inner regions of the airport terminal, although they are not at the moment members of the tightly encapsulated group aboard the aircraft itself. But airport terminals, especially larger ones, are virtually self-contained, and can be conceived of as extensive encapsulated groups. Indeed, it is possible to travel completely around the world, even conduct overnight business meetings at stopovers, without ever seeing more of the cities or the countries than the inside of the airports. Those passengers will soon enter yet another encapsulated group, their connecting airplane, and will repeat the later phases of the passenger enactment process. Experienced passengers ensure that the number of plane changes they must make is minimal and, if changes are mandatory, confine them to the same airline or to one in close proximity to their previous offloading point.

When persons are on the outbound leg of a round trip, they take with them out of the airport the second half of their tickets. In a sense they have become passengers "on leave" from the encapsulated group. Shortly, they will reenact the entire process of entry into the passenger role. The airline will want to know, when they confirm their tickets, where they are staying during their visit. Their ground transportation may even be linked to the airport terminal by arrangement.

People generally leave airports as rapidly and as directly as they can. They have families to join, appointments to keep, vacations to

begin. Their reasons for having subjected themselves to me~
the airplane encapsulated group and for accommodating t
role are no longer operating.

CONCLUSION

As a matter of course, citizens in urban societies enact member roles in the people pipelines of powerful bureaucracies. Those roles usually include the expectation that the enactors will passively and compliantly be processed through the system—for example, students enrolling at a university, clients applying for welfare or unemployment benefits, patients entering a hospital, customers ordering a telephone, and potential draftees registering with selective service. Urban transportation systems are particularly good illustrations of people pipelines. Individuals enact the passenger role because they want to travel somewhere.

Some people pipelines contain encapsulated groups. Encapsulated groups are collectivities of individuals who voluntarily or involuntarily are clustered together in close proximity (though not necessarily socially cohesive) by ecological constricitons, mechanical boundaries, or equipment design for the purpose of attaining some goal or reaching some destination.

Airplane passengers were processed through a people pipeline and, when they were actually aboard the plane, were members of an encapsulated group. Enacting the passenger role involved several stages: making reservations; arriving at the airport; checking in; boarding the plane; taking off, flying, landing; offloading; and departing from the airport. Each of those stages contained elements or conditions that fostered passenger passivity. Novice passengers, feeling confused and unknowing, generally acquiesced to the processing. They let others or the established procedures make decisions for them. They compliantly took the passenger role. Experienced passengers usually engaged in behaviors that gave them greater autonomy in the people pipeline and the encapsulated group. That autonomy particularly concerned choices or activities that enhanced privacy, personal space, comfort, convenience, and prestige. Sometimes they distanced themselves from the passenger role, sometimes they manipulated it. They tended actively to make rather than passively to take the role.

Being an airplane passenger involves a routine role conducted in everyday life. There is nothing very dramatic or unusual about it. It, like most roles in people pipelines and encapsulated groups, is so ulturally and historically commonplace that it is taken for granted. However, such roles often are much more complicated and demanding than people notice (Garfinkle, 1967; Mehan and Wood, 1975; Cicourel, 1968). They contain many behavioral expectations, some of which limit the freedom of the actors. Those actors, when they have the requisite knowledge and the opportunity to examine the behavioral expectations in light of their own preferences and self-concepts, modify even routine roles in such a way as to maximize autonomy.

7

FILLING A ROLE VOID
Volunteers in a Disaster Work Crew

Sometimes people are suddenly and involuntarily thrust into situations in which nearly all of their usual role enactments become inoperative. A calamity of some kind disrupts the social structure in which they occupy positions and, consequently, causes a role void. Routine behavioral expectations become muddled. The ability to predict and control events or interactions becomes problematic.

Community disasters, whether natural or human-made, are examples of role-voiding calamity. The social fabric of the community is shredded by such disasters as earthquake, flood, tornado, explosion, fire, or environmental poisoning. One's usual work and community roles, unless disaster related, are temporarily suspended. Leisure roles are rendered irrelevant. Family roles usually remain intact, but take on a situational urgency related to safety or survival. Direct victims of the disaster are of course the most seriously affected, but those community members who were not victims still experience role disruption.

Depending on the kind and extent of the disaster, the community sooner or later returns to normal. Physical structures are rebuilt and social structures are reestablished. The usual everyday roles again operate routinely.

This chapter is a modified version of my previously published paper, "Social Psychological Functions of Ephemeral Roles: A Disaster Work Crew," *Human Organization* 27 (Winter 1968): 281-297. Used by permission. Not for further reproduction.

When disaster strikes and everyday roles are temporarily voided, people in the community, according to some observers, seem to run amok. Their responses are confused, uncoordinated, undisciplined, and maladaptive (Glass, 1959; Crawshaw, 1953; Tyhurst, 1951). Other observers have concluded that disaster behavior, although it may seem different from everyday activity, actually is just as purposive, organized, and adaptive (Quarantelli, 1960, 1977; Quarantelli and Dynes, 1977; Drabek and Stephenson, 1971; Taylor et al., 1970).

In Chapter 6, novices in people pipelines and encapsulated groups were described as being confused about appropriate role behavior. More experienced individuals were able to establish autonomy, control, and predictability in those settings. Boots in the recruit training center (Chapter 2) and sailors aboard ship (Chapter 3) followed the same pattern; the more they knew about the system, the more autonomy they were able to exert.

This chapter will outline how some individuals who lived in a community ravaged by a tornado created temporary disaster roles, thereby filling a role void and putting a sense of order back into their social worlds. The example of a disaster volunteer work crew will illustrate that people, no matter how severely their routine role sets might be disrupted, can innovatively maintain personal autonomy, control, and predictability. If the usual role-supporting social structures are fractured, they inaugurate new ones. Those innovations serve not only the self-concepts of the stricken individuals, but facilitate the reestablishing of predisaster social structures.

At 7:15 p.m. on Wednesday, June 8, 1966, a full-scale tornado ripped along a diagonal midline from the southwest to the northeast corner of Topeka. There were 17 people killed, 550 injured, and 2500 rendered homeless. Property damage was estimated at over $100 million.

Though in "Tornado Alley" and a part of the U.S. Midwest's "cyclone culture," Topeka had not previously been struck by tornado. The community was profoundly shocked and disrupted by the disaster. Local formal organizations first were stunned, then were mobilized. Disaster relief agencies began functioning. Recovery activity began immediately for search, rescue, and first aid to victims. That activity, conducted in collaboration with police, fire, civil defense, and National Guard personnel, was completed about 12 hours after the tornado impact. Subsequently, in accordance with Wallace's (1957) "cornucopia theory" of postdisaster events, volunteer help and contributed materials began flooding the community. An ad hoc emergency relief organization evolved from the surge of altruism (Taylor et al., 1970).

During its 14-day life span, the relief organization coordinated the work of approximately 10,000 volunteers and distributed tons of food, clothing, and household items. Many of the volunteers joined the disaster recovery efforts as members of such social entities as religious organizations (for example, 2000 Mennonites), military bases, fraternal and civic organizations, towns and cities neighboring Topeka, and the Job Corps. In addition, there was an undetermined number of spontaneously formed work crews that functioned for various lengths of time and were not associated with the emergency relief organization.

The volunteer work crew I studied represented those groups that: (1) had not been formed prior to the disaster; (2) were at least loosely associated with the ad hoc emergency relief organizations; (3) consisted of Topeka residents from areas outside of the tornado's direct path and whose homes had not been destroyed or seriously damaged; (4) were composed of individuals with no preemptive role obligations to help relatives, friends, or neighbors. Exact figures were not available, but it was reliably estimated that 25 such crews, averaging about 8 members each, existed during the course of the recovery effort. The volunteer work crews (hereafter called VWCs) did not emerge until Friday morning, June 10, almost 36 hours after the storm's impact. Apparently, before individuals could form a VWC, they needed time to assess primary role obligations and to verify the safety of relatives and friends. Once that was done, they had the opportunity to address their own role voids and to act accordingly.

I gathered data about the volunteer work crew as a participant observer and by informal interviews with crew members and other pertinent actors. The interviews were conducted within three weeks after the crew had disbanded. At the time, I was residing in Topeka, the tornado-stricken community. Though not a direct victim, I lived three blocks from the tornado's destructive path. During my participation in the crew I kept detailed field notes. Until after the VWC was dissolved, none of the other members knew that I was observing and recording the group processes. I cannot claim to have been a dispassionate and detached observer nor originally to have joined the VWC for data-gathering purposes. It is more accurate to say that I, as one of the people who enacted the role of VWC worker, happened also to be interested in how role voids are filled.

THE VOLUNTEER WORK CREW

The VWC of which I was a member was organized at 10:30 a.m. on Friday, June 10, in the "headquarters" emergency relief organization.

Table 1   The Core Members of the Volunteer Work Crew (VWC)

VWC Role	Days Worked*	"Civilian" Occupation	Age
Contactman	1, 2, 3	social psychologist	30
Climber I	1, –, 3	heavy equipment operator	48
Sawman I	1, 2, 3	civil defense employee	31
Climber II	1, 2, 3	undergraduate student	20
Monsterman	1, 2, 3	house painter	40+
Roper I	1, 2, –	extension worker	38
Rigger	–, 2, 3	writer	25
Roper II	–, 2, 3	clinical psychologist	43
Sawman II	–, 2, 3	commodities inspector	50+
Monster Assistant	–, 2, 3	house painter	40+

*1 = Friday; 2 = Saturday; 3 = Sunday.

It disbanded at 7:20 p.m. on Sunday, June 12. Membership in the VWC ranged from four people (when the crew formed) to fourteen (mid-Saturday). Ten individuals were "core" members who remained with the VWC during at least two of the three working days. The group worked in a low-income residential section of Topeka. The primary task was to remove fallen tree limbs and trees from a total of more than forty houses.

A list of the ten core members of the VWC, the days on which they worked, their ages, and their "civilian" occupations are presented in Table 1. Each member is identified by the VWC work role he enacted (all were male). I was Contactman.

In interviews, all of the VWC core members expressed feelings of restlessness and a need for *action* of some sort after the tornado struck Topeka. This urge to activity has been well documented. Moore (1958: 313) cites the prevailing sentiment following disaster—"For God's sake, *do something!*"—and adds that the demand for activity was met not only on an impromptu basis, but subsequently in more organized and directed ways. Menninger (1952: 129) describes the vague feeling, personal threat, and keen desire to want to do something—anything. He sees this urgency as a tension state from which people seek some outlet and suggests that the nature of a postdisaster assignment is of little importance as long as individuals feel that they are doing something. Several other writers have reported similar observations (Wolfenstein, 1957; Janis, 1958; Withey, 1962; Kardiner, 1941), some emphasizing that the urge to act varies according to the degree of involvement in the disaster, particular personality characteristics, and the length of time from disaster impact.

The feelings of unrest and the urge to act can be interpreted as a response to what Taylor et al. (1970) have called the postdisaster "role moratorium." People want to fill the void that has resulted from the catastrophic disruption of their usual roles. They want to reestablish some semblance of social order and solidarity for themselves (Turner, 1967).

The members of the VWC converted the urge to "do something" into direct action. They created and enacted a set of temporary roles that offset their disaster-induced role void. The temporary roles emerged in and through the VWC, as a result of interaction among its members, during the three-day period of its existence.

THE FIRST DAY

By midmorning on Friday, the individuals who would become Contactman, Climber I, Climber II, and Sawman I were feverishly cutting, hacking, and pulling at the debris on and around homes near the Emergency Relief Center. There was little conversation beyond asking for a tool, or for help with a too heavy tree branch, or to share a curse. Two young men quietly drifted in, were acknowledged by a nod, worked for about half an hour and then left, their departure as inconspicuous as their arrival. Their visit had no noticeable impact because the men were not a group in any organized sense at this stage. They had come to the Emergency Relief Center because it seemed the place to go and "do something." But the center was not yet established enough to guide their action, so they had gone outside and begun to clear debris.

The four individuals worked fiercely in proximity with one another, but their interaction was minimal and entirely incidental to the task of attacking the mounds of debris around them. Climber I recalled: "My arms were aching quite a bit, because I hadn't used an axe in a long time. But I didn't care. It was worth it to see the chips fly." Climber II later noticed a long scratch on his forearm, and wondered how or where he had got it. Contactman remembered

feeling exhilarated by the hard physical activity, and pleased by the fact that I was sweating profusely . . . almost the same kind of feeling one gets when, after a period of nervousness before a football game, he charges into the game and plays hard. . . . I was using a small saw for some time, and suddenly I discovered I couldn't release my grip on the handle; my hand had cramped into a clenched fist.

Sawman I noticed that "rather than let the tools do the work, we were in there bending our backs and working harder than necessary." The opportunity for uncomplicated and physically difficult labor, particularly when the work served in some way to "fight back" at the tornado's awesome damaging power, was cathartic for the VWC members on this and the following days. Rigger, who joined the crew the second day, remembered "the work felt good. It felt the way I wanted it to feel, and I could allow myself to respond to the whole range and texture of feeling that I had denied myself since the tornado."

"Attacking" the debris was, for the four men, a way of testing their capacities, of redefining destruction they could not stop into destruction they could in some way control. Their "irrational," disorganized, and unsystematic battle with fallen tree limbs matched what to them was "irrational," disorganizing, and wanton tornadic devastation. Uncomplicated and rigorous physical tasks have been observed by others to have therapeutic value for individuals emotionally affected by disaster (Menninger, 1952).

Though the men were at this time "doing something" as individuals, it was comforting to be working in the presence of like-actioned others even if names were not exchanged and verbal communication was minimal. "If I had been working all by myself," commented Sawman I, "I would have felt kinda foolish, maybe, trying to do something alone with all that mess. Having the other guys there made me feel sort of stronger, I guess." Contactman was reminded of "the fear you sometimes feel when standing watch alone on a black night at sea—a fear that vanishes when you remember there are unseen shipmates around you." Tyhurst (1951) suggests that during recoil from disaster, group behavior is based on the urge to seek out and be with others to meet dependency needs rather than for the sake of forming stable groups. The dependency is associated with the need to ventilate, to get angry, and to express oneself in some way. Membership in the VWC, particularly during the first day, provided both a channel for catharsis and the comforting proximity of others. The proximity afforded the opportunity to create temporary roles.

In the early afternoon, the VWC members hurriedly ate a lunch of sandwiches and coffee from a roving Salvation Army van and returned to work. About an hour later, Contactman, trying to find some larger handsaws, walked the short distance back to the Emergency Relief Center. A bright yellow civil defense wagon, rigged with an A-frame winch, was parked there. Contactman found its yellow-helmeted driver, and the VWC core membership was expanded by one.

The power wagon had a marked impact on the VWC. First, it expanded the scope of operations beyond walking distance. The truck was also equipped with useful tools, cables, ropes, and an extension ladder. With its A-frame winch, it could lift or drag tremendous chunks of debris far beyond the members' individual or collective strength. Quickly dubbed "the Monster" (hence the driver's title of Monsterman), the machine became part of the VWC's cathartic activity. Roper II, who joined the crew the next morning, commented:

> I felt that, like working with the crew, the crazy machine was at least partially an equalizer to the damage that had been done. I think that's what we felt, all of us—that singly, what the hell, a tree on a guy's porch is more than a match for us; but given this piece of equipment we could, instead of working with helpless anger, pull those goddamn trees out of the way and get them off people's houses and porches. This was an outlet to the helpless feeling that you have when you see so much desolation.

Contactman recalled:

> It was very clear that the machine had been anthropomorphized by us, and was really another member, a rather formidable member, of our work crew. When the Monster was straining at a heavy load, we would shout encouragements to it and help it by tugging on ropes we had tied to the debris. If it were successful, and it always was, we would run over to it and pat it on the hood or slap it on the roof and fenders. I remember comments about the Monster lifting trees whose weight was beyond the winch's rated potential—I think we felt the Monster, like the rest of us, was being tested beyond its limits, and it gave us confidence, somehow, in seeing it succeed.

The power truck provided the VWC with a focus for more organized groupness. The members developed in functional work roles around the best utilization of the machine. Consequently, toward the end of the first work day, there was a rudimentary division of labor. As a job neared completion, Contactman would scout in advance of the truck, spot homes endangered by debris, and speak with the owners. Monsterman drove the truck and operated the power winch. Climbers I and II scrambled on rooftops and up trees, setting the hook of the winch. Sawman I moved in with his power saw whenever rapid cutting was needed. Roper I, who joined the VWC late that afternoon, affixed guide or hauling ropes whenever necessary. If any member was not, at the moment, performing his specific work task, he would carry, clear, lift, or pull as the job demanded.

Though anonymity was still in practice, verbal communications markedly increased as the afternoon wore on. This increased interaction was stimulated by the presence and performance of the Monster, by the experience of evolving and defining work roles, and by the decreased need for more isolated and personal vengeance on the tornado. The hours of physical labor and the encouraging ameliorative power of the Monster served to reassure and reorient, at least in part, threatened and confused individuals. They could look beyond the haze of their own emotions to the individuals with whom they were working. The VWC was reaching the point when, as Rigger later interpreted, the members "were far enough removed from their initial response, or lack of response, to the tornado so that they could feel free to work together and be together and form a group together now."

At 7:45 p.m., the VWC received word that the mayor had established an 8:00 curfew, and all volunteers had to be out of East Topeka by that time. Monsterman protested, "But we're just getting going now. Why do we have to quit! There are some spotlights on the truck." Roper I complained, "We just start getting something done and some lousy regulation stops us." The group immediately discussed plans for "getting the same guys together tomorrow." The first hour generally agreed upon was 7:00 a.m., but because of transportation problems, the crew settled for 8:00 a.m. Begrudgingly, they packed up and went back to the Emergency Relief Center.

As the sunburned, grimy, and sweaty crew members entered the center, they became aware of the striking difference between their appearance and that of the inside office volunteers. Looking at his torn clothing and at his fatigued comrades, Climber I laughingly remarked, with pride and satisfaction, "We look more like disaster victims than volunteer workers!" The startling contrast and the attention and comments from non-VWC volunteers served to support group identity. The members separated briefly to put away tools, wash up, and get in line for food. However, one by one, they headed for the same table, where they began to talk excitedly about the challenges the day had brought and how they and the Monster had met the challenges. They teased each other about being "so out of shape that you won't show up tomorrow." After the meal, when the members were leaving, they polled each other, making certain of the time and place for tomorrow's meeting. It was agreed that in the event anyone was late, Contactman would leave word at the center's front desk about the VWC's location so that the prodigal member could find, as Monsterman put it, "where he belonged."

THE SECOND DAY

By 8:30 Saturday morning, Contactman, Climber II, Roper I, and Monsterman had tools and were ready for work. Friday's other two core members, Sawman I and Climber I, had not yet arrived. Though there was discussion about waiting for them, the group decided to "leave word and shove off."

Three new core members joined the VWC as preparations for work were being made on the second day: Roper II, Monster Assistant, and Sawman II (see Table 1). In addition to them, three other helpers, among them Roper II's son, asked to come along and stayed with the crew for part of the day. These and other noncore VWC members will be referred to as "ancillary" members.

The VWC had a particular work location in mind. Toward the end of Friday, they had noticed a three-story house with an enormous tree blown over onto, and in some places through, its peaked roof. The owner of the house had asked the crew to help him the next day, and they had agreed it was "a job with real challenge." Upon arriving at the site, the crew looked the problems over more carefully, trying to determine where to begin. The task was awesome as the tree was at least 75 feet high, had a circumference of about 8 feet, and was heavy with twisted, broken, and dangling limbs. It had been blown onto the house with such force that part of the wooden frame structure had been moved an inch or two from the foundation. Most of the tree's roots had been ripped from the ground, and the house seemed to be providing the major support for tons of tree. The VWC members were impressed by the danger of the job and the delicacy required to prevent further damage to the house. Bravado was set aside as the crew members made imaginary cuts here, winch pulls there, and calculated the angles of fall.

During these moments of planning, Sawman I arrived and was warmly welcomed by Friday's core members. "I was really afraid I wasn't going to be able to find you fellows," he said, and then looking up at the tree, added, "God, you sure picked a winner, didn't you!" Rigger (the last of the core members to join on the second day) heard about the VWC from people at the center. He found the crew, was welcomed into their deliberations, and began verbally sketching a system for segmenting the tree into small chunks (from the top down) and lowering them by winch cable and rope, using the lower branches as booms and pulleys. The crew decided the procedure was "worth a try" and to "give it hell!" Extension ladders were set, and the Monster was moved into position.

As the hours went by, the functional work tasks and the associated temporary roles became sharper and more familiar. Contactman contacted, Climber II climbed, Rigger rigged, Sawmen I and II sawed, Ropers I and II roped and guided, and the Monster tugged and lifted—successfully. Great pieces were cut from the tree and guided to the ground without further damage to the house. As each segment hit the ground, often after much straining and many "close calls," the VWC applauded themselves, the Monster, and the boom-pulley technique, which by then was institutionalized as "Rigger's Law."

The cathartic activity of the day before was shaped into role behaviors, and the associated expectations stimulated the evolution of specific positions within the group. The division of labor crystallized, and with it group cohesion and solidarity increased. Having created functional roles for themselves in the VWC, the self-confidence of the members was bolstered, and their feelings of control over the environment were reassured. The activities of the VWC—shouts to one another, scrambling in trees and on rooftops, the roar of the Monster's engine, the screams of the two power saws, the thuds of axes, and the crash of falling branches—attracted the attention of neighbors and passersby. Though at this time there was little interaction between them and the VWC, the presence of onlookers further firmed the group as an entity. If any member was asked who he was, he identified himself as "a member of this volunteer work crew" rather than by name or "civilian" occupation.

Late that morning, five uniformed Boy Scouts (actually two men and three boys) joined the VWC as ancillary members. Upon arrival, the Scout leader, looking for an assignment, shouted, "Who's the straw boss of this outfit?" Most of the VWC members turned to look at the uniformed inquirers momentarily but continued their work. Contactman, who was the closest to being an informal foreman, set down the branch he was carrying with Roper I and explained, "We're a team; there is no straw boss." Monster Assistant added, "That's right! We've got too much to do. We haven't got time for straw bosses!"

With that introduction, the Scouts began piling the fallen branches and clearing the yard. Though they worked as hard as any core member, they remained alien to the group (as did, to a lesser extent, all ancillary members). Their uniforms identified them as members of another social order in the world "out there" beyond the VWC. The Scouts seemed satisfied with and confident in their customary, predisaster role. By their very presence they inadvertently seemed to be imposing their predisaster organization, confidence, and satisfaction on the VWC members who wanted to evolve and were evolving their own roles and organization. The Scouts wanted to locate the typical structure and know where the boss was. The Scout leader was puzzled by Contactman's failure to introduce himself as "a doctor from the Menninger Foundation" (a fact that the Scout leader had learned from another ancillary member). Later, the Scout leader suggested that "the crew split up, half to stay at this place and finish up, and the other half to move on." This was a sensible suggestion from the logistics viewpoint, but it was protested by the VWC core members. The Scouts, who could easily divorce themselves from the VWC, moved on freely anyway.

Though never fully accepted by the VWC, the Scouts further defined group boundaries and roles. At the same time, the Scouts, highly formalized and smacking of secondary associations, were reminders that eventually the temporary VWC roles would phase back into broader and more complex community roles.

At lunch time, the VWC members got sandwiches and coffee from a Red Cross food truck near the work site, and sat on the freshly severed chunks of tree to eat their meal. By now, some of the anonymity of the individual members had faded. Many of the core members used each other's first names. Last names and "civilian" occupations were unknown except in those few cases where core members had been acquainted before. What was clearly known by all was the temporary role of each individual. Roper II observed:

We, you know, felt so close . . . I think we learned a way of working, you know, like the guy who could drive the Monster. There was the driver and there was the guy who could kind of size up the situation and another guy sort of assumed the task of talking with the people in the house. I think certainly very specific roles emerged that were quite appropriate to what we had to do. It's interesting, I still don't know the names of the guys . . . It didn't seem appropriate to ask . . . It seemed irrelevant.

More bluntly, Sawman I commented about the anonymity:

I felt like, well, I may not know his name but I know that I can rely on him and that he ain't gonna drop this tree on me or something like that . . . the name wasn't important . . . I didn't pay any attention to who the people were or what their status was in the community or anything like that . . . it didn't make any difference.

Anonymity apparently is the rule rather than the exception in disaster recovery. Menninger (1952) noted that social status disappeared entirely in volunteer work crews, and that bank presidents and day laborers worked at the same job side by side. Form and Nosow (1958) referred to the large number of unnamed others who were instrumental in recovery efforts. The anonymity in the VWC reflected the fact that proper names, as identifications in and links with a community complex that was fractured and disrupted, had little meaning. In fact, they served to remind VWC members of the disruption and of their own role void. Another identity, based on the created temporary roles that linked the members with comforting comradeship, growing competency, and a sense of control seemed far more appropriate—at least for now.

The temporary VWC roles were the products of past and present experiences of the enacting members. Accustomed modes of behavior, more on the first day than the second and more on the second day than the third, were set aside. Names and statuses were waived. But as the VWC roles evolved from their initial cathartic function toward more complex social behavior, other past experiences became more relevant. This phenomenon was manifest at lunch on the second day when the group members, most of them veterans, talked about the similarity of some of their military experiences with those in the VWC. They talked especially about their "old outfits" and some of the "gang" they worked for or fought with. They exchanged humorous stories and tales of success under adversity. The emphasis was on aspects of the informal organization of the military and their similarities to the dynamics of the VWC (see Chapter 3). Nonetheless, the temporary roles were gradually being broadened, similarities were being seen with other community roles, and social pseudopods were being extended back into the *status quo ante.*

Still, the VWC members were not yet ready to accept formalization as such. After lunch, the crew returned to work at the site of the massive tree. Contactman went back to the Emergency Relief Center to check on the availability of plastic windows and roof covers for the tornado victims. By this time, the center had become markedly more organized than the day before. Several other work crews now were in the field, and a dispatcher was responsible for their whereabouts. Contactman went up to the dispatcher's desk, was asked the location of the VWC, and was handed a list of names and addresses of people who had called in for help, or whose homes had been assessed by survey teams to be endangered by debris. Contactman was then given a pin and a cardboard badge proclaiming him to be a "Group Leader." He got the roll of plastic he had come for and, outside the center, threw the badge into a trash container, later reflecting, "The badge seemed ridiculous . . . like wearing a necktie in a nudist camp. . . . If I were the group leader, and no one was really, it would have been known to the crew by my actions . . . not by a badge pinned on me by somebody back inside the Center."

At 4:00 p.m., the VWC had completed the job on the huge tree. With comments about "being ready now for anything," the crew moved on to the addresses given to Contactman by the center dispatcher. The first two addresses did not exist. The third was a home completely flattened by the tornado, and the fourth had no tenants. Monsterman complained: "What the hell is with those people back at the Center? Don't they know what's going on?" Sawman I advised Contactman to "throw away that damned list, and let's keep finding our own jobs." "We can't let this crew and the Monster go to waste," urged Rigger, "and we know better than anyone else what we can handle." So it was agreed that the crew would operate autonomously, checking back with the center periodically for emergencies or "jobs that were worth a crew like us." All of the members were happy to be out in the field where they could "really help people" instead of "back where all the red tape was." Of the ten core members, seven initially had associated themselves with formal organizations after the tornado and were not satisfied either with the organizations' response or with their own participation. They found what they were looking for in the VWC, and they did not want it "fouled up by red tape."

The VWC worked on several more houses before the 8:00 p.m. curfew. The jobs were not so dramatic as the first one, but were still difficult, challenging and, according to Monster Assistant, "the way we liked 'em." During this period, an unelaborate but noticeable argot developed along with an increase in humorous exchanges among the members—both indices of growing group solidarity. Monsterman had a seemingly inexhaustible supply of colloquialisms that became part of the crew's work language. Tools, ropes, the cable hook, or whatever was in demand at the moment became a "pea-picker"—for instance, "that pea-picking rope." Axes, in honor of Climber I (a Native American), were "tomahawks." The members kidded each other, particularly immediately before or after a difficult or dangerous act: "Let it fall on your head, then it won't hurt anything!" "Don't worry about scars, you can't look any worse than you already do!" "Let's leave him up in the tree, he looks so natural there!" The humor may appear deprecatory, but by voice inflection, timing, and intent it was supportive in teasing a man out of his fear. Furthermore, the kidding, since no one became angry despite its personal nature, indicated the openness of the members to one another and their belongingness in the group (see Chapters 4 and 5). There was also much general mirth associated with both successes and mistakes. Contactman remembered: "Sometimes, especially at first, we must have looked like the Keystone Kops."

Toward the end of one of the afternoon's jobs, Contactman, as was the pattern, left in his car to locate the next job. Roper II accompanied him. After finding a house endangered by hanging branches and talking with the occupants, they returned to where they had left the Monster, but it was gone! Contactman reported:

> We were stunned by the fact that the Monster was gone, along with the rest of the work crew. The streets were a turmoil of trees, debris, and equipment, and it was difficult to see the entire length of a block. We attempted to search the area by car, but still couldn't locate the Monster. We felt a sense of personal loss, and were genuinely concerned. Finally, after almost half an hour of searching, we spotted the ungainly but lovable shape of the Monster on a street that had previously been blocked at both ends by other trucks. They had moved to get out of the way of power company workers. We hurried to the Monster and our arrival was like a family reunion. We welcomed each other and then everyone was teased about not being able to find the way around in an elevator. The other members had been looking for us, and we for them!

The group had also demonstrated feelings of solidarity and loyalty at lunch when they expressed concern about Climber I, who had failed to show up for work. Sawman I, who arrived a little late that morning, commented: "I was afraid that I was going to be late. I stopped to help some guy cut a little tree off his porch, and it took longer than I thought it would. I hurried, though, because I knew I had to get over to our crew. I didn't want to miss them!"

The modal dynamics of the VWC on the first day had been individual and cathartic; each member took comfort from the presence of the others, but interpersonal interaction was minimal. By the end of the second day, the members had "come out of themselves"; and the group was valued for itself. The modal dynamics then centered around the group's development as reflected in the division of labor, creation of the temporary roles, increased interpersonal interaction, elaboration of argot and group humor, and intensification of core member loyalty to the VWC. Rigger sensitively reflected upon these dynamics:

> After some trial and error, the members of the crew found themselves accepting those particular jobs which seemed to suit either their abilities

or inclinations and, strangely enough, everyone seemed to have a place. . . . My own motives underwent some sort of metamorphosis as the group became more unified. At first, I seemed to be concerned with proving myself . . . in order to wipe out the frustration. . . . As time went on, though, this feeling changed substantially, particularly after the evolution of "Rigger's Law." . . . I found then that I took to the rooftops or treetops not as an exhibitionist but out of an unfamiliar sense of responsibility for the group's success with each project.

The VWC finished its last job that day about 7:45 p.m. It had been a particularly dangerous problem, the tree crushing and yet supported by the front porch and roof of the house. The VWC moved the nine residents, including a man in a wheelchair, out of the building before going to work. After considerable effort, the crew was again successful. The tree, carefully trimmed of its broken branches, was manipulated away from the house and dropped safely with a crash. The members cheered, then noticed the hour and decided it was time to quit.

The decision to stop work was easier than on the first day because the crew was at a good breaking point, having just "finished off a big sucker." They were tired after handling a dozen major jobs in nearly twelve hours of labor, and of course some members had worked the previous day or days. But the most important factor contributing to the acceptance of quitting time seemed to be that today had been a *good* day. The group, as Roper I expressed it, "was swinging." The other members, taking stock of the day's activities while packing their gear into the vehicles, agreed. Sawman I capped the discussion: "Well, there's no job we can't handle now—not after today!" Enthusiastically agreeing with Sawman I, the VWC headed back to the Emergency Relief Center.

As on the night before, the physical appearance of the VWC was in sharp contrast to the inside-office center volunteers. Now, however, there were more workers present from other crews. But the members of our particular VWC again all sat at the same table, laughing and joking as they recounted the day's exploits and "close calls," and compared jobs in terms of techniques and unique problems. A task-oriented group history had accumulated and was being shared and reinforced. As the meal continued, the crew decided to meet at the center by 8:00 a.m. the next morning (Sawman II still argued for 7:00 a.m.) and to leave word at the desk for latecomers. The members encouraged one another to be there. "We better show up," laughed Monster Assistant, "nobody else could stand to work with Monsterman." Sawman I commented more seriously, "It wouldn't be the same working in another crew." "Yeah," Climber II amended explosively, "who else could make the Monster work miracles!" With that, the VWC members said goodnight, and went home.

During the second day two other interrelated phonemena emerged. The VWC began to delimit more specifically the jobs they would or would not undertake and also began to notice and comment on the reactions of their "clients." These phenomena, indicating that the members were now starting to look beyond the group, would be central to the dynamics of the third day.

THE THIRD DAY

At 8:20 a.m., Sawman II, Roper II, Climber II, Monsterman, Monster Assistant, and Contactman left the Emergency Relief Center for their first job of the morning. Rigger and Sawman I, after checking at the center for the crew's whereabouts, joined the rest about thirty minutes later, and were warmly greeted. Climber I arrived shortly thereafter, explained his absence the day before (had to operate a bulldozer for his employers—"It wasn't like working with the gang here"), and was welcomed back.

Contactman recalled: "The group seemed a good deal more relaxed today, though we set about our tasks with the same, if not more, industriousness." They completed four jobs efficiently in less than an hour—jobs that would have taken an hour each the previous morning and that would have been impossible when the crew was first formed. Sawman I commented: "The third day, well, it just wasn't any work at all. It had become more or less a science by then." The crew worked as a coordinated team around the Monster, and had become quite expert in the application of "Rigger's Law."

The VWC was increasingly selective about the jobs they undertook. Though exceptions were made, especially when victims approached the crew for some special kind of help, generally "our kind of job" was a home: (1) hazarded by broken or felled trees of large size; (2) still inhabited by occupants who wanted help; and (3) where the crew would not "waste its precious equipment on minor jobs," or "waste manpower on small stuff the people could do themselves." The expertise of the VWC was recognized and cherished by the members. They realized that the Monster was a rarity among equipment available for use on private property, and they preferred jobs that maintained the division of labor and the temporary roles they had evolved.

Contactman had a list of addresses given him that morning by the dispatcher at the Emergency Relief Center. When he suggested that the VWC go to some of those addresses, Monsterman complained, "Did you get that list from those guys back there who draw all the pictures and wave their hands back and forth in the air?" The crew laughed, but Contactman explained that the center had become more organized, their surveys more accurate, and that his own earlier scouting indicated that some of the jobs on the list really were "worthy of our group." The VWC thus began to accommodate itself to the center's scheduling, but still insisted, as Rigger emphasized, "We go our own way if we see people who want and need the kind of help we can give." Nonetheless, the ties between the VWC and the center (which in turn was enmeshed with the communitywide disaster effort) were becoming stronger. As a further example, the shortwave radio in Sawman I's panel truck, which was linked with the same radio circuit as the center, was used more on this third day than on the previous two days to inquire about legal, Red Cross, and Public Health aid for victims, and to ask for tools and equipment for the crew or for food, clothing, candles, and plastic storm windows for people in need. The VWC was moving toward increased specificity of purpose and increased formality. It resembled more closely and articulated more fully with secondary associations in the community social complex.

The VWC's increasing awareness of "clients" and their needs was another indication that their attention was expanding beyond themselves as individuals and beyond the crew. Sawman I recalled that Sunday was

> the first time when it had really gotten through to me, when I paid attention to the people relying on us to do the work. . . . The crew was just finishing up one house and was going to move next door. I went over there and plunked my fanny down on the porch to rest for a minute and to work on my saw. . . . I got to talking to the people on the porch and this was the first I had thought about what they were like, those people we helped.

The need for solitary catharsis was gone. The group was solid, the temporary roles were comfortable, predictable, and automatic. The work was more systematized and routinized. Satisfied with themselves and with the VWC, the core members could now look farther afield. They noticed the degrees of gratitude and ingratitude among the tornado victims they helped. They complained about a few instances of exploitation or "being ordered around" by house owners. They became angry at some "big, healthy guys parked on their butts drinking beer while we worked on their houses" and at "that idiot who took movies of us up in his tree instead of helping us." They were touched by "the old lady who cried when we had to cut down the remnant of a tree 'that grew up with the children,'" and by the impoverished family that offered to share with them what they had for their evening meal—a few Red Cross sandwiches. Bit by bit, armed with returning confidence, the VWC members opened themselves again to the broad spectrum of their predisaster roles and experiences.

Late that afternoon, the VWC was proceeding to 123, an address specified by the Emergency Relief Center dispatcher as "a place needing a power winch to move a large tree trunk from a house." Driving a circuitous route around blocked streets, the crew encountered another volunteer work crew from the center. The crews exchanged enthusiastic greetings and brief tales of exploits. "Where are you headed?" the other crew inquired. "To 123," we responded. "What?" protested the other crew. "We were just there, and did a damned good job, too!" Hackles were raised as the two crews, both proud of their accomplishments and perhaps both evolved through the same dynamics, brushed in competition. Contactman hastened to explain that the VWC was going to the house to remove a tree trunk because "we have the Monster, here." "Oh, that's different! We trimmed it all off, but couldn't move the trunk. We got it all ready for you. Good luck!" There was shared laughter again and hearty farewells as both crews, assured of their integrity, moved on toward their respective destinations.

East Topeka was, even more than the day before, a mass of public utility workers—gas, electric, light, water, road, and telephone service vehicles and equipment edged through the streets, their modern machines clearing, repairing, and reconstructing wherever they went. In the midst of such efficiency and power, the VWC became increasingly aware of its ultimate obsolescence. The "pros" were moving in, as the following incident illustrates.

A property owner stopped the VWC on its way to 123 and asked if they would "please cut the branch off up there that's dangling over where my kids like to play." The branch was beyond reach of the crew's extension ladder, the tree appeared unclimbable, and none of the members could throw a rope that high. As the crew pondered whether or not their limited equipment could do the job, a U.S. Forest Service bucket truck came down the street. The VWC stopped it, and the rangers agreed to go up in the bucket to sever the threatening limb. Contactman recorded:

> The forest ranger was lifted with ease by the bucket apparatus and, with quick dexterity and a special trimming power saw, clipped down the dangling branch and several other potentially dangerous limbs in only a few minutes' time. All of our crew stood watching the operation in awe. That job would have taken us almost an hour if we could do it at all, and

the whole while we would have been sweating out ways of manipulating the falling branches away from the house so they wouldn't do any damage.

Roper II remarked, "Look at that guy; he's dropping those branches at the bottom of the tree like stacked cordwood. He's *almost* as accurate as we are." "Well, they may be able to do it faster," argued Sawman II, "but it's a lot easier for them than it was for us. We can be *proud* of what we did!" Rigger added, "They do a good job, but they don't do a *human* job." Monster Assistant laughed, "It looks as though automation is going to put us out of a job!"

The temporary quality of the VWC roles became quite clear to the members, as did the competence and efficiency of a formal organization—competence and efficiency that may have been disrupted by the tornado, but that had now returned for all of us to see. The VWC laughed at its "obsoleteness," but took comfort in the fact that they had been "pioneers," a "crew with a soul," and "the first in the area, before all those fancy tools." The crew agreed that "there's still lots of work we can do without that kind of equipment." They then continued toward the task awaiting them at 123.

At 123, they plotted the cross-cuts to be made and the rope and cable strains involved in removing the large tree trunk wedged into the side of the house. Decisions were made, techniques applied, and within less than twenty minutes "that big sucker" was on the ground. A single shingle was the only additional damage to the house during the removal process. The VWC cheered itself, and Sawman I proudly exclaimed, "Hell, what's left for us now!" But as the crew members eyed the ominously darkening skies and felt the wind quicken, the words lost some of their bravado.

The VWC moved off in search of another job. Spotting the volunteer crew they had met earlier they decided to "handle the big stuff" on the lot where the other crew was working. The crews labored side by side for about thirty minutes. They did not merge, although they exchanged brief comments about their earlier activities. At 6:30 p.m., the other crew left the area.

The weather was getting heavier, lightning was rapidly approaching from the southwest. While Climber II dug through Sawman I's truck for an axe, the shortwave radio crackled a storm warning for the Topeka area, and the mayor used the circuit to discuss with other disaster officials what to do in the event of a tornado siren alert. Climber II relayed the information, posing a dilemma for the VWC, which was then halfway through a hazardous tree. They decided "we

have to finish it, or we'll leave it more dangerous than we found it."
With thunder and lightning all around the crew worked frantically in
the rain. The axes seemed dull, and the saws terribly slow. Climber II,
who had taken up a station by the radio, bellowed, "The military is
moving out of East Topeka; one of their men got hit by lightning." The
VWC worked even more furiously. The tree finally fell to the ground
precisely where the crew had planned, and they moved into further
segment it. Climber II screamed, "The Center has ordered us out of
here—there has been an unconfirmed tornado touchdown just south of
Topeka!" Contactman advised, "That's all. Let's get out." While crew
members hurriedly loaded their equipment, they expressed concern for
each other's safety with such warnings as "drive carefully" and "take
cover if you see a funnel." After brief good-byes, the group split up and
the members went off in several different directions, most of them to
their homes to "look after the family" (Hill and Hanson, 1962; Form
and Nosow, 1958).

Spawned by one tornado, the VWC was hastened toward its demise
by the threat of another that never developed. There were no plans for
getting together the next morning, and the VWC would not meet
again. The group's interpersonal ties did not break easily, however.
Sawman I, Rigger, and Contactman (strangers before the tornado)
visited each other on occasion after the VWC disbanded. During the
interviews for this study, the members talked warmly about their comrades, the Monster, and the group's experiences. All of the members
interviewed expressed the notion that they would have liked to get the
VWC together again the weekend following its disbanding, but somehow they "just couldn't work it out." The temporary roles were no
longer functional. They had done their job, and the enactors, with
renewed faith in themselves and in society, were back in their predisaster community roles. Their innovative VWC roles were now only
something to talk about, or write about.

CONCLUSION

When communities are stricken by disaster, everyday social structures and roles are disrupted. People's self-concepts, since they are
role-bound, similarly are affected. The severity and scope of the disruption depends on the extensiveness of the disaster.

The volunteer work crew members attempted to fill the role void
they experienced as a result of the tornado by creating temporary
disaster roles for themselves. Those roles emerged from interaction

among the VWC members and evolved during the crew's three-day existence, but were influenced by their previously enacted roles (or the failure of them in the disaster setting).

On the first day, the VWC, not yet really a cohesive group, primarily provided the participants with an opportunity to "do something." That activity facilitated a release from disaster-induced feelings of fear and frustration. Since it was conducted in the company of others, it also provided the opportunity for rudimentary interaction among the participants. As the day went on, the interaction became less rudimentary and VWC roles began to emerge.

During the second day, the VWC became a cohesive unit. The members interacted far more fully, confidently, and openly than on the first day. They saw themselves as VWC members, and further developed the work roles they had innovated within the crew. Those roles constituted a division of labor around the task of clearing debris, especially trees, from tornado victims' houses. In support of the temporary roles, and because of them, the crew members developed a sense of group history, loyalty, and humor, and created a simple group-specific argot.

The third and last day in the life of the VWC saw the members refining their division of labor and temporary roles almost to the point where the behaviors became routinized. They broadened their perspectives beyond the VWC, now noticing their "clients," other work crews, and the relation between the VWC and the Emergency Relief Center. The temporary roles had evolved from relatively undifferentiated cathartic activity to the point where the VWC members, sensing the encroaching obsolescence of the VWC for themselves and for the community, could facilely phase back into the everyday predisaster social structures and roles.

The VWC members might have appeared, especially during the first day, "irrationally" to have been engaging in exhausting, overcompensating, and inefficient physical labor. Indeed, the work was hard, but it was rational and purposive both socially and psychologically. Turner (1967) reports that when disaster causes a breakdown in organic solidarity, there must follow a temporary period of mechanical solidarity. Organic solidarity is what is seen in the everyday social organization of urban societies and communities (Durkheim, 1947). It involves an elaborate division of labor and large networks of interlocking statuses and roles. People identify themselves and others in terms of differences among those statuses and roles. Mechanical solidarity is more typical of "primitive" societies, where the division of labor is less complex (Durkheim, 1947). People identify themselves and others not according to differences in statuses and roles, but in terms of their common experiences and feelings of sameness.

After a disaster, according to Turner (1967), there is a resurgence of mechanical solidarity based on the common feelings and experiences shared by people in the disrupted community. If the disaster is severe, people are faced with the task of rebuilding solidarity from the beginning.

The VWC dramatically demonstrated mechanical solidarity for the purpose of social rebuilding. The feeling of commonality among the members was first generated by the shared experience of difficult, undirected, physical labor. As the members created and refined temporary roles, the VWC evolved beyond mechanical solidarity. Over the three days, a division of labor emerged, and with it a prototype organic solidarity that set the stage for the ultimate obsolescence of the VWC and the members' complete return to the everyday urban setting.

Turner (1967: 66) emphasizes that mechanical solidarity must be enacted if it is to serve a regenerative function:

> It is as if people felt called upon to make a display of solidarity and were not satisfied merely with taking its presence for granted. The period of conspicuous mechanical solidarity is not simply an event preceding the reemergence of organic solidarity, but a necessary stage before the division of labor can be reimplemented.

In the VWC, the members invented and enacted temporary work roles. Those roles were malleable enough not only to serve mechanical solidarity, but to support the evolution from mechanical to organic solidarity within a short time span.

When the social systems that support their usual roles are rendered inoperative, individuals autonomously can find ways to make new roles. Those creations not only help the innovators maintain their self-concepts and sense of competence, but facilitate the rebuilding of the social *status quo ante*.

8

ENJOYING AN EPHEMERAL ROLE
Participants in a
Friendly Poker Game

Virtually everybody in any given society enacts a work and a family role. Most people enact a marriage role. Those roles are dominant in everyday life. In addition to work, family, and marriage roles, people also usually elect to enact leisure roles, roles in voluntary groups, and a wide variety of part-time or short-term roles, many of which can be considered to be "ephemeral roles." An ephemeral role is a temporary or ancillary position-related behavior pattern chosen by individuals to satisfy social-psychological needs incompletely satisfied by the more dominant and lasting roles they regularly must enact in everyday life positions.

The notion of ephemeral role assumes that people cannot or do not fully accommodate their own inclinations, or societal expectations, by enacting the dominant roles associated with earning a living, being a family member, or being a spouse. The term "needs" in the definition of ephemeral role is not rooted in arbitrary psychological traits. It refers to the perceptions that individuals have about how they ought to act in order to be consistent with their own self-concepts and with their understanding of the behavioral expectations that other people have

This chapter is a rewritten version of my previously published paper, "The 'Friendly' Poker Game: A Study of an Ephemeral Role," *Social Forces* 49 (December 1970): 173-186. Used by permission.

for them. It also assumes that individuals are inclined to expand their role sets in such a way as to enhance their autonomy and feelings of competence.

In this chapter, I will use a game, specifically a poker game, as an example of an ephemeral role. The players will be shown to have developed and enacted that role because it provided them with satisfactions not readily available in the more dominant roles they routinely enacted.

Games, forms of play with agreed-upon sets of rules, have long been considered by social scientists to assist in the socialization and personality formation of the individual. The structure and dynamics of various games often reflect the values, behavioral expectations, and kinds of social control in a particular culture (Caillois, 1961; Erikson, 1950; Huizinga, 1955; Piaget, 1951; Strauss, 1959; Sutton-Smith and Roberts, 1963; Zurcher and Meadow, 1967; Mead, 1934).

Card playing, and particularly poker, is a popular game in the United States (Crespi, 1956; Lukacs, 1963; Martinez and LaFranci, 1969). Though poker is available in commercial gambling establishments (Bergler, 1957; Herman, 1967a, 1967b; Edwards, 1955), the participants in a friendly game are by no means professional gamblers. Their game is not part of a commercial enterprise. They get together regularly, take their participation seriously, and usually thoroughly enjoy themselves. Theirs is not a work role, as in the case of professional gamblers. Theirs is an ephemeral role, elected because it provides them with satisfactions not available in the more dominant roles of work, family, and marriage. They create and control their role in the friendly poker game.

For twelve months I attended, as a player, the twice-monthly game of a poker group that had been meeting for over ten years. I did not take any notes during the games, nor did I use any recording devices. Though such techniques would have enhanced the reliability of the study, they would have disrupted the games. I outlined my observations immediately following adjournment of the sessions, and dictated a narrative based on the outline within eight hours. The other players did not know that I was observing their role behavior.

I did not join the game in order to conduct research on it. I enjoy poker, and have played in friendly games off and on during most of my life. However, after the first game with this group I felt that the social dynamics of the group and the role satisfactions gained by the players were important to record and analyze. This friendly game was not significantly different from others in which I had played, nor was it significantly different from other friendly poker games. At that particular point in my poker-playing career, it occurred to me that such games might be a special role-making phenomenon.

The day after my last game with the poker group (the day before I left to take a job in another state), I interviewed all the regular players about their reasons for playing, the criteria for selecting and socializing new members, and the development of group rituals and argot. I showed the regular players what I had written about the poker group and asked them to correct any misperceptions.

THE PLAYERS

The seven "regular" players who attended almost every game during the period of my observations were all college-educated, married, professional men: a lawyer, a college coach, a high school coach, an engineer, a sociologist, a social psychologist (me), and an insurance broker. Four had been playing poker together for over ten years, and two others for over five years. They ranged in age from early thirties to late forties, and all were in the middle-salaried socioeconomic bracket. Four had been reared and educated in the midwestern city (population, 125,000) where the game took place, and where all of the players currently resided. When the friendly game first formed, the players had been associated with a small local college. Three of the current players were still employed by the college, each in a separate department. A second common characteristic of the founding members and four of the current members was experience in coaching scholastic athletic teams.

Since three of the regulars had to leave the group because of job transfers or time conflicts, the remaining members were actively recruiting new players. Those invited during the course of my observation included an accountant, a rancher, a sports writer, a high school teacher, and a purchasing agent. I had been brought into the group by the sociologist, who was a co-worker at a local psychiatric research facility.

THE SETTING AND STRUCTURE OF THE GAME

The games were held twice monthly, between 7:30 p.m. and midnight on Monday nights, in rotation at each of the regular players' homes. One of the players hosted the game in a den, the others in dining rooms, kitchens, or spare rooms. Three had purchased green felt-covered poker tables; the others used whatever large table was available. The playing table was surrounded by smaller tables containing ashtrays and bowls of chips and pretzels. Hot coffee and soft drinks were available throughout the game, but no alcoholic beverages were allowed, nor was eating of food other than chips or pretzels. However, after the completion of the "last deal around the table," which started at midnight, the hosting player was responsible for a meal of hors d'ouevres, sandwiches, and desserts.

The evening's leisure was divided into three major components: (1) the informal discussion while waiting for all the players to arrive and the poker chips to be distributed, (2) the game itself, (3) the meal following the game. During the game it was understood that there were to be no "outside" interruptions. There were no radios or televisions playing, no wives serving beverages, no children looking over shoulders. The atmosphere was quite relaxed and the dress casual (although on occasion some of the members arrived in suit and tie following a business meeting). There was no apparent seating preference around the table except that if there was an empty chair, it generally would be next to a new player.

At the beginning of the game each player purchased $3.00 worth of chips (blue, 25¢; red, 10¢; white, 5¢). He had the option to buy additional chips at any time, although frequently cash was introduced in place of chips. The host player was responsible for being the banker, and also responsible for dragging a dime or so out of each pot to defray the cost of the postgame meal. The betting limit was established at 25¢, with a three-raise limit. Drawing "light" (borrowing money) from the pot or purchasing chips by check was tolerated.

The general rules of poker were closely followed, but the games played under "dealer's choice" were more varied than in a commercial poker setting. Use of the joker or naming of "wild cards" was forbidden. Often the draw and stud game were dealt with the stipulation that the high hand split with the low hand, or the high hand split with the low spade. Rarely, low ball (where low hand wins) was played. Each player seemed to have one or two favorite games that he dealt regularly and that were called "his" games by the other players.

BECOMING A MEMBER:
SELECTION AND ROLE SOCIALIZATION

The criteria by which a new player was judged for membership revealed much about the group dynamics and functions. Two regular players reflected about these criteria:

> A fellow coming into the game almost must feel like he's walking into a closed group, because we've been playing together for quite a while. I

guess some newcomers leave the game sometimes feeling "will they ever ask me back again" or "I don't want to play with that bunch of thieves again." Sometimes we have fellows join us who we decide we don't want to come back. In particular, we don't like people who slow up the game, or bad players who get wiped out. They have to be capable of playing with the other players, or we don't want them.

In our game the group is the thing. We invite people in who we think are nice persons, and who we can be friends with. That's the important thing. But he has to be more than a nice person. He has to be able to play poker with the rest of us. It's no fun to sandbag a sucker! So to get invited to sit in regularly, we've got to like the person, and he's got to know what he's doing so that he adds to the game and doesn't subtract from it. The group has to be kept in balance. One dud can throw the whole thing out of focus. Another thing, too. In our group, he has to be able to take a lot of teasing, and maybe give out some too. We have a good time teasing each other.

The new player therefore had to be friendly and experienced enough to learn, compete, and maintain the pace and stability of the game.

Lukacs (1963: 58) has observed that "there are a thousand unwritten rules in poker, and continuous social standards and codes of behavior." The new player was, as a prerequisite of invitation, expected to know the basic rules and etiquette of poker. He was to be socialized, however, in accordance with the group's idiosyncratic expectations. He was to learn the local rules of the game, the style and tempo of play, and the patterned interactions. In other words, he was not going to be taught how to play poker, but how to be a member of this poker group.

Many of the socialization messages were verbal instructions from the regular members, particularly with regard to betting rules, games allowed, quitting time, and borrowing money. Other socialization messages were more subtle, though no less forceful. The player who slowed the pace of the game might hear the drum of fingers on the green felt or an annoyed clearing of the throat. The player who talked too lengthily about a topic unessential to the game might be reminded that it was his deal, or his turn to bet.

The new player would be strongly reinforced for role behavior that conformed to the group's expectations by verbal compliment, camaraderie, or a simple but effective "Now you've got it!" One new player, for example, unwittingly disrupted the group's unwritten strategy, that of killing large raises from a strong hand by exhausting the three-raise limit with nickel bets. Three of the regular players immediately made pleasant comments about the "lack of insurance" in that particular hand. They did not directly admonish the new player for not having enacted his part of the "insurance." When on a later occasion he did

carry out the strategy, he was immediately reinforced by a hearty
"Good play!" from two regular players.

At no point during the entire period of observation did any of the
regulars show overt anger at a new player's violation of group expectations. They did on a few occasions invoke what appeared to be their
most severe sanction, an absence of response, cutting the errant player
momentarily from group interaction. When, for example, a new player
challenged a dealing regular's choice of game, the dealer dealt and the
rest continued to play their cards as if the new person had not said a
word. On another occasion, when a new player angrily threw down his
cards in disgust, two of the regulars quietly gathered them up, handed
them to the dealer, and there was otherwise a total absence of response.
(See Goffman, 1956, for a description of emotionally "flooding out"
from group interaction.) If someone suggested a game he played that
was not in the group's repertoire, he would be met with a lack of
enthusiasm that was more crushing than any verbal negation could
have been.

One of the regular players commented about the "silent communication that takes place" within the group:

> We've been playing together for so long that we can read each other's
> expressions for the opinions that we have about something. If one of the
> fellows who's new or who is just sitting in for the night does something
> out of line, there's a quick and silent communication that takes place,
> and almost simultaneously we know what to do about it. We tease him
> or we give him instructions or something.

Sometimes the regulars united in humorously expressed sanctions
of another player's behavior. One new player had committed the cardi-
nal sin of criticizing the play of regular members. He had also lectured
on the "right way to play poker." As if on cue, a regular deliberately
checked his bet and, when the bet came around to him again, laughingly announced he was going to raise (an act that actually was forbidden by the group, as the bettor knew). The new player exploded: "You
can't do that! You can't check and then raise! What kind of game is
this! Where did you learn to play poker?"

A second regular, with straight face, replied, "We always do that!
We do some strange things in our group!"

A third added, "Yes, sometimes we allow ourselves to take back our
discards if we think they can improve our hand."

A fourth added, "Well, but we have to match the pot first!"

Shortly thereafter, when the new player won his first pot, a regular
again with straight face asked for 25 percent of the pot to put into the

kitty, since "it is a custom that you always donate one-fourth of your first pot in this game." The new player, who was not asked to return, was effectively excluded from the group interaction, even though he was present for the remainder of the evening.

One regular explained how novices were covertly appraised:

> It's hard to put your finger on it, but there's a secret evaluation of a new player during the game. You know, we look at each other, and seem to be able to come to a conclusion about whether or not we want him to come back and play with us again, even before the game is over. Sometimes we talk about the player after the game, or during the week if we see each other before the next game. But most of the time we know even before that.

Of six new players (including me) invited to "sit in for a night," three were asked to return. Each of those "accepted" had manifested during their first night role behavior that corresponded to group expectations and that was openly reinforced. In two cases, the new players were welcomed to "our group" at the end of the session and told where the game would be held two weeks hence. The third was informed by telephone after some of the regulars had "talked it over," and agreed to invite him back. When the regulars felt unsure about inviting a new player back, or when they were certain that they did not want to invite him back, there was no postgame discussion of the next meeting.

A new player who was being accepted could be observed increasingly to identify himself as a member. During the early hours of the game he would ask questions about specific rules that "you fellows have." In the later hours he might phrase his questions differently, asking what "we" do in certain situations.

The regulars clearly seemed to enjoy instructing a new player, overtly and covertly, about their expectations. In fact, his receptivity to those socialization messages was a key criterion for acceptance. A regular expressed how he felt about the socialization process:

> I think there is a certain enjoyment in teaching the rules of our game to people that can learn them. It's kind of a pride. Maybe it's a simple pride, but it's still a matter of pride to be able to show other people how to play in our game, when you know all the rules, but they don't.

Once accepted as a regular member, the individual retained that status even if circumstances precluded his further participation. I was present when a member announced he was being transferred to a different job. The players were eating their postgame meal, when he said:

> I may as well tell you fellows this before you find out from somewhere else. I won't be able to play anymore because I got orders to go to Wisconsin. I hate to tell you this, because I hate to leave my contacts here with all my friends, and especially I hate to leave the poker club.

The group was silent for several seconds, and a few players stopped eating. Finally, one said, "That's too bad." Several inquiries were made about the specifics of his transfer, and players commented that he would be missed. One added that "the gang won't be the same without you." They talked briefly about the "breaking up of the group," and discussed the importance of starting to recruit new people for permanent positions. As they left, they warmly said good-bye to the departing member, and several of them earnestly asked him to "get in touch" whenever he visited the city. "Remember," encouraged one, "there will always be a chair open for you in the game." The offer of an "open chair" was similarly made to two other regular members who subsequently had to terminate their attendance; one of them has played when he was in town at the time of a scheduled session.

A returning regular member was not immune from socialization, however. During my participation, one returned to "sit in for a night" after an absence of two years. Throughout the evening he inadvertently violated some of the group norms. He started to bet beyond the limit, and he began to deal a game not in the repertoire. One of the other regulars smilingly reminded him of the norms, and said, "You've been away so long you've forgotten our standing rules." The visitor was gently being resocialized.

BENEFITS OF MEMBERSHIP:
SATISFACTIONS FROM THE EPHEMERAL ROLE

Participation in the friendly game provided the members with several rewarding role-related experiences, including opportunities for: scripted competition; self and situation control; event brokerage; normative deception and aggression; microinstitutionalizing; and retrospective conquest.

Scripted Competition: "Knocking Heads"

The criteria for acceptance as a regular member included one's ability to "hold his own" in the game. He was not to be "easy" or a "pigeon," but rather should be able to "put up a fight" and maintain the "balance" of the play. The new player was expected to be a competitor, to have "guts" and not be a "feather merchant."

Zola (1964) has pointed out that the importance and relevance of competition to gambling varies with the social context in which it occurs. Competition among the players seemed to be a carefully scripted and central dynamic in the friendly game. Competition involved money, but also, more importantly, accomplishments of skill, daring, and bluffing, as two regulars indicated:

> We cut each other's throats while the game is going on. We forget about it after, but it's that very competitive part of the game that I enjoy so much. Maybe it's a carry-over from my sports days, but I just like to compete. There aren't many places anymore where I can really get eye to eye with someone and "knock heads." A hand starts and you try to get other players to drop out. Then there's just two or three of you left, and you really start putting the pressure on. You can really slug it out, but it's only a game, and you forget about it when you leave the table.

> It's sort of like when you were a kid, and you were testing yourself all the time. Poker is like the good old days; you get a chance to test yourself.

Several other writers have reported that competition in gambling, whether against others or "the system," provides individuals with opportunities to demonstrate self-reliance, independence, and decision-making abilities that for one reason or another are unavailable to them in their major life roles (Herman, 1967a; Bloch, 1951; Crespi, 1956; Goffman, 1967). All of the regular players were employed in bureaucracies. It may have been that their jobs made impossible the kind of competition, the kind of "testing" that they desired—particularly in the case of those members who had histories of athletic competition. Within the friendly game they could carefully and normatively script for themselves satisfactory and safe competitive experiences.

Self and Situation Control: "Showing Skill"

Each of the players was expected to possess considerable skill in dealing, betting, playing his hand, and bluffing. A player who noticeably showed skill was pleased with his accomplishment, whether or not he won the hand. Regulars rewarded his demonstration of skill with compliments and verbal recounting ("instant replay") of the action.

Skill was closely related to competition, as illustrated by the following quotes:

> I like to keep a mental file about the way people play. I like to think about how a person acts when he has something, and how I might act myself when I have something, and try and change that periodically. I think about how someone played a hand last time, and then try to figure out what he has by the way he's playing this time. You decide how to play your hand by the way you see others playing. That's the real skill in the game.

> It's a beautiful thing to see a guy play a hand of poker well. It's better, of course, if you are the one who's doing it, but it's still nice to watch somebody else make a good bet, play his cards right, and then win. I don't like to lose, but if I've got to lose, I'd much rather lose to someone who's showing some skill in the game than to somebody who just steps into it.

Crespi (1956: 106) points out that "skill players of necessity play frequently and by preference with others who are also highly skilled," and that they "seek to demonstrate their mastery of the necessary skills and, if possible, their skill superiority." Zola (1964: 255) concurs when he observes that in the horse parlor "the handicapper gains and retains prestige not because of monetary profits or preponderance of winners, but because he demonstrated some techniques of skill enabling him to select winners or at least come close."

Skill, as it appeared in the friendly game, seemed also to be related closely to control over other players, over self (for instance, "poker face"; resisting temptations to bet or draw cards impulsively), and to a large extent over luck. Lukacs (1963: 57) considers "the uniqueness of poker to consist of its being a game of chance where the element of chance itself is subordinated to psychological factors, and where it is not so much fate as human beings who decide." Zola (1964: 260) extrapolates this interpretation to gambling in general, and feels that it "occasionally allows bettors to beat the system through rational means, and thus permits them to demonstrate to themselves and their associates that they can exercise control, and for a brief moment that they can control their fate. . . . [It] denies the vagaries of life and gives men a chance to regulate it." Skill in this sense indeed has a rational character, but also seems to have a kind of magical quality.

Event Brokerage: "Feeling the Action"

The poker group did not tolerate disruption of the "pace" of the game. Some players commented about the rapid series of "thrills" that were strung together in a night's playing—the thrill of the "chance" and the "risk." Gambling, according to Bloch (1951: 217-218), allows the player to "escape from the routine and boredom of modern industrial life in which the sense of creation and instinctive workmanship has been lost. Taking a chance destroys routine and hence is pleasurable." Bergler (1957: 117) writes of the "mysterious tension" that is "one of the pivotal factors in deciphering the psychology of gambling. . . . This tension is a mixture, part pleasurable, part painful. It is comparable to no other known sensation."

Goffman (1967: 155, 185) sees gambling as being most thrilling when it requires "intense and sustained exercising of relevant capacity," and when, as "action," "squaring off, determination, disclosure and settlement occur over a period of long enough time to be contained within a continuous stretch of attention and experience." Each hand of poker met the criteria for "action" and the requirement for "intensive and sustained exercising of relevant capacities" (skill and competitiveness). Central to this process was the opportunity for the player to make decisions concerning his participation in the play, decisions that were perceived to influence the outcome of his "action." Herman (1967a: 101) writes that the function of money, in the context of the gambling institution, is primarily to reify the decision-making process, establishing "the fact of a decisive act" and "verifying the involvement of the bettor in the action."

Both Goffman and Herman, in their discussions of "action" and "decision making," refer to commercial gambling establishments. However, these factors, particularly as they relate to the stimulation of players and their experiencing of "thrill," were clearly manifested in the friendly game. A regular explained, "We don't eat sandwiches and things like that during the game, and we don't shoot the bull, because it causes a break in the action." Another remarked, "It's like a new game every hand. There's a new dealer, you get a new set of cards, and it's a whole new ball game. You get your new cards dealt to you and you've got to think all over again what you are going to do this hand." Each player was a broker of events potentially thrilling to himself and his colleagues.

Normative Deception and Aggression: "You're a Liar!"

To "bluff" in poker is to attempt by a pattern of betting, physical cues, and playing the cards to deceive other players about the quality of your hand. In poker, the bluff is

> not only occasional but constant, not secondary but primary. Like certain other games of chance, poker is played not primarily with cards but with money; unlike other games the money stakes in poker represent not only our idea of the value of cards, but our idea of what the other player's idea of the value of cards might be [Lukacs, 1963: 57].

Goffman (1961b: 38-39) observes that "assessing a possible bluff is a formal part of the game of poker, the player being advised to examine his opponents' minor and presumably uncalculated expressive behavior."

Bluffing is related to the dynamics of competition, skill, decision making, and action. Each player attempts to "fake out" the others. By giving the appearance that the cards randomly dealt to him are really something other than what they appear to be, he tries symbolically to control fate. With each succeeding hand the player must decide whether to try to "run one by" or to "play them straight."

Shortly after I joined the poker group, I was shown a cartoon sketch of the players that one had drawn. The drawing caricatured the regulars at play. They were addressing one another and, strikingly, every comment referred to self, others, or the whole group "lying." In the friendly game, to "lie" or "speed" meant to bluff, and the performance of this act, successful or not, brought great pleasure to all, as indicated by the following interview responses:

> I really enjoy slipping one by the other guys. . . . Putting one over on them—that's *really* a great feeling. I get a kick out of that.

> I like the teasing that goes on in the game. You can say things there to people that you couldn't say elsewhere. I tell one of the other players he's a damned liar, for example, and he might take offense at that under other circumstances. But here it's almost a form of endearment. You'll say something to the rest like "nobody here is telling the truth. Everybody is a phony." Well, some of the guys may hit you on the head with something if you said that anywhere else.

To be called a "liar" or to be accused of "speeding" was a compliment, a sign that one could engage in the intense personal interaction that bluffing stimulated. The game, and particularly the bluff, established the kind of "focused gathering" that Goffman (1961b: 17-18) describes as providing a "heightened and mutual relevance of acts; an eye to eye ecological huddle" quite generative of a gratifying "we rationale."

Regular members often discussed their ability to catch one another "speeding," and the cues that would give fellow players away:

> When he puts a big stack of chips on his cards like that, I know he's bluffing. . . . When he puffs his pipe like that, he's trying to speed. . . . He's got that funny look in his eye. . . . When he says, "I don't know why I'm doing this" or "I must be stupid to stay in this," you better look out!

Lukacs (1963: 57) comments, "Since the important thing to poker is not the cards but the betting, not the value of the player's hands but the player's psychology, as one gets to know the habits, the quirks, the tendencies, the strengths, the weaknesses of the other players, the play becomes increasingly interesting."

To be caught "speeding" and then teased as a "liar" seemed to be a *rite de passage* for a new man. On his first night, a new player was caught attempting to bluff and lost to a better hand. The men burst into laughter, and a regular loudly commented, "Now you're a member of this thieving group! You've been caught lying! Trying to speed, huh? Now you're one of us!" The new man was asked to return for subsequent sessions. The "liar" in the poker group seems honorifically similar to the "handicapper" in horse playing (Zola, 1964: 255).

On the other hand, not to have the capacity or inclination to bluff, or to be considered "honest," was flatly an insult. A new man in exasperation asked during his first and only night why it was that everyone dropped out whenever he initiated a bet or a raise. A regular player shook his head and responded, "Because you are too honest." This was said unsmilingly, and was based on the new man's tendency to bet only when he had cards to validate the size of his bet. He was not inclined to bluff or "lie." He was *too* predictable. One didn't have to read subtle cues or study the pattern of his play in order to approximate whether or not he was "speeding" or "for real." Potentially, he was a "pigeon" who would destroy the group "action."

Ironically, a player had to be caught bluffing if others were to know that he was a "speeder." Once caught and appropriately teased, he established his potential for "speeding" and further stimulated the intense personal interaction, competition, and opportunity for cue-reading skill that generated from the bluff. In essence, the "speeder" contributed to the uncertainty in the game and to cognitive imbalance for the players. The resolution of this uncertainty and cognitive imbalance seemed to be pleasurable and thus rewarding.

When a regular player was caught in a particularly gross bluff, there were comments from others about historically memorable "lies," and the former culprit, if present, was again teased for his attempt. Usually someone would add, "Well, that's a time we caught him. Nobody knows how many times his lying is successful!" The uncalled winner does not have to show his hand in poker, so players were never really certain when he was bluffing. A common poker strategy used occasionally in the group was deliberately to be caught bluffing so that on subsequent occasions the relation between betting and hand strength was less clear.

The "lie" can also be interpreted as an opportunity to engage safely in behavior that might be considered "deviant" according to norms outside the friendly game (for a relevant treatment of group norms for deviance, see Erickson, 1962: 307-314). "Honesty" became a negative attribute and "dishonesty" became a positive attribute. A fellow player could be called a "liar" and he would laugh. To have called him such in public would probably have invited anger. Within the game, delimited aggression and deception were normative and functional.

Microinstitutionalizing: "Almost a Law"

Ritual, magic, and tradition, complexly interrelated, have often been described as central components in human play. That component complex is present in poker, and was dramatically apparent in the friendly game. In addition to the more explicit rules governing play discussed above, there were instances of at least implicit "rules of irrelevance." According to Goffman (1961b: 19-21), rules of irrelevance are an important aspect of focused interactions. They strengthen idiosyncratic norms and the cohesion and "separateness" by declaring irrelevant certain characteristics of the participants or setting that may have considerable saliency in the world "outside."

In the friendly game, even though a player's occupational status may have had some influence in his being invited, that status became irrelevant. For example, I was asked by a new man what my occupation was. Before I could answer, another regular player laughingly but nonetheless forcefully exclaimed, "Right now he's a poker player, and it's his deal!"

Although all the regulars were married, family roles were also deemed irrelevant. One might talk about family problems or items of mutual interest in the "socializing" before the game began or during the meal after the game, but certainly not during the game. The mere presence of wives or children was prohibited, and even the thought of allowing wives to play was, as one regular player summarized it, "horrible!" Another commented, "My son would like to come and watch us, but I won't let him. It's kind of an invasion of privacy, and you don't want *people* to be butting in at times like that."

During the game, virtually all topics of conversation not appropriate to the action were deemed irrelevant. "My wife asked me what we talk about when we play cards," observed a regular. "I tell her we don't talk about anything, we play cards. She can't understand that because they gossip when they play bridge. But they aren't really playing a game then." On one occasion a regular player worriedly interjected, "My God, how about this war in Vietnam?" The others were silent for a few seconds, then one answered, "Whose deal is it?" The player who had commented about the war continued his statements, and quickly was interrupted by another who somewhat sternly though not angrily advised, "I didn't come here to hear you give a speech. I came here to play poker. I could give a speech myself, you know." "Who will sell me some chips?" inquired another, and the game continued.

Along with the accepted and expected verbal interactions of teasing and "game talk," the players enjoyed, indeed institutionalized, a regular member's occasional references to the sagacity of his grandfather as a poker player. Whenever he was facing a particularly difficult decision, he would lean back in his chair, puff on a cigar (all but one of the players smoked either pipes or cigars during the game), and reflectively comment, "Well, my grandfather used to say" (for example) "never throw good money after bad." Often other players would make similar statements when they were faced with problem situations. The "grandfather" quotes had reference to betting, bluffing, soundness of decision, or competition. The content of the messages might accurately be described, as suggested by an interviewee, as "a poker player's *Poor Richard's Almanac.*" The quotes seemed to be an important mechanism for bringing into the friendly game, as a lesson of a wise, "pioneer" man, considerations of the Protestant Ethic. The advice of "grandfather" was often cited to new players, thus serving a socialization function.

The verbal rituals, rules of irrelevance, and various behavioral taboos seemed to support valued group dynamics. The no alcohol rule, for example, was adopted early in the group's history when an inebriated player had disrupted the pace. Similarly, the no eating rule was inaugurated when players were observed to drop cards or get them sticky. A number of specific games or methods of playing split-pot games were outlawed because they had in the past caused anger among players.

Although the players stressed the use of skill, particularly as a manifestation of control over fate, they also invoked what Malinowski (1948: 38, 88) called "practical magic," primarily in an attempt to control the flow of cards or to change their luck. They would, for example, talk to the deck, urging it to give them good cards; rap the table with their knuckles just before receiving a card; slowly "squeeze out" a hand dealt to them, particularly after having drawn another card or cards, in order to "change the spots"; make a "fancy cut" as a luck changer; bet a hand "on the come" or "like you had them," as a means of guaranteeing getting the card or cards desired; deal a different game in order to "cool off" or "heat up" the deck; get up and stretch, or get a cup of coffee, in order to "change the way the money is flowing on the table"; stack their chips in a "lucky" way. On one occasion a player reached over and disordered another's chips, laughingly saying, "That should change your luck! You're winning too much!" (For a discussion of such behavior among craps shooters, see Henslin, 1967.)

The most striking example of magical behavior within the friendly game was the clearly understood and always followed rule that a player must bet fifteen cents, no more and no less, on the first face-up ace he received in a hand. It was agreed that if one did not follow this rule, he would "insult the ace" and would inevitably lose. No one seemed to know where the "rule" originated, but all followed it and made a point of instructing new players to do likewise. Three members specifically referred to the fifteen cent rule when interviewed about "special rules." "I don't know why we do that," commented one, "but that's our precious ritual. I do remember one time I forgot to bet it that way, and by God I lost!" The second thought betting fifteen cents on the ace was "a funny rule, but still a rule." The third referred to the fifteen cent bet as "almost a law. It's stupid, I guess, but it makes the game more fun." In this case, the magic served not only the function of insuring against possible loss but also as another contributor to group cohesion. It may have been a "stupid" law, but it was "our" law.

The meal following the game might be considered a ritual feast. The strict poker rules and interactions were loosened, and the players discussed various topics deemed inappropriate during the game itself.

Retrospective Conquest: "If I Had Only . . . "

In the friendly game, winners necessitate losers. Unlike forms of betting games in which the participants play against the "house," not every player in poker can win.

The most a member could win or lose was approximately $30.00. Generally, there was one "big winner," one "big loser," and the rest were distributed in between. One regular player was a "big winner" more often than the others, but not enough to disrupt the balance of the group. There was no consistent "big loser." All of the members were in approximately the same income bracket, and thus winning or losing $30.00 had a similar impact on them. Goffman (1961b: 69) points out that if betting is low relative to the financial capacities of the players interest may be lacking in the game and they may not take it seriously. If, conversely, players feel that betting is too high, then interest may be strangled by concern for the money they could lose. The regulars understood the impact of someone who "couldn't afford to lose" or "didn't care about losing." In their view, the former "makes you feel guilty if you win," and the latter "is no challenge, because if he's not really losing anything, you're not really winning anything." It was important that the financial conditions of the players be such that they maintained the equilibrium of the group.

The players knew that someone had to lose and inevitably at times it would be themselves. All agreed it was better to win than lose, but losing was not a disgrace so long as one did so through no lack of skill. For the member who had "played well" but nonetheless ended up a loser at the end of the evening, the group offered and accepted several rationalizations, most commonly sympathizing about a plague of "second-best hands." This meant that the loser had played his cards well, "knocked heads" to the very end, and then come up with a slightly inferior hand. In essence, the cards were being blamed for his loss. It was no fault of his, because he "played well." When a player of this quality lost, luck was the culprit. But, when he won, it was by virtue of his skill; luck had nothing to do with it.

The regular members looked with disfavor upon anyone who won by luck alone. A skillful player might invest some money early in a hand, but should not consistently "ride the hand out" hoping subsequently to be dealt some good cards. He should assess the odds, appraise through observation of cues and actions the quality of others' hands, and, if evidence warranted, should decide to drop out and take his temporary loss.

Those who had lost a hand were often seen to "relive" the play. They would utter such statements as: "I figured that you . . . "; "If I hadn't thrown away those . . . "; "All I needed was another spade and . . . "; "I thought you had three of a kind because you were betting . . . " Zola (1964: 256) observed this phenomenon, which he calls "the hedge," in the horse parlor, and described it as a means of maintaining some status even when losing. The loser would give a series of reasons why he lost, and how he wouldn't have if he had done some minor thing differently.

Goffman (1967: 247) points out instances where in competitive interactions "both parties can emerge with honor and good character affirmed." This opportunity was clearly provided in the friendly game for those players who would "knock heads." There was potential in that situation for a "good winner" and one or more "good losers."

If a regular player clearly had made a blunder, he would be teased by the others. Often the blunderer in defense would narrate a blunder historical for the group, whether made by himself or some other player. "Remember the time when Joe bet like crazy on his low hand because he thought the game was high-low split, and it was high hand take all!" Considerable detail would be shared about the nature of the epic mistake. The current blunderer effectively would have anchored his own current error on a point somewhere less gross than a historical one. The regulars appreciated and were comforted by the fact that all of them made mistakes. As one interviewee pointed out, "Nobody likes to play poker against a machine."

The player who had lost despite his skill might choose some other form of rationalization. He might consider the evening to have been "cheap entertainment," or "the cost of some lessons in poker." He might indicate that it was "his turn to lose tonight," or he had "let the host win." Nobody ever really complained about losing (although frustration was expressed concerning "second-best hands"). "I have more fun *losing* in this group," commented a regular member, "than I do *winning* at roulette, or something like that."

The amount of money won or lost was discussed only in the most offhanded manner. Specific figures were seldom mentioned, only estimates given, and then only sporadically and without pattern by different players. A regular reflected:

> At the end of the evening the game is over. Who cares how much you win or lose on one evening because each of us wins or loses, and it

balances out. It's each hand during the game that counts, and whether you win or lose that hand. The overall thing doesn't mean as much.

The money, out of the context of group interaction, seemed unimportant.

CONCLUSION

The regular participants in the friendly poker game perceived themselves to be in a "different world" when they were playing. They had created and maintained idiosyncratic roles, norms, rituals, rules of irrelevance, group boundaries, and the associated emotions. They were able to choose and socialize new players. Anyone or anything that disrupted the group dynamics or reduced the satisfactions experienced was eliminated or avoided. The players testified to their awareness that the poker group was "separate" from their other, broader, day-to-day social roles and relationships:

> I look forward every other Monday to getting away from it all. I can do that when I'm playing poker with the guys. I forget about my job, and other problems that I have, and I can just sort of get lost in the game.

> It's a chance to get away from our wives and families. Every man needs a chance to get away from that once in a while.

> When that first card hits the table, it's like we're on an island, you know, all to ourselves. Nobody bothers us. You're your own man! I miss it whenever we have to cancel a game for some reason or another.

The friendly game seemed, as did Zola's (1964: 248-249) horse parlor, to allow the players to effect "disassociation from ordinary utilitarian activities."

Goffman (1961b: 36, 67-68) describes a "gaming encounter" as having social participants involved in a focused interaction, and as such having a "metaphorical membrane around it." When the poker players had all arrived, they formed the metaphorical membrane, and the friendly game became "a little cosmos of its own" (Riezler, 1941: 505). Within the group boundaries, each member acted the ephemeral role of poker player, providing him the opportunity for scripted competition, self and other control, event brokerage, normative deception and aggression, microinstitutionalizing, and retrospective conquest. More specifically, it provided him with the following opportunities for satisfaction: to share in the establishing and/or maintaining of a personally relevant group structure and interaction pattern; to compete vigorously but safely with equals; to bluff, tease, or otherwise "one up" equals; to demonstrate and be admired for skill in betting and playing; to become deeply involved in intense but controlled personal interaction; to read, analyze, and utilize cues emitted from other players; to control and become immersed in action, including a series of thrills and the exhilaration of "pace"; to enjoy the fellowship of a chosen and mutually developed primary group; to exert control over self, others, and luck or fate; to capture or relive some of the competencies and freedoms of youth; to reaffirm his "masculinity" (a somewhat archaic concern, but important to the players and perhaps still relevant considering contemporary changes in sex roles); to enjoy legitimized deviancy; to implement, in rapid succession, a great number of significant decisions; to declare as irrelevant norms and roles that society at large deems mandatory in favor of idiosyncratic group norms and roles; and to escape the routine and "ordinary" social dynamics of everyday life.

The players entered and left the metaphorical membrane and ephemeral role through two buffer zones structured into the friendly game. The first buffer zone was the pregame socializing period during which players waited and discussed various topics until everyone had arrived. The transition from everyday social interaction to the contrived interaction in the game, the "easing" into the ephemeral role, was facilitated by this short delay. Players who had arrived late and thus missed the socializing period were heard to comment, for example, "Give me a second to shift gears," or "Let me put on my poker hat."

The other buffer zone, the meal after the game, served a similar function. The players then were behaving as members of any other group sitting down to have a snack together. The topics of conversation were unrestricted, and only rarely and briefly were any comments made concerning the game itself. During that period of the evening, the players were being "eased back" into their day-to-day complex of social roles.

Those who could not make the transition into the ephemeral role were disruptive to the group. This happened on only two occasions that I observed. The first occasion involved a new player whose home had some months before been destroyed by a severe tornado. Shortly before the game had begun, a tornado watch had been announced for the area; the sky was heavy with clouds and the wind was noticeably increasing. The new player kept looking over his shoulder and out of the window, rose several times to walk to the front porch and look up at the sky, and twice dropped out of the game to phone his wife (see

Chapter 7 for a discussion of the dominance of family roles during threat of disaster). A regular player commented, in an uncriticizing manner, "Your mind is wandering, isn't it?" The distracted player himself commented that since he was "so nervous" it might be a "good idea" for him to go home. The group quickly agreed with him, and he left. A minute or so later a regular player announced, "Okay, let's settle down and play some poker," and the game went on.

In the second incident, a regular player seemed to be distracted throughout the game. He told short jokes, talked about "irrelevant" topics, and generally slowed down the pace. "What the hell's the matter with you?" inquired another. "Why are you so talkative tonight?" The reasons for his behavior were not clear until later, during the meal, when he announced that he was being moved to another area and would no longer be able to participate. He apparently had found it difficult to enact fully the ephemeral role, since he realized he would no longer be part of the friendly game. His distraction by the world "out there" had distracted the other players. As Goffman (1957: 47-60) observes, in a gaming encounter "the perception that one participant is not spontaneously involved in the mutual activity can weaken for others their own involvement in the encounter and their own belief in the reality of the world it describes."

The regular players in the friendly poker game had found a way to create and enact an ephemeral role, to make a role, that gave them considerable satisfaction. They were not able to get that satisfaction from their routine, dominant roles, although those dominant roles influenced their choice of an ephemeral role. Ironically, the poker role that they created and maintained had to be taken, with considerable conformity, by new players. They had established their own "mini-history," their own group culture. Indeed, the manner in which the new players, during group interaction, took the poker role determined whether they would be invited back as regulars. The opportunity to socialize the new players was an important part of what the regulars enjoyed about the game. Creating the role in itself was an important act. Being able to guide others in the enactment of the innovative role enhanced that act.

Being a regular in the friendly poker game is only one example of an ephemeral role. The members of the volunteer work crew described in Chapter 7 can be considered as having developed and enacted such a role. They were faced with the temporary disruption of their dominant everyday roles. They were challenged to create, to make, a substitute role to fill the void. Other people, not in a disaster situation, routinely elect ephemeral roles to round out their everyday role repertoires. They do so to fulfill the expectations that they have for themselves as part of their self-concepts and to accommodate the behavioral expectations of others whose judgments they think important. Chapter 9 presents another example of the autonomous choice of an ephemeral role.

9

DEVELOPING ROLE BALANCE
Civilians in the Naval Reserve

In Chapter 8, I described participation in a friendly poker game as an ephemeral role, that is, as a part-time role chosen by the players to augment the satisfactions they derived from the dominant roles associated with their work, families, and marriages. Ephemeral roles often provide greater opportunity for creativity and autonomy than dominant roles. Perhaps even more importantly, they enable people to develop complex role repertoires, each component of which contributes a special element of satisfaction. Ideally, the sum of the satisfactions derived from dominant and ephemeral roles yields a full and rich accumulation of role satisfactions (Cummings and El Salmi, 1970; Sieber, 1974; Snoek, 1966).

How and why do people create or choose particular ephemeral roles? What influences the amount of time and energy they will invest in enacting those roles? How do they establish a workable balance of satisfactions among dominant and ephemeral roles? This chapter addresses those questions, using the example of civilians who have chosen to enact ephemeral roles as Naval Reservists.

This chapter is a rewritten version of my previously published paper, "The Naval Reservist: An Empirical Assessment of Ephemeral Role Enactment," *Social Forces* 55 (March 1977): 753-768, and also draws upon "The United States Naval Reservist: Some Observations on Satisfaction and Retention," a paper I published with John F. Patton and A.M.B. Jacobsen in *Armed Forces and Society* 6 (Fall 1979): 82-110. Used by permission.

Dominant roles can be considered as "operating" or "model." Operating dominant roles are those currently enacted by the individual and usually reflect the statuses associated with work, family, and marriage. Model dominant roles have been enacted in the past, and for some reason have been abandoned, yet they have provided satisfactions such that they influence the individual's enactment of ephemeral roles. Model dominant roles also might be based in reference groups to which the individual aspires membership (Hyman, 1942; Shibutani, 1955; Merton and Kitt, 1950; Newcomb, 1950; Sherif, 1948).

The individual, wanting more than the satisfactions associated with operating dominant roles, elects an ephemeral role to provide that satisfaction. The choice can be influenced by a previously enacted dominant role that has given enough satisfaction that it serves as a model. The ephemeral role chosen or created is similar to the model dominant role, but is not so extensive as to be dominant. Following Heider's (1958) view of social perception, it can be argued that there must be a balance in overall satisfaction derived from the model dominant, the operating dominant, and the ephemeral roles if one of those roles is not to be enacted to the exclusion of the other two. The operating dominant role and model dominant role should be close in overall satisfaction for the individual, but the operating dominant role provides a greater number of specific satisfactions. The model dominant role and the ephemeral role should be close in overall satisfaction, but the ephemeral role provides a greater number of specific satisfactions. The operating dominant role and the ephemeral role should be close in overall satisfaction, but the operating dominant role provides a greater number of specific satisfactions. The greater the difference in overall satisfaction between the operating dominant role and the ephemeral role (in favor of the ephemeral role), the more time and energy the individual will spend enacting the ephemeral role.

THE NAVAL RESERVE

When I gathered data for the study presented in this chapter (1974), among the approximately one-half million men and women in the Naval Reserve there were 139,000 designated in drill status. They "drilled" for training purposes with a Reserve unit a specified number of days or weekends per year, and served on active duty for training approximately two weeks per year. Most received pay for their participation. All earned credit toward retirement and were granted limited insurance, medical, and exchange benefits. They were subject to call to active duty in the event of national emergency.

Drilling Reservists have an interesting role array. Nearly all of them have served as active duty members of the Navy, usually for a minimum of two years. Following release from active duty, they have continued, as drilling Reservists, to be members of the military, and at the same time are civilians. They carry with them not only civilian membership cards, but a military identification card and instructions indicating their duty station in the event of national mobilization. Military uniforms hang in their closets along with civilian attire. The agenda of their activities includes enactment of numerous civilian roles and, unlike most other persons, the enactment of a military role. To the list of civilian organizations and associations with which they have contact, Reservists add military organizations and associations (Kreh, 1969). Thus, drilling Reservists can have three identifiable statuses, each involving role enactments that can comparatively be assessed for balance of satisfactions: previous full-time active military duty (a model dominant role); civilian occupation (an operating dominant role); and Reserve participation (an ephemeral role).

Not all drilling Reservists would be enacting an ephemeral role by their participation. Some are in the drilling Reserve because they must satisfy contractual requirements under an enlistment program (which may have been undertaken in order to avoid draft into the Army). They are mandatory drillers "counting the days" until they can be discharged from the Reserve. Those individuals would not view past, full-time active duty as a model dominant role. They did not like it, nor did it influence their choosing to enter the drilling Reserve. They were obliged to accept participation. Some others may have enjoyed active duty, and were influenced by that experience (thus using it as a model dominant role) to elect participation in the drilling Reserve. But the Reserve did not live up to their expectations, and they planned to get out as soon as possible.

Those Reservists whose participation in drill serves as an ephemeral role would clearly show an overall balance of satisfactions with active duty, Reserve drill, and civilian occupation. They would also clearly reveal several specific satisfactions better provided in ephemeral role enactment (Reserve drill) than in the model dominant role (active duty) and in the operating dominant role (civilian occupation). Those Reservists for whom drill does not serve as an ephemeral role would show an overall imbalance of satisfactions in favor of civilian occupation, and would reveal few if any specific satisfactions better provided in active duty or Reserve drill than in civilian occupation. Both those Reservists who enact Reserve drill as an ephemeral role and those who do not will report more specific satisfactions in civilian occupation than in active duty, but the differences for the ephemeral role enactors will not be so great.

THE ASSESSMENT OF
EPHEMERAL ROLE ENACTMENT

The Questionnaire

From 2 pilot studies conducted with a total of 500 officer and enlisted Reservists, a 141-item, structured, self-reporting questionnaire was constructed. The questionnaire contained a network of items concerning military and civilian characteristics and included 3 scales: the Active Duty Satisfaction Scale (ADSS), the Naval Reserve Satisfaction Scale (NRSS), and the Civilian Occupation Satisfaction Scale (COSS). The scales had 14 Likert response items in common. The items asked the Reservists to express the degree of satisfaction (completely satisfying, mostly satisfying, average in satisfaction, mostly unsatisfying, completely unsatisfying) that he or she experienced (concerning past active duty, Reserve participation, and civilian occupation) in general and with: own authority, own responsibility, status (prestige), use of own talents and abilities, supervisors, comradeship, recognition for own work well done, opportunity for promotion, training, facilities or equipment, pay, fringe benefits, and sense of own accomplishment. The items were found in pilot studies to represent salient and recurrently cited sources of respondent role satisfaction. Those satisfactions also were mentioned frequently in the literature on military service (Janowitz and Little, 1959; Janowitz, 1960, 1964, 1971; Little, 1971; Moskos, 1970; Stouffer et al., 1949). The literature on the sociology and psychology of industry includes all of those role satisfactions among lists relevant to the work setting (Argyris, 1957, 1964; Dalton, 1959; Dubin, 1968, Katz and Kahn, 1966; Miller and Form, 1964; Roethlisberger and Dickson, 1964).

Having identical satisfaction items in the three scales would reveal the relative balance of satisfactions experienced by respondents in each role: past full-time active duty (model dominant role), measured by the ADSS; Reserve drill (ephemeral role), measured by the NRSS; and civilian occupation (operating dominant role), measured by the COSS. The comparability of the scales also would indicate how individual satisfactions in each of the three role enactments complemented or compensated each other on an item-by-item basis.

The respondents' reports of satisfaction concerning past, full-time active duty were retrospective, and were no doubt influenced by the resolution of cognitive dissonance (Festinger, 1957) and selective memory. However, the respondents did, as drilling Reservists, spend approximately two weeks each year on active duty for training. Thus they were at least somewhat refreshed about active duty, though in a temporary Reserve context.

The Sample

The questionnaire was administered under standardized conditions to Reservists in the San Francisco and Los Angeles areas during a regularly scheduled drill late in February 1974. A total of 967 officers and 2287 enlisteds in 135 Reserve units completed the questionnaire. The sample was representative in proportion of ranks and rates to the nearly 9000 Naval Reservists in the areas. However, the interpretations in this chapter are not intended to be generalized to Naval Reservists, but to examine the process of role balancing.

As project director, I was centrally involved in the construction of the questionnaire and the sample for the survey research. However, the survey research resulted from my participant observation as a Medical Service Corps officer in the Naval Reserve. For three years prior to the development of the survey, I kept notes on what I saw as pertinent to understanding the satisfactions derived from enacting the Naval Reserve role. The questionnaire, and the scales it included, reflected those key aspects. The interpretations of the questionnaire data and the illustrative quotes in this chapter are based on my having "been there."

THE BALANCE OF ROLE SATISFACTIONS

To provide sharper analytical categories of satisfaction with participation in the drilling Reserve, and thus enhance assessment of the function of ephemeral role enactment, the respondents were divided into "more satisfied Reservists" (those who scored at or above the median of the distribution of scores on the NRSS) and "less satisfied Reservists" (those who scored below the median). It was not reasonable to cluster officers with enlisted respondents, since studies of the military have indicated that officers generally are more satisfied with participation. Separate distributions of NRSS scores were established for officers and enlisteds, yielding four analytical categories of Reservists: "more satisfied officers" (MSO), scored at or above the median of the distribution of NRSS scores for officers; "less satisfied officers" (LSO), scored below the median; "more satisfied enlisteds" (MSE), scored at or above the median of the distribution of NRSS scores for enlisteds; "less satisfied enlisteds" (LSE), scored below the median. The four categories, MSO, LSO, MSE, and LSE, will be used throughout this chapter and in the tables. The phrases "more satisfied Reservists" or "less satisfied Reservists" will indicate that officer and enlisted respondents concurred in their view of a satisfaction (or lack of it), and can be merged for interpretive purposes.

Summaries of the responses of the Reservists to the fourteen identical ADSS, NRSS, and COSS items can be compared in the manner presented in Tables 2, 3, 4, and 5. The total scale mean scores are displayed in Table 2; the individual item mean scores are displayed in Tables 3, 4, and 5. The differences between item mean scores often are very small, and would not be statistically significant. However, the pattern of differences is more important than the differences in any single scale item.

Tables 2 and 3 show that the NRSS total mean and item mean scores are notably and consistently higher for MSO than for LSO, and for MSE than for LSE. That finding was anticipated, given the fact that the more satisfied Reservists were separated from the less satisfied Reservists at the NRSS median. Had any of the item mean scores of LSO been higher than those of MSO, or any of the LSE higher than MSE, the NRSS validity could have been questioned.

Table 2 shows that, for the more satisfied Reservists (MSO and MSE), there is little difference in ADSS, NRSS, and COSS total mean scores. That finding demonstrates, as anticipated, the relative balance in overall satisfactions among the model dominant, operating dominant, and ephemeral roles if one is not to be enacted at the expense of the other two. MSO and MSE do report slightly more overall satisfaction with civilian occupation than with Reserve drill or active duty, which seems reasonable, but not so great a difference to eliminate drill as an ephemeral role or active duty as a model dominant role. In contrast, the less satisfied Reservists (LSO and LSE) reveal a marked imbalance in overall satisfactions, favoring civilian occupation over Reserve drill and active duty. Reserve drill can be operating as an ephemeral role for MSO and MSE; it is not likely to be operating as such for LSO and LSE.

Ephemeral role enactment is further illustrated with the comparisons of ADSS, NRSS, and COSS individual item mean scores. Table 3 indicates that MSO found Reserve Drill to be in eight ways more satisfying than active duty; MSE, seven ways; LSO, only two ways; LSE, only one way. In Table 4, MSO are shown to have reported civilian occupation to be more satisfying than active duty in ten ways; MSE, eleven ways; LSO, eleven ways; LSE, fourteen ways—every satisfaction measured. Table 5 indicates that MSO found Reserve Drill

Table 2   Mean Total Scores for the ADSS, NRSS, and COSS

	MSO	LSO	MSE	LSE
ADSS	55.0	51.1	50.3	42.5
NRSS	56.3	41.7	50.3	35.1
COSS	57.2	54.4	52.9	51.3

NOTE: For the fourteen identical scale items, the maximum mean scale score is 70; the minimum is 14; the range is 56. The higher the mean score, the higher the satisfaction.

to be more satisfying than civilian occupation in six ways; MSE, five ways; LSO, one way; LSE, no way.

Thus the more satisfied Reservists reported, as anticipated, a greater number of specific satisfactions with ephemeral role enactment (Reserve drill) than with the model dominant role (active duty) and the operating dominant role (civilian occupation). Civilian occupation, however, provided a greater number of specific satisfactions to the more satisfied Reservists than either active duty or Reserve drill. Though active duty might have served as a model dominant role, influencing them to choose the Reserve as an ephemeral role, and though Reserve drill might have offered some satisfactions incompletely (or less well) provided in the operating dominant role of civilian occupation, the latter was still the more satisfying of the alternatives. The more satisfied Reservists did not wish to return to active duty (though a few stated they might, if the civilian job situation became unfulfilling), nor did they see Reserve drill as ever taking more than a fraction of the total time in their everyday lives. Reserve drill was for them an ephemeral role, and only an ephemeral role.

Reserve drill was not an ephemeral role for the less satisfied Reservists. They reported virtually no specific satisfactions better provided in Reserve drill than in civilian occupation (LSO reported pay, which for officer Reservists is, when calculated as dollars for hours worked, rather competitive). They noted several ways in which active duty provided more satisfaction than Reserve drill, but only because it was the lesser of perceived evils. Civilian occupation satisfactions overshadowed those remembered in active duty.

MSO and MSE spent, on the average, three hours per week on Reserve activities *in addition to* the normal drill time; LSO and LSE spent, on the average, no additional time. As anticipated, the greater the difference in overall satisfaction between the operating dominant role and the ephemeral role (in favor of the ephemeral role), the more time the actor spent in the ephemeral role.

Table 3 Comparison of NRSS and ADSS Item Mean Scores

Mean Item Scores*	MSO			LSO			MSE			LSE		
	NRSS	ADSS	Sign	NRSS	ADSS	Sign	NRSS	ADSS	Sign	NRSS	ADSS	Sign
Satisfaction with:												
In general	4.2	4.1	+	3.2	3.9	–	3.8	3.6	+	2.5	3.2	–
Authority	4.2	4.1	+	3.0	3.9	–	3.6	3.5	+	2.4	3.0	–
Responsibility	4.1	4.3	–	2.9	4.1	–	3.6	3.8	–	2.4	3.3	–
Status	4.3	4.1	+	3.1	3.9	–	3.7	3.5	+	2.5	2.9	–
Use of talents and abilities	4.1	3.8	+	2.6	3.5	–	3.4	3.6	–	2.0	2.9	–
Supervisors	4.3	3.6	+	3.4	3.3	+	3.9	3.4	+	2.9	2.9	o
Comradeship	4.5	4.3	+	3.8	4.1	–	4.1	4.1	o	3.4	3.7	–
Recognition for work	4.3	3.9	+	3.2	3.5	–	3.9	3.6	+	2.7	2.9	–
Promotions	4.1	4.1	o	3.0	3.6	–	3.9	3.7	+	3.0	3.0	o
Training	3.6	3.9	–	2.5	3.6	–	3.2	3.7	–	2.0	3.1	–
Facilities/equipment	3.2	3.7	–	2.3	3.4	–	2.8	3.6	–	2.0	3.1	–
Pay	4.3	3.5	+	3.7	3.2	+	3.8	3.2	+	2.9	2.7	+
Fringe benefits	3.3	3.9	–	2.5	3.6	–	3.2	3.5	–	2.3	3.0	–
Sense of accomplishment	3.8	3.9	–	2.5	3.5	–	3.4	3.5	–	2.1	2.8	–
Totals of differences and directions of differences			8+ 1o 5–			2+ 0o 12–			7+ 1o 6–			1+ 2o 11–

*The maximum item score is 5; the minimum is 1; the range is 4. The higher the score, the higher the satisfaction.

Table 4 Comparison of ADSS and COSS Item Mean Scores

Mean Item Scores*	MSO			LSO			MSE			LSE		
	ADSS	COSS	Sign	ADSS	COSS	Sign	ADSS	COSS	Sign	ADSS	COSS	Sign
Satisfaction with:												
In general	4.1	4.3	+	3.9	4.1	+	3.6	4.0	+	3.2	3.9	+
Authority	4.1	4.2	+	3.9	3.9	o	3.5	3.8	+	3.0	3.7	+
Responsibility	4.3	4.4	+	4.1	4.2	+	3.8	4.1	+	3.3	3.9	+
Status	4.1	4.2	+	3.9	4.0	+	3.5	3.8	+	2.9	3.7	+
Use of talents and abilities	3.8	4.3	+	3.5	4.1	+	3.6	3.9	+	2.9	3.7	+
Supervisors	3.6	4.0	+	3.3	3.8	+	3.4	3.7	+	2.9	3.7	+
Comradeship	4.3	4.1	–	4.1	3.8	–	4.1	4.0	–	3.7	3.9	+
Recognition for work	3.9	4.1	+	3.5	3.9	+	3.6	3.7	+	2.9	3.7	+
Promotions	4.1	3.8	–	3.6	3.7	+	3.7	3.4	–	3.0	3.4	+
Training	3.9	3.8	–	3.6	3.7	+	3.7	3.6	–	3.1	3.6	+
Facilities/equipment	3.7	4.1	+	3.4	4.0	+	3.6	3.9	+	3.1	3.7	+
Pay	3.5	3.9	+	3.2	3.6	+	3.2	3.6	+	2.7	3.4	+
Fringe benefits	3.9	3.7	–	3.6	3.5	–	3.5	3.6	+	3.0	3.3	+
Sense of accomplishment	3.9	4.3	+	3.5	4.1	+	3.5	3.8	+	2.8	3.7	+
Totals of differences and directions of differences			10+ 0o 4–			11+ 1o 2–			11+ 0o 3–			14+ 0o 0–

*The maximum item score is 5; the minimum is 1; the range is 4. The higher the score, the higher the satisfaction.

165

Table 5 Comparison of NRSS and COSS Item Mean Scores

Mean Item Scores*	MSO			LSO			MSE			LSE		
	NRSS	COSS	Sign	NRSS	COSS	Sign	NRSS	COSS	Sign	NRSS	COSS	Sign
Satisfaction with:												
In general	4.2	4.3	–	3.2	4.1	–	3.8	4.0	–	2.5	3.6	–
Authority	4.2	4.2	o	3.0	3.9	–	3.6	3.8	–	2.4	3.7	–
Responsibility	4.1	4.4	–	2.9	4.2	–	3.6	4.1	–	2.4	3.9	–
Status	4.3	4.2	+	3.1	4.0	–	3.7	3.8	–	2.5	3.7	–
Use of talents and abilities	4.1	4.3	–	2.6	4.1	–	3.4	3.9	–	2.0	3.7	–
Supervisors	4.3	4.0	+	3.4	3.8	–	3.9	3.7	+	2.9	3.7	–
Comradeship	4.5	4.1	+	3.8	3.8	o	4.1	4.0	+	3.4	3.9	–
Recognition for work	4.3	4.1	+	3.2	3.9	–	3.9	3.7	+	2.7	3.7	–
Promotions	4.1	3.8	+	3.0	3.7	–	3.9	3.4	+	3.0	3.4	–
Training	3.6	3.8	–	2.5	3.7	–	3.2	3.6	–	2.0	3.6	–
Facilities/equipment	3.2	4.1	–	2.3	4.0	–	2.8	3.9	–	2.0	3.7	–
Pay	4.3	3.9	+	3.7	3.6	+	3.8	3.6	+	2.9	3.4	–
Fringe benefits	3.3	3.7	–	2.5	3.5	–	3.2	3.6	–	2.3	3.3	–
Sense of accomplishment	3.8	4.3	–	2.5	4.1	–	3.4	3.8	–	2.1	3.7	–
Totals of differences and directions of differences			6+ 1o 7–			1+ 1o 12–			5+ 0o 9–			0+ 0o 14–

*The maximum item score is 5; the minimum is 1; the range is 4. The higher the score, the higher the satisfaction.

166

As Tables 3, 4, and 5 indicate, the more satisfied Reservists, in their ephemeral role enactment, were better satisfied with status (officers only), supervisors, comradeship, recognition for work, promotion, and pay in the Naval Reserve than they were with those same factors in civilian occupation.

The officers enjoyed the prestige associated with the Naval Reserve ephemeral role. (From a Commander: "In civilian life I am a GS-9 civil servant. Big deal. There must be a million other GS-9s in the country, and there's nothing very special about being one. Not much prestige, you know? But when I go down to the Reserve Center in uniform, with that gold braid on my hat, that *is* something special. Hell, I even wear my uniform out to dinner sometimes, with my wife, before I go to drill. I like the feeling it gives me, a feeling of pride, when people notice the uniform and the rank.")

Both officers and enlisteds were able to relate to Reserve supervisors in a way they generally could not in civilian occupation. (From a First Class Petty Officer: "Whether you're giving it or receiving it, during Drill an order is an order. It is good for a change to have a clear idea what you're supposed to be doing, or what you want somebody else to do, and to see it get done. Reservists have learned how to supervise both in their jobs and in the Navy, and that's a good combination. I really like my Reserve bosses better than my job bosses; they seem more decisive.")

The more satisfied officers and enlisteds could experience the intense comradeship shared by military personnel. (From a Chief Petty Officer: "I don't know about any club or work gang where you got so much in common with others as you do in the Reserve. You've been in the same wars, eaten the same chow, put up with the same shit, had the same good times, and talk the same talk. You got friends at work, but you got *buddies* in the Reserve. There's a big difference, you know.")

Officer and enlisted Reservists were able to be rewarded tangibly and immediately for work successfully completed in the Reserve. (From a Lieutenant Commander: "The Navy, both regular and Reserve, is great for letting you know when you screw up, but they're also great for letting you know when you have excelled. Whether it's the traditional Navy 'Well done!' or a letter of commendation, or a medal, it's usually quick and loud and a thrill. In civilian life, the rewards are usually a money bonus, or a prize of some kind, and are a lot less dramatic.")

The more satisfied Reservists could find greater satisfaction with the Reserve promotion system than with the civilian. (From a Captain: "I've loved every Reserve promotion I have gotten along the way. I received many promotions in my company over the years, and they were okay, but not the same as Navy promotions. In the Reserve, you know exactly what it takes to get promoted; it's more predictable. And when you get the nod, there's an impressive ceremony, you get another stripe, more noticeable privileges, and everyone knows you have moved up a notch. To be promoted from Second to First Vice President was nowhere near so enjoyable for me as being promoted from Commander to Captain.")

Finally, both officer and enlisted Reservists were able to get some added income. (From a Lieutenant: "My Reserve pay works out to a little under ten dollars an hour. That's better than my job salary, and more like the pay I'm really worth.")

CONCLUSION

Ephemeral roles are chosen by individuals to augment the feelings of satisfaction they get, or incompletely get, from enacting dominant roles. Their history of model dominant roles influences which ephemeral roles are created or chosen. The person remembers the satisfactions experienced in a model role, and hopes to find them in a similar ephemeral role. The ephemeral role enactment thereby provides satisfactions not met in the current operating dominant role(s). There should be an overall balance of satisfaction among the model dominant, operating dominant, and ephemeral roles, lest one be chosen to the exclusion of the other two. But there should also be several specific satisfactions better provided by the ephemeral role than by model dominant and operating dominant roles. The operating dominant role, however, provides more specific satisfactions and generally gives the enactor slightly greater satisfaction than the ephemeral role, or it is likely to cease being dominant and operating.

Many of the Naval Reservists were using that activity as an ephemeral role. Past, full-time active duty in the Navy represented a model dominant role, Reserve drill an ephemeral role, and civilian occupation an operating dominant role. When the Reservists were divided into categories of greater or lesser satisfaction with Reserve participation, and their responses to the ADSS, NRSS, and COSS compared, the results were as anticipated. The more satisfied Reservists showed an overall balance of satisfaction derived from past active duty, civilian occupation, and the Reserve. They also reported several specific satisfactions better met in the Reserve than in past active duty or civilian occupation. The less satisfied Reservists showed an imbalance of overall satisfaction, much in favor of civilian occupation. They reported almost no specific satisfactions better met in past active duty or the Reserve than in civilian occupation. The more satisfied Reservists generally were enacting Reserve drill as an ephemeral role, and had been influenced in that selection by past active duty as a model dominant role. The less satisfied Reservists generally were not enacting Reserve drill as an ephemeral role, and had not been influenced by active duty as a model dominant role.

Of the more satisfied Reservists, 78 percent planned to stay in the program; 63 percent of the less satisfied Reservists intended to get out as soon as possible. Why did 22 percent of the more satisfied Reservists intend to drop the Reserve if it was functioning as an ephemeral role? Why did 37 percent of the less satisfied Reservists intend to remain if it was not functioning as an ephemeral role? Those reversals could have been caused by the statistical impreciseness of dividing the Reservists into categories of "more" or "less" satisfaction at the median of the NRSS scores. A Reservist one point above the median was by definition more satisfied; a Reservist one point below was by definition less satisfied. The reversals could have reflected the complexity of the role repertoire that was being enacted by the Reservists. Individuals can simultaneously enact more than one ephemeral role, each of which provides some special satisfactions not met in their operating dominant roles. But no one ephemeral role alone does the job. A combination of them adds to augment the satisfactions of dominant role enactment. The reversals could have been due to the fact that some of the respondents had decided to remain in the Reserve even though it no longer served as an ephemeral role for them (for example, "I'm just putting in my time for the next three years until I am eligible for retirement from the Reserve"). Or it could have been due to the fact that some of the respondents intended to leave the Reserve even though it still was serving as an ephemeral role for them. Other ephemeral roles had become more attractive, and there was not enough time to enact them all (for example, "I like the Reserve, but I've become an officer in the Rotary Club, and had to make a choice between the two. So I chose to drop the Reserve.").

As anticipated, many (40 percent) of the less satisfied Reservists were mandatory drillers. They were not enacting drill as an ephemeral role, because it was not voluntary for them, and they derived insufficient satisfaction from it. However, 13 percent of the more satisfied Reservists also were mandatory drillers. It is likely that some of the respondents who entered the Reserve because of contractual obligations found important satisfactions in participation, and thus were enacting an ephemeral role.

Whenever possible and when they think it appropriate, people create or elect ephemeral roles. Those enactments provide them with special feelings of satisfaction and enable them autonomously to develop expansive and personally rewarding role repertoires. Their creation or choice of particular ephemeral roles is consistent with their self-concepts and past role experiences. It is also guided by their perceptions of other peoples' expectations for their behavior.

Ephemeral roles can either be taken or made, depending on the degree of flexibility in the social setting. The ephemeral role of Naval Reservist, in itself, mostly has to be taken. There is not much opportunity for creating a new Naval Reservist role given the fact that it is lodged in a powerful and culturally valued institution. However, as in all role taking, people participate in interactions that shape the behavioral specifics of the enactment and put their own mark on it. Enacting even the most rigid of ephemeral roles, one that must be taken literally as given, can be a creative act. The individual autonomously chooses that role, rigid though it may be, in order to fill what he or she feels is a gap in his or her role repertoire. The actor purposefully develops or accumulates a satisfying pattern of enacted roles, some dominant and some ephemeral, some rigid and some flexible. Over time and depending on circumstances, he or she drops and adds roles to the repertoire, and modifies those within it. An ephemeral role might become so satisfying that it is made into a dominant role. For example, on weekends, an individual enacts an ephemeral role as a member of an amateur rock band. She likes it so much that she quits her job as a bank teller and becomes a full-time musician. She has made what was an ephemeral role into a dominant one.

10

REACTING TO DISRUPTION
OF ROLE BALANCE
Naval Reservists in
a Marine Field Exercise

In Chapter 9, I used the example of drilling Naval Reservists to illustrate how individuals creatively establish a balance of satisfactions among the dominant and ephemeral roles in their repertoires. In this chapter, again using the example of Naval Reservists, I explore how circumstances can disrupt that balance and how people might respond when that happens.

I had administered the fourteen comparable items of the Naval Reserve Satisfaction Scale (NRSS) and the Civilian Occupation Satisfaction Scale (COSS) described in Chapter 9 to the members (five officers and twenty enlisteds) of a Naval Reserve medical unit. Most of the members had been drilling together for eighteen months, since the time the unit was established in 1975. As would be expected from what is known about ephemeral roles, and as is shown in Table 6, most of the respondents reported greater overall satisfaction with civilian occupation (the dominant role). However, they identified several specific

This chapter is a rewriting of an earlier version of the paper, "Role Satisfaction, Situational Assessment, and Scapegoating," which I published with Kenneth L. Wilson in *Social Psychology Quarterly* 44 (September 1981): 264-271. Used by permission.

satisfactions better provided by their participation in the Naval Reserve (the ephemeral role). Though the respondents' role repertoires contained many components, only the civilian and military roles were isolated for this study.

A medical unit in the Naval Reserve usually is less "military" or "gung ho" than other units. The members typically are highly educated and are oriented more toward medicine than toward military ritual. The officers in the respondent unit all had advanced degrees; the enlisteds were college graduates or university students. Nonetheless, as indicated in Table 6, there were differences among the members in their degree of military orientation, as suggested by the balance of the satisfactions they derived from the Reserve and occupational roles. Some of the respondents were more "civilian" and some more "military." The unit's training climate in monthly Reserve drills was flexible enough to accommodate the varying orientations. During those times, there was no serious challenge to the respondents' balance of civilian and military role satisfactions. The unit retention rate was high; members were content with their participation.

One month after I administered the NRSS and the COSS to the unit, it was unexpectedly mobilized for seventeen days of training duty in support of a U.S. Marine amphibious exercise. The unit was to provide both real and simulated medical service to combat Marines in the field during a massive "war game." Ordinarily, the unit members would have served twelve days of annual training duty in a Navy medical facility. In principle, participation in the unit mobilization was voluntary. However, members who did not participate would jeopardize their paid positions in the Reserve.

I was one of the drilling Reserve officers (not the commanding officer) in the unit and participated in the Marine exercise. During the seventeen days, I kept notes on my observations and informally interviewed other unit members and key actors. They knew I was a social scientist who had studied and was studying the Naval Reserve. Because I already had data on the unit members' balancing of civilian and military role satisfactions, I formulated the following hypothesis before we joined the Marine maneuvers:

> The more satisfied the participants were with the Naval Reserve (ephemeral) role, the more favorably they would assess participation in the Marine field exercise. Conversely, the more satisfied they were with the civilian occupational (dominant) role, the less favorably they would assess participation in the exercise.

Table 6 Balance of Satisfactions Between the Reserve (Ephemeral) Role and the Occupational (Dominant) Role (N = 25)

Number of Ways Better	Number of Respondents Who Reported Reserve Role Is on Balance More Satisfying than Occupational Role	Number of Respondents Who Reported Occupational Role Is on Balance More Satisfying than Reserve Role
14	0	2
13	1	0
12	1	2
11	0	1
10	0	1
9	1	0
8	0	2
7	1	1
6	0	2
5	1	1
4	1	1
3	1	1
2	1	1
1	1	1

During the first regularly scheduled drill weekend following the Marine exercise, I asked the unit members to respond to two questions assessing their satisfaction with that exercise and, because it had become an important issue, with the unit leader's performance during it. The questions were: "How satisfied were you with being a participant in the field operation with the U.S. Marines?" and "How satisfied were you with the performance of the commanding officer during the field operation with the U.S. Marines?" The possible Likert responses were: completely satisfied; satisfied in general; satisfied a little; neutral about satisfaction; dissatisfied a little; dissatisfied in general; and completely dissatisfied.

After I had summarized and interpreted my observations about the field exercise in writing, I shared them with the unit members. They corrected or elaborated upon my perceptions.

ROLE IMBALANCE AND ASSESSMENT OF THE SITUATION

When they joined the Marine maneuvers, the members of the Naval Reserve medical unit encountered a stark contrast between the relatively relaxed, rather civilianized monthly drill setting and the military rigors of the field exercise. Instead of starched white or pressed blue uniforms, the unit members wore Marine fatigues, boots, helmets, and combat packs. Instead of noon breaks for hot meals, they ate cold field rations. Instead of going home in the afternoons after drill, they lived in the field 24 hours a day and slept in tents. This was not the hospital or laboratory setting with which most of the unit members were familiar. Instead of having low-keyed lectures, demonstrations, discussions, and debates on medical matters, the participants had to respond without question to military orders. Often those orders seemed without purpose, were subsequently reversed, and led to hours of fruitless waiting. Sometimes there appeared to be little logic or coherence to the field exercise.

I am not suggesting that the exercise was wholly unproductive training for the unit. To the contrary, it reminded or informed the members about the seeming chaos in large-scale military operations and how to perform professionally amid that chaos. Nor was it unlikely that at least some of the unit members would, in the event of national emergency, be assigned for active duty with the Marines. A few of the members had already served in that capacity. But this was supposed to be Reserve training duty, not recall to active duty. It was supposed to be part of the ephemeral role enactment, not the enactment of a dominant military role. There was supposed to have been opportunity to maintain the balance of satisfactions between the Reserve and the civilian roles. There was little such opportunity during the field exercise. The situation and the supervisors demanded exclusive enactment of the Marine military role.

Table 7 shows that there was only partial support for the hypothesis that the more satisfied the participants were with the Naval Reserve (ephemeral) role, the more favorably they would assess participation in the Marine field exercise and, conversely, the more satisfied they were with the civilian occupational (dominant) role, the less favorably they would assess participation in the exercise.

For the most part, there was, as predicted, a downward linear trend in favorable assessment of the exercise from those members who had reported more satisfaction with the Reserve role to those who had reported more satisfaction with the civilian role. In Table 7, the pluses represent ways in which the Reserve role provided more satisfactions than the civilian role. The members in the category +14/+9 had, in their responses to the NRSS and the COSS, noted between fourteen (all) and nine ways that the Reserve gave them greater satisfaction than civilian occupation. The category +8/+4 indicates between eight and

Table 7   Role Balance and Assessment of the Field Exercise

Direction and Degree of Role Balance*	Number of Respondents (N = 25)	Assessment of the Exercise (Average)**	Distribution of Individual Assessment Scores
+14/+9	3	7.0	7, 7, 7
+8/+4	3	5.0	6, 5, 4
+3/−3	6	2.0	1, 1, 1, 2, 3, 4
−4/−8	7	3.6	3, 3, 3, 4, 4, 4, 4
−9/−14	6	3.0	4, 4, 3, 3, 2, 2

*A plus indicates preference for the Reserve role. A minus indicates preference for the civilian occupation role. The numbers indicate the degree of preference, derived by totaling the NRSS and COSS item responses for each member (see Table 6). The distribution of role balances is clustered for ease of presentation.
**The maximum item score is 7; the minimum is 1. The higher the score, the more favorable the assessment of the field exercise.

four ways that the Reserve role was more satisfying. The minuses represent ways in which the civilian role provided more satisfactions than the Reserve role. Among the unit members, those in category +3/−3 had the closest balance of satisfactions between the Reserve and civilian roles. They ranged from three ways in which the Reserve role was more satisfying to three ways in which the civilian role was more satisfying. Those members in category −4/−8 had reported that the civilian role was from four to eight ways more satisfying than the Reserve role. The members in category −9/−14 had noted between nine and fourteen (all) ways that civilian occupation was more satisfying.

As shown in Table 7, the unit members in category +3/−3 gave the most unfavorable assessment of their participation in the Marine field exercise. Perhaps that finding should have been expected, and the hypothesis should have been stated accordingly. The +3/−3 members did have the closest balance of satisfactions between their Reserve and civilian roles. Theirs was the most fragile role balance, the one most easily disrupted. But why did they assess the Marine field exercise even more unfavorably than those members who had reported the most satisfaction with their civilian occupational role? My participant observation and informal interviews during the exercise yielded some explanations of that result.

The three members whose scale scores indicated the strongest satisfaction with the Reserve role (+14/+9) thoroughly enjoyed and favorably assessed the rigors and the military ritual in the field. As one of them (+12) enthusiastically exclaimed, "The bugs, the heat, the dirt, the stink, the rotten food, and the fatigue are a challenge! This is a picnic compared to being a medic in real combat. I actually get a kick out of this." Throughout the exercise, those men were the first to take initiative on military matters. They were "red hots," seemingly attempting to be more Marines than the Marines. The field situation was quite compatible with their role orientation, and they liked it. But they were not disparaged by the unit members less "gung ho" than they, because the "red hots" actively helped their colleagues ease field stresses by showing them how to live in the field. The next most Reserve-oriented members (+8/+4) also were receptive to the field operation, though not so flamboyantly as the +14/+9 members. "I see this stuff as necessary training, and important in that regard," said one (+5), "but I do my best work in a Navy hospital, not in a surgical tent." The field situation was not incompatible with their role orientation, and they assessed it favorably.

The members whose scale scores indicated the strongest satisfaction with the civilian occupational role (−9/−14) were visibly unhappy about the field exercise, as were the −4/−8 members. However, they evaluated the experience as average or sightly below average. The field situation was incompatible with their civilian role orientations, but they were resigned to it. They expected an unpleasant situation, got it, and thus saw the operation as "typical Navy horse shit," which could be evaluated as providing the "usual" level of satisfaction. Like the members who predominantly favored the Reserve role, those who predominantly favored the civilian role were not exposed to inconsistencies between their expectations for and the realities of the field exercise. Their role balances essentially were undisturbed. "Of course this duty sucks," stated one member (−10). "So what else is new? I'll put up with this just like I put up with the rest of the Reserve. I need the money until I finish college."

The −9/−14 and less so the −4/−8 members seemed effectively able to withdraw from the field situation. A few of them did so literally, by disappearing into the bushes whenever possible. Some of the others frolicked within the setting—for example, they made clandestine raids on the Marines' supply of field rations; parodied the operation like the actors in the fictionalized MASH movie; made their field uniforms as nonregulation as feasible; and attempted to surrender to the "aggressor" forces. "This is a war game, isn't it?" proclaimed a −14 member. "So let's play games."

The members whose scale scores indicated about equal satisfaction with the Reserve and civilian roles (+3/−3) clearly had the most difficulty accommodating the intense militarism of the Marine field exercise. As shown in Table 7, they were the unit members least satisfied with the operation. Unlike the +14/+9 and +8/+4 respondents, they were not able to find enjoyment in the experience, or even to justify it as worthwhile training. Unlike the civilian-oriented –14/–9 and –8/–4 respondents, they were not able to withdraw from the situation or to "play games" with it. They had been maintaining a balance between their Reserve and civilian occupational roles. The field situation had disturbed that balance. It was not consistent with the members' expectations for participation in the Reserve. It was *too* military, too "gung ho." A +1 unit member with twelve years' service explained his disappointment:

> I joined the Reserve because there are things I like about being a sailor. But there are things I like about being a civilian too. If I didn't, I would go on active duty in the regular Navy. The thing with the Reserve is, you can have it both ways, some Navy, some civilian. I enjoy that. But this field exercise is no good. It reminds me about what I don't like about the service instead of what I like. It just goes too far into the John Wayne stuff for me.

Another member (–1) complained:

> I joined the Navy Reserve, not the goddamn Marine Corps. Look at me, I look like a goddamn Grunt (infantryman). I don't even look like a sailor! If I knew it was going to be like this, I wouldn't have taken off the time from work.

The +3/–3 members very negatively assessed the situation that had caused the imbalance of role satisfaction. Their assessment of the field experience was even more negative than that of the members whose role orientation was decidedly civilian. They participated fully in the activities of the field exercise, often with notable competence. But there was a perfunctory quality, nearly robotlike, to their involvement. Additionally, they continually complained about the field exercise, more than did any of the other unit members. Their complaints, shared among themselves and made to anyone else who would listen, were far more frequent and intense than the "bitching" considered routine among military personnel engaged in unpleasant activities.

The behavior of the unit members suggested that in a given social situation, role embracing or role distancing (Goffman, 1961a) may not be easy options for some enactors. For example, the field exercise demanded that the +14/+9 members exclusively perform the military role, which was more satisfying to them than the civilian role in their repertoire. They readily embraced the military role. The exercise demanded that the −9/−14 members similarly perform the military role, which, however, was much less satisfying to them than the civilian role in their repertoire. They readily distanced the military role. The exercise demanded that the +3/−3 members exclusively perform the military role, which was about equally as satisfying to them as the civilian role in their repertoire. They found it difficult either to conform with or to distance the military role. It was not (as with the +14/+9 members) so much more satisfying than the civilian role that it could be embraced. It was not (as with the −9/−14 members) so much less satisfying than the civilian role that it could be distanced.

The behavior of the unit members also suggested that the degree of commitment to different roles in a repertoire may make conforming or deviating from the norms of a given situation difficult options for some enactors (Becker, 1960). The field situation called for exclusive performance of the military role from the +14/+9 members. Since that was the role to which they were most committed, they were able to conform fully to the situational norms. The −9/−14 members, less committed to the military than the civilian role in their repertoires, were able to deviate from the situational norms. But the +3/−3 members, equally committed to the civilian and military roles, were able neither fully to conform nor fully to deviate from the situational norms.

Since the +3/−3 members had difficulty embracing or distancing from the intense military role, and since they could not readily conform to or deviate from the norms of the field situation, they needed to find other solutions. One obvious remedy would have been to leave the distressing field situation. But that was legally prohibited. Another option, soundly to condemn the situation and to complain about it, has been discussed. I observed a third alternative during the field exercise—making someone in the problematic situation a scapegoat.

ROLE IMBALANCE AND SCAPEGOATING

Scapegoating is popularly defined as "the action or process of casting blame for shortcomings or failure on an innocent or at most only partly responsible individual or group" (Woolf, 1975: 1031). Sociologists and social psychologists have suggested several functions of scapegoating. Adorno et al. (1950) and Rokeach (1960), for example, report scapegoating to be a defense mechanism centrally used by persons who manifest authoritarian personalities or closed cognitive structures. Allport (1954) sees scapegoating as part of the process of prejudice, intended to elevate or maintain the social status of the bigot. Reflecting Freud's (1946) notion of projection, Frazer (1957) depicts the scapegoat as a convenient repository for the misgivings group members have about themselves and their own performances. Influenced by Durkheim's (1947) conceptualization of a collective conscience, Klapp (1962) interprets scapegoating as a device that reaffirms dominant societal values and contributes to overall social control. Daniels (1970) has argued, based on her findings from a study of sensitivity training sessions, that the emergence of a scapegoat serves to stabilize small groups and to legitimize the purposes of the institutions that sponsor the groups.

Situationally generated imbalances in a role repertoire also can be associated with scapegoating. During the first week of the seventeen-day field exercise, the unit members responded in a consistent manner to the situation. Those whose role balance was strongly oriented toward the Reserve enthusiastically engaged in the operations. Those whose role balance was strongly oriented toward civilian occupation whenever possible withdrew from or avoided the operations. Those whose role balance was approximately equally balanced between Reserve and occupation engaged in the operations, but steadily groused about them.

The strongly Reserve-oriented and the strongly civilian-oriented members responded to the situation during the entire field exercise in the same manner as they had during the first week. During the second week, however, the grousing of the +3/−3 members began sharply to be directed against the commanding officer (CO) of the unit, who had enthusiastically entered and was thoroughly enjoying the Marine exercise. They began to blame the CO for their dissatisfaction with the situation. They concluded (erroneously) that he had volunteered the unit for the Marine exercise. Although the CO himself was strongly oriented toward the military (+14 in role balance), had previously been a Marine, and was generally considered to be "gung ho," he had not been derided by any of the unit's members during the weekend drills. There was enough flexibility in that situation to accommodate the role balances of all the members. In the field exercise the flexibility was gone and the +3/−3 members derided the CO for it. He was being held responsible for disturbing their balance of military and civilian role satisfactions. A −2 member complained: "The guy's gone crazy out here. Look at him! He thinks he's Douglas MacArthur or somebody! He's forgotten he's really a civilian. Worse, he's forgotten that we're really civilians!"

Actually, the CO was behaving no differently in the field than he did during weekend drills. But the +3/−3 members, in the constrictions of the field setting, interpreted his enthusiasm for the military and for the operation as villainous. The CO became a scapegoat for the discomfort generated by their situationally caused role imbalance. He became defined as a deviant in the context of the Marine exercise and against the background of a challenged civilian/military role balance.

The +3/-3 members attributed to the CO nearly every miscue the unit experienced in the exercise. When trucks did not arrive for transportation, it was because "Attila the Hun wants us to march the ten miles." When the unit members were assigned such nonmedical duties as tent raising, latrine digging, and guard duty, it was because "the CO wants to make real men out of us." When it was learned that the forces of which the unit was a part were losing the simulated battle, it was because the CO had "volunteered our asses for cannon fodder." The CO in reality had little or nothing to do with such miscues. In fact, he was nearly powerless in the field exercise, and most of the unit members knew it. The +3/-3 members, however, faulted him even for his powerlessness, which was seen as "giving in to the Grunt Colonels."

As happens in virtually all scapegoating, the CO was caricatured by the scapegoaters. Upon seeing the CO camouflage his helmet with leaves, a -3 member strapped an entire small bush to his back, and paraded around the bivouac area. Several of the CO's mannerisms were parodied. For example, his command to the unit to "mount and move" during an evacuation drill became a source of comic competition among the +3/-3 members for issuing similarly brisk commands: "go and blow"; "box and band"; "turn and burn"; "poop and shoot." The CO's exhortation that the unit was "going to war" as it prepared for a simulated attack was adopted mockingly as a general descriptive for almost any activity. Even going to the latrine was defined as "going to war." When the CO matter-of-factly inquired of a unit member, "How's it going, sailor?" the phrase became a jocular inquiry among the +3/-3 members. Crawling through the dirt toward some vague objective, one member would shout to another, "How's it going, sailor?"

The scapegoating inclinations of the +3/-3 unit members were further indicated by comparing the NRSS/COSS scale scores of all members with their postexercise assessments of the unit leader (measured by the Likert item). Table 8 shows that, as with the members' assessment of the field experience, there was a linear downward trend in favorable assessment of the leader from those members who had reported more satisfaction with the Reserve role (+14/+9, +8/+4) to those who reported more satisfaction with the civilian role (-4/-8, -9/-14).

Those members who had indicated a close balance of satisfactions with the Reserve and civilian occupational roles assessed both the field

Table 8   Role Balance and Assessment of the Unit Leader

Direction and Degree of Role Balance*	Number of Respondents (N = 25)	Assessment of the Leader (Average)**	Distribution of Individual Assessment Scores
+14/+9	3	7.0	7, 7, 7
+8/+4	3	5.7	7, 5, 5
+3/−3	6	2.7	2, 2, 2, 3, 3, 4
−4/−8	7	4.0	3, 4, 4, 5, 4, 4, 4
−9/−14	6	3.7	4, 4, 4, 4, 3, 3

*A plus indicates preference for the Reserve role. A minus indicates preference for the civilian occupation role. The numbers indicate the degree of preference, derived by totaling the NRSS and COSS item responses for each member (see Table 6). The distribution of role balances is clustered for ease of presentation.
**The maximum item score is 7; the minimum is 1. The higher the score, the more favorable the assessment of the unit leader.

situation and the unit leader more unfavorably than did the members who had indicated most satisfaction either with the Reserve role or with the civilian role.

It was my impression as a participant observer in the field exercise that the unit members validated Klapp's (1960) conclusions about the social construction of heroes, villains, and fools. The members who were most oriented toward the military tended to see the CO as a hero. One of them (+12) described the CO's behavior in the field exercise as being

> like General George Patton. There was no nonsense about him. He got the job done. Not everybody in the unit liked his style, but I respect it. I would want him in charge if I were going into combat.

The members who were about equally oriented toward the military and civilian roles tended to see the CO in the field as a villain. One of them (−3) complained:

> That bastard deliberately got us into this exercise. I'll bet he volunteered the unit so he could get promoted.

The members who were most oriented toward the civilian role tended to see the CO as a fool. One of them (−12) exclaimed:

> Who cares about Dr. Strangelove! Screw him. Let that clown do his "Sands of Iwo Jima" number. He's ludicrous. He doesn't realize the 1950s are over and he's an anachronism.

Apparently, the configuration of people's role orientations, and the manner in which those orientations are accommodated in a social setting, can influence the labeling of the responsible leaders as heroes, villains, or fools.

Within a month after the Marine field exercise, five of the members left the unit. Two of them (–12, –14) quit the Naval Reserve. Three (+1, –1, –3) transferred to another unit. Also, the commanding officer of the unit (+14) applied for appointment to full-time active duty with Navy medical operations in support of the Marine Corps. Although that outcome could have been influenced by other factors, it was fully consistent with the findings of the study. The field situation convinced the –14 and –12 members to shuck the Reserve ephemeral role. It had interfered with the satisfactions they derived from their civilian role. The +1, –1, and –3 members did not want to leave the Reserve because they derived role satisfaction from it. The transfer to another unit minimized the chance that they might again have to endure the role frustrations they experienced in the Marine exercise. The +14 CO had so enjoyed the field experience that he decided to guarantee more of it. He was willing to abandon his dominant civilian occupational role altogether, and to make the Reserve ephemeral role dominant.

CONCLUSION

The balance of satisfactions that the Naval Reservists had established between their civilian occupational (dominant) and Reserve (ephemeral) roles had been readily maintained during their weekend drills. When their unit was mobilized for seventeen days' training duty in the Marine field exercise, that role balance was disrupted. The situation called for total enactment of a rigorous military role, a circumstance the Reservists did not anticipate unless recalled to active duty in time of national emergency (when they understood that their ephemeral role would become dominant).

Those Reservists who derived more feelings of satisfaction from the Reserve than from civilian occupational roles enjoyed and favorably assessed the field exercise. Those who derived more satisfaction from the civilian than the Reserve role tolerated the exercise, though they did not assess it favorably. The exercise was consistent with their expectations for the military role. The Reservists who had the closest balance of satisfaction between their civilian occupational and Reserve roles were the most distressed by the field exercise and assessed it most unfavorably. Theirs was the most delicate and vulnerable role balance.

In many social situations, people who are seriously distressed with a role enactment can leave the setting and abandon the role, or at least they can effectively distance themselves from it (for example, the hashers in Chapter 5 and the airplane passengers in Chapter 6). None of the Reservists could leave the field, unless he was willing to hazard powerful legal punishment. Those who were strongly oriented toward the civilian role were able to withdraw, to distance themselves, from the role demands of the field. Those who were strongly oriented toward the military role embraced the field experience. The Reservists who had the closest balance of satisfactions with the military and civilian roles faced a dilemma. They did not want to distance themselves from the Reserve role, because they liked it. But they did not like that role enough to allow it, in the field situation, to become so dominant. They were trapped by the situation. Those Reservists responded by negatively assessing and by scapegoating the unit leader. They attributed to him the role frustrations they were experiencing in the field.

Scapegoating was, in this instance, one way of dealing with disruption of role balance. It was creative in the sense that it was an emotionally satisfying solution, but (like the hashers' hostile reactions to role conflict described in Chapter 5) it cannot be considered a productive solution. Another human being, the unit leader, personally suffered because of the scapegoating. He saw, felt, and was puzzled and troubled by it.

When the Marine field exercise was completed, some of the unit members elected alternatives consistent with what they had experienced in that setting. Two who were most oriented toward the civilian role quit the Reserve. They had enough of the military role. One who was most oriented toward the Reserve role applied for active duty in the military. The exercise convinced him that he wanted the Navy as a dominant role. Three who had close balances of satisfaction between the civilian and Reserve roles transferred to other units where they thought they could better maintain the balance between their dominant and ephemeral roles.

When people create balance of satisfaction among components in their role repertoires, they can be intensely disturbed when a new situation in which they find themselves disrupts the balance. It is to be hoped that they can autonomously resolve that stress with better techniques than scapegoating.

11

RESOLVING ROLE MARGINALITY
An Indigenous Leader
in a Poverty Program

The extensive role repertoires that people create and accumulate sometimes operate in situations where the actors experience feelings of role
marginality. One of their role enactments bridges contradictory expectations different groups of individuals have for them. That circumstance is related to but not the same as role conflict, where two or more
roles the actors simultaneously enact generate disparate expectations
from significant others or where the expectations they have for themselves differ from the expectations other people have for them (for
example, the hashers in Chapter 5).

The social science literature contains several examples of role marginality, including: line supervisors in the workplace, marginal between
management and line employees; the senior noncommissioned officer
in the military, marginal between commissioned officers and junior
enlisted personnel; the recent migrants to a society, marginal between
their new society and that from which they migrated; and the person

This chapter is a shortened and rewritten version of what I previously published as
"The Leader and the Lost: A Case Study of Indigenous Leadership in a Poverty Pro-
gram Community Action Committee," *Genetic Psychology Monographs* 76 (August
1967): 23-93; and as Chapter 13, "Walking the Tightrope," in *Poverty Warriors: The
Human Experience of Planned Social Intervention* (Austin and London: University of
Texas Press, 1970). Used by permission.

whose role enactment cuts across the behavioral expectations associated with different cultural groups (Stonequist, 1937; Park, 1928; Siu, 1952; Slotkin, 1943; Thomas and Znaniecki, 1927; Kerckhoff and McCormick, 1955; Hughes, 1949; Dickie-Clark, 1966; Roethlisberger, 1945; Wray, 1948; Gardner and Whyte, 1945).

In 1964, the legislative bodies of the U.S. government passed and funded the Economic Opportunity Act, more popularly known as the War on Poverty. The act mandated "maximum feasible participation" of the poor in programs undertaken to ameliorate poverty and its societal underpinnings (Rubin, 1967; Moynihan, 1968). To facilitate such participation, neighborhood action groups were to be established in low-income areas. Those groups were to elect officers (indigenous leaders) who lived in the area, identify specific poverty-related needs, and develop pertinent antipoverty programs fundable by the Office of Economic Opportunity (OEO).

The Topeka Office of Economic Opportunity (TOEO) was established in 1965 by an OEO grant. The TOEO included twelve "target neighborhood committees" (TNCs) as antipoverty action groups that represented constituencies of low-income citizens in the city.

The elected TNC indigenous leaders were to speak and vote for their neighbors in all dealings with the TOEO, including TOEO staff deliberations and meetings of its board of directors. The indigenous leaders were among the members of that board. The role of TNC indigenous leader was by definition and in practice marginal between, a bridge between, the poverty intervention expectations of the low-income residents and those of the middle-class TOEO staff and board members.

One of the twelve TNCs represented Topeka's Native American (Indian, as they preferred to be called) community. As this chapter will show, Mr. A, the chairperson of the Indian TNC, experienced especially intense role marginality. His constituents (mostly Prairie Potawatomi) not only were poor, but were struggling to maintain their ethnic identity against a long history of arbitrary encroachments by the U.S. government (Clifton, 1965; Clifton and Isaac, 1964; Leon, 1965; Searcy, 1965a, 1965b; Vogt, 1957). They understandably doubted the intentions of the federal, mostly Anglo supervised, OEO program.

I had been awarded a grant to study the social-psychological impact of the Topeka OEO poverty intervention effort on its participating poor, particularly the indigenous leaders. For nearly two years, my research associates and I attended as observers all the activities of the TOEO, including the Indian TNC. I also had the opportunity both formally and informally on a continuing basis to interview the TOEO staff, the TNC indigenous leaders, and the TOEO board members. The content of those interviews was recorded systematically in field notes. All of the TOEO participants knew that I was studying the impact of their involvement. At the end of the research project, I showed Mr. A what I had written about his role marginality. He validated or corrected my perceptions.

THE ELECTION OF THE "CHIEF"

On October 5, 1965, the Indian group held its sixth meeting at the Indian Mission, a neighborhood church. This meeting, as had been the previous five, was called and chaired by the TOEO assistant director. The Indian group still had not identified itself with the TOEO, nor had the participants viewed themselves as a TNC. Those who had participated in the previous meetings did so for a number of reasons, none of which seemed to be aligned with the goals of the poverty program. Some came because they were "curious about what this was all about." Others attended because "it was a nice opportunity to spend some time chatting with friends who lived across town." A few sat in on the meetings because "it was fun to needle a government man a little bit." The assistant director hoped that tonight's meeting would be different from those held earlier. He had a feeling that "the Indians are, I think, beginning to see the opportunities that the program has to offer, and I think that they may be about ready to elect themselves some officers. Also, I think they're beginning to trust us, and to see that maybe we aren't like the bad picture they have of government officials." During the week prior to this evening's meeting, the assistant director had made personal contact with about twenty Indian families, felt that he had begun to establish rapport with some of the Indians, and that they were beginning to have confidence in him. He hoped the meeting to start shortly would reveal, more than any of the meetings before, the beginnings of the Indian TNC.

The meeting was scheduled to begin at 7:30 p.m. At 7:45 p.m., the assistant director suggested that we "get the show on the road." There were fifteen people in attendance, six of them women. All of the members besides the assistant director and myself were at least part Indian. The assistant director stated that "the purpose of the meeting tonight is to find out if you are interested in this program, and if you are, for you to elect officers." He reemphasized to the group that the TOEO was not a welfare program, and anything that was to be accomplished would have to be started and supported by the people here. He asked if there were any questions.

During the assistant director's five-minute talk, the people listened attentively. When he asked for questions, they continued to sit silently and look forward attentively. One of the men asked the assistant director, "Well, what are we supposed to do now?" The assistant director responded with the suggestion that they think about electing officers. Another of the men said, "Maybe we should think about this some more." He then asked if there was any literature on the program. The assistant director, responding in the affirmative, went out to his car and got some pamphlets for the participants. The Indians read the pamphlets, and asked the assistant director to describe more specifically what the "programs are that have been started by your office." The assistant director reminded the group that programs were not "started" by his office, but that his office only helped carry out the ideas of the TNCs. A clear difference could be seen between the expectations that the Indians had for the TOEO, and the expectations that the TOEO had for the Indians and other target neighborhood residents. The Indians, at this stage, still viewed the TOEO as a government agency, and saw the assistant director as a "good guy who will help us get what we've got coming from this War on Poverty program." The Indians were judging the TOEO in accordance with their long-standing experience with the U.S. government—an experience that was based firmly on paternalism. On the other hand, the TOEO, reflecting the rationale and goals of the War on Poverty, expected the Indians, as it expected other target neighborhood residents, to become actively involved as participants in the antipoverty efforts. They were to assess and vocalize their needs, to select feasible programs to meet these needs, and to use the TOEO as a service. A key component in this conflict of expectations was the process of active beneficiary participation in a social-amelioration organization, as opposed to traditional passivity to and dependence on such organizations.

One of the men asked the assistant director, "Why don't we just write down on a piece of paper the programs that we want, and then you send these back to Washington for us?" The assistant director explained that it wasn't quite that simple, and if they wanted a day-care center, a Neighborhood Aide Program, and so on, they would have to become active in demonstrating the need, planning, and carrying out a number of the specifics for the program. The same man added, "Well, you know we've never had to do much planning for things like that. Usually, somebody else does the planning for us. Where do we begin?" The assistant director suggested that they talk with their friends and neighbors and try to put together a list of specific needs that the Indians might have, such as employment, housing, and education.

"Why do we need this here TOEO anyway? Why don't we just send this list of needs directly to Washington?" inquired a man. Another answered, "Washington's a long way from here. Maybe if we got together with this OEO thing here in Topeka, then anything we write down would carry a lot more weight." "Yeah," another commented, "maybe we had better string along with this deal." "Say," asked a third, "you said that there were some other committees already going great guns. What're they doing?" The assistant director explained about the daycare centers, Neighborhood Aide Program, Neighborhood Center Programs, and so on, fostered by other TNCs. "Those ideas came from them?" the man persisted. The group was visibly impressed with this, and it seemed that the program, at this instant, became more believable to them. "Those other committees that have gotten these different programs, you say they already have officers?" asked an Indian woman. The assistant director replied in the affirmative. An Indian man then urged, "Well, let's get us some officers too!" All the group members agreed vocally to the suggestion, but then the action dramatically ceased.

Several dynamics worked to engender this silence. First, the participants were not familiar with the procedures for nomination and election. Clifton and Isaac (1964) and Searcy (1965b) have reported that the Prairie Potawatomi had relatively little experience with tribal self-government, hence with the procedures associated with such self-government. Second, as a later interview with a participant indicated, there was some feeling of clumsiness about electing a leader—"You know, we just don't *elect* chiefs." Third, and again revealed in later interviews with the participants, there is a devaluation of volunteering for leadership among the tribes from which the Topeka Indians come. One of the respondents explained that he had quite early learned the lesson of not "trying to be the big-shot leader." He amplified his reasoning with an example:

My father told me that if you made it obvious that you wanted to be Number One man, then you would give other people a feeling that you thought you were better than they were, and that would be the worst kind of bad manners that there are.

Another respondent supported this view:

Grandpa gave us good advice whenever we wanted to play sports in high school. He used to tell us "Don't be *too* good at football, or anything else. Don't make people think you're showing off. If you're playing in a game, stay far enough out in front so you can win the game, but don't make anybody else look bad! I suppose there's nothing wrong with winning, but don't forget that it might be one of your brothers who is going to lose." We listened carefully when he told us about things like that.

A third respondent concurred also:

> I can remember when I used to run in track meets, and I was as fast as the wind. I remember usually being able to win easily, but lots of times just staying a couple of feet ahead of the second man so that I'd cross the tape first. Then after the race was over, I'd turn to him and say, "Boy, you sure gave me a tough time," and I could see that he'd feel good about it. I'd do this even though I knew I could have run away from him at any time.

There thus appeared to be a complex and somewhat ambivalent attitude toward leadership when that leadership involved competitive activity or active pursuit. It appeared to be another matter if leadership was thrust upon an individual by his peers. "If your people turn to you and make you a leader," commented an Indian respondent, "then you have no choice but to be a leader. To refuse, even though you may not want to be a leader and have done nothing purposely to get it, would be the same thing as telling your brothers that you think your opinion, the opinion of one man, is better than all theirs." Apparently, the important element was, according to these respondents and my observations, that the individual should not appear to want to be a leader and should not overtly compete with others for that status.

After a rather lengthy and awkward silence, broken only by considerable foot shuffling, shifting in seats, and coughing, the assistant director explained briefly the standard nomination and election procedure and called for elections, saying, "Don't any of you think you've got some leaders here?" There was another shorter pause, and then finally one of the older men present was nominated for chairperson. He stood, and said very seriously, "I consider this a great compliment to be nominated as a leader, but I have to decline because my health is not good." He in turn nominated another man, who thanked the group but declined because he didn't "really have enough time."

A few minutes before, while the assistant director had been explaining to the group the procedures for nominating and electing officers, Mr. A, a 48-year-old heavy-equipment operator, had gotten up from his chair and stepped outside the door "to have a cigarette." He stood quite near the entrance, well within earshot of what was going on inside. Mr. A had attended the fourth meeting of the Indian group and on both occasions had been the most outspoken, aggressive, and skeptical of the participants. He was an intelligent and articulate individual, with a quick and keen sense of humor. Mr. A was one of the individuals with whom the assistant director had developed a personal friendship and a mutual respect.

After the first two men had declined nominations for chairperson of what was now becoming the Indian TNC, and while Mr. A was still standing outside smoking his cigarette, a man suddenly said, "Wait a minute! I know who a good man for the job is! It's Mr. A. He's a fighter, he is, and he'll be a good representative for us. He knows what's going on too! I put up Mr. A for the job!" The group called Mr. A back into the church and told him that he had been nominated. They asked him if he would accept the nomination and he replied, in a soft voice and with a shrug of his shoulders, "I guess so, if that's the way you want it." He was elected by acclamation, and seemed visibly pleased as his friends congratulated him. Mr. A later informed me that he had gone outside "because I had a feeling I might be nominated by the people, and I didn't want to be around if I was." He also said later that he thought at the time of the nomination meeting that "the job of chairman might be worth a try, but I'm not going to work very hard to get it." It was clear that he didn't actively pursue the nomination, and, in fact, left the room before the nomination began. In this way, perhaps, he was able successfully to resolve a conflict between wanting to "take a crack" at being the chair and whatever ambivalence he had toward actively pursuing or accepting a position of leadership and authority. There was little doubt that he was pleased that the people had elected him, even though, as he said in his brief acceptance speech, "I'm still not quite sure what the hell we're going to do, but if we hang on, maybe we'll find out."

The election of the vice chairperson was a far simpler matter. It seemed that once the chair was established, anything else was secondary. Only one man was nominated. He accepted and was elected by acclamation. For secretary, the group nominated Mr. A's wife, who accepted and was elected by acclamation.

The Indian TNC was now formally established as part of the TOEO, with all the rights of representation and vote due any other TNC. The newly elected chair discussed a time for the next meeting with the assistant director and the group. The reconvening date was set for two weeks later. Mr. A then adjourned the meeting. There was another round of handshaking, congratulating, and a strong indication of "we feeling" within the group. As the participants filed out of the door of the Indian Mission, one of the men turned to the newly elected chairperson and loudly said, "Good night, Chief." Mr. A beamed.

THE COMMITTEE BEGINS TO FORMALIZE

The day after Mr. A had been elected chair of the Indian TNC, he began, as he reported, "going around to the houses of Indians that I know personally and talking up this OEO Program with them." He said that he chose to go to their homes personally because he "knew from working with his people before that sending memos or announcements about something was a waste of time. The fact of life is this—if I can get people to come out to these next couple of meetings, it's mostly because they're my friends, not because they believe that the Program is going to do them any good."

At 7:45 p.m., on the evening of October 17, 1965, Mr. A called to order the seventh meeting, held in the Indian Mission and attended by thirty people. He told the group, "I'm not much of a talker, and I'm not quite sure how to go about this. As a matter of fact, my wife told me that I'm like the bottom half of a double boiler—I make a lot of steam, but I don't really know what's cooking up above." Mr. A then called upon the assistant director to explain again "what OEO is all about, and what the Indians can do about it."

Following the brief talk by the assistant director, Mr. A introduced one of the evening's speakers, an Indian who was the director of a program to stimulate Indian participation in OEO programs throughout eight midwestern states (not including Kansas). The speaker outlined what the Indians were doing, particularly dwelling upon the victory of the United Council of Tribes in South Dakota in a recent land dispute. He impressed his audience, stating, "You see what Indians can do if they get together—they can even beat the state."

Mr. A then introduced an officer from the local chapter of a national Mexican-American organization, who described some of the self-help activities of his chapter. When the officer had finished, Mr. A commented, "There's another example of how working together will get you somewhere. We owe it to ourselves as friends and tribesmen to help one another out. It's the only way that we can get along and get ahead!" Mr. A was hammering at the friendship obligations of one Indian to another. He was aware that he could not immediately start talking about specific problems without first building a base of acceptance for the TOEO within his group. "You've got to offer the Indians something more than just a bunch of program talk, at least at first. You've got to offer them, when they attend the meeting, something that's more important to them—like friendship. Then gradually, maybe they'll start talking about the specific things in the TOEO on their own—and it will come from them, not pushed down on them from above."

Mr. A's strategy, and the stimulation from the testimony of the invited speakers of the evening, had the hoped-for effect. One of the participants asked, "Well, if we're going to get together, we might as well see what this OEO operation has that we can use. Why don't we write down all our needs and then take up these needs as subjects in future meetings? Maybe that way we can develop our own programs." There was general agreement within the group about that. It was the first indication of the development of an agenda for meetings to come. Mr. A followed up the suggestion by telling the group he would accept those lists any time the people wanted to give them to him. He said, "This'd be something quite a bit more than getting a 'tough luck' slip to go see the chaplain and then getting nothing but a bunch of words in return. Here's a chance that maybe we can do something for ourselves."

One of the participants inquired, "What about paying dues? Maybe we ought to pay 50¢ a year, or something." Mr. A responded that he didn't think this was necessary. He felt that "the purpose of this organization doesn't call for dues." The man began to argue with Mr. A and said, somewhat derogatorily, "Well, Mr. Chairman, sir, you can't expect people to be interested if they're not going to pay a little dues." Mr. A continued to disagree, saying, "We only want people here who are interested. We don't want their money. We don't want anything more from them than just their participation." The questioner smiled and said somewhat softly, "Okay, Mr. Chairman, okay." This was the first show of disagreement between a follower and the leader. In a subsequent interview, Mr. A remembered this incident quite well, and said, "You know, that was the first time I felt uncomfortable being the chairman." This incident was to be a harbinger for later role marginality stresses he would experience as an indigenous leader.

Mr. A suggested to the group that they get some of the coffee and cookies that had been provided. Then, looking a little bewildered, he blurted out, "I don't know how to end this thing!" He asked the assistant director, "What do I do now?" The assistant director explained to him the procedures for adjourning the meeting, and Mr. A began to do just that, until he was loudly interrupted by several members of the group. "Wait a minute! What about setting a time for the next meeting?" Mr. A apologized and the group agreed to hold another meeting two weeks hence. The participants had expressed a genuine desire to continue having their TNC meetings.

Mr. A adjourned the group at 10 p.m. The meeting had lasted for two and a half hours. After some postadjournment chatting with a few of the participants who remained after the others had left, Mr. A suggested that "we all go home now, and then see what'll happen at the next meeting."

THE COMMITTEE LOOKS FOR A PROJECT

Mr. A again spent considerable time prior to the eighth meeting of the Indian TNC making personal visits to the homes of Topeka Indians, attempting to get them to come to the next meeting. He and the vice chairperson had also attended, as voting delegates from the Indian TNC, their first meeting of the Economic Opportunity Board. Though Mr. A was silent throughout the meeting, he took several notes and commented afterward: "I'm amazed at the scope of this organization, and the number of people and agencies that are involved in it. We may have something here!" He was a little concerned, though, about the pace of the meeting:

> All these motions and votes on different proposals and things go so fast that you hardly have time to think about them. You just get finished being asked to vote on one proposal, and before you really understood what that vote was all about, another vote comes along. I wish they would slow down a bit! At first I thought it was just that I was stupid, but then I talked to some of the other Committee officers and I found that they felt the same way too.

> I hope the Topeka OEO and the agency people don't forget that this is all kind of new to us. Another thing that worried me too. Every time there was a vote, everybody voted "yes." Nobody ever voted "no." I hope it wasn't because a lot of people just didn't understand what was going on. I know that was the case with me. A couple of times I voted "yes" and didn't know what the hell I was voting about, but went along with the rest of the people.

In early November, Mr. A arrived at the Mission for the eighth meeting of the Indian Committee several minutes before the scheduled starting time of 7:30 p.m. Nineteen people were in attendance—ten men and nine women. Raising his voice, Mr. A said, "Let's see if we can get the ball rolling. I reckon we're all here now, so this meeting comes to order. We *are* all in order, aren't we?" (The group laughed softly.) Mr. A briefly reviewed what had happened at the last meeting. He emphasized that the important lesson learned was "we have to get together if we're going to get anything done." He asked the group if they had written down the specific needs they felt that the Indians had. Several of them said that they had talked about these needs, but hadn't yet written them down, and so Mr. A distributed paper and pencils and asked them to "put them in black and white." He stopped for a second, laughed, and then said, "We've done a lot of talking but we haven't had any concrete ideas. I've got one concrete idea now—there's coffee up here, come up and help yourself." (The group laughed.)

Mr. A continued, "These meetings are going to be very informal, so if anybody has anything to say, just say it, speak right up. You're going to have to go along with me for a while, because I really don't know how to run a meeting." Several of the members of the group discounted his last remark saying, "You do okay, Chief!" "Yeah, you do fine." "Keep up the good work, Mr. Chairman." Mr. A seemed pleased with this response and said, "Well, this is a group affair, and we've got to work together, if we're going to get anywhere."

Members of the group then offered some suggestions for programs that the Indians could pursue, and Mr. A read a few others from the papers that he was collecting. These included suggestions of ways of providing jobs for high school dropouts, training programs for adult Indians, a counseling program for Indian high school students still in school, legal aid, and a few others. The assistant director explained to the Indians, "All of the programs you have mentioned so far are already going in Topeka, and so there is not much need in setting up new ones." Mr. A shook his head and said:

> Boy, getting these poverty programs going is going to be tough. It looks as though the Indian's too late again. You know, speaking of the Poverty Program, I heard an interesting joke the other day that probably tells us why the Poverty Program's so tough to get started. This government guy asked a down-and-outer what can be done to get him out of poverty. The guy tells the government man that he can put him on one of those committees and pay him for it. The government man then asks the down-and-outer, "What will you do then?" "I'll move out of the neighborhood," says the guy. "Well, if you move out of the neighborhood," says the government man, "then you won't qualify for the poverty money anymore."

The group laughed appreciatively and Mr. A added, "You see, this is kind of a round robin thing, and we have to figure out some way to stop it from going around in circles." One of the men then raised a question, "Say, is this Poverty Program here in Topeka going to be like that one in Kansas City? I've heard that in that Job Corps thing, only rich boys got the jobs." Mr. A quickly answered, stating vehemently:

> No, I don't think that's going to happen here. The guy who was the head of that Job Corps Program here in Topeka talked to us at that board meeting the other night, and he convinced me that they're being very

careful about that here. Also, I don't think there are any guys here who
are trying to latch onto the Poverty Program for high salaries. The
biggest problem that we're going to have here in Topeka is getting
people interested and getting the programs to reach the people. I think
that the TOEO may have trouble doing that.

At this point Mr. A was actually defending the TOEO. There was
not much doubt that Mr. A was still somewhat skeptical that the
program would work the way it promised to work, but he thought it
definitely was worth a try, and that it shouldn't be attacked until it had
been given a fair chance. "I don't know," Mr. A added as an after-
thought, "sometimes I get the urge just to go up to one of the agency
officials like the employment people, grab them by the neck, and
threaten to beat the hell out of them unless they get Indians better jobs.
I remember once I had to jerk a principal of a school across his desk
before I was able to get him to understand my problems and my kid's
problems." Mr. A then smiled somewhat sheepishly, looked at the
assistant director, and said, "But I guess that's not the way to do
things. At least that hasn't worked very good in the past. Maybe with
this OEO organization to help us, we can have a louder voice and get
more done. I don't know."

An Indian man startled everyone by demanding in a loud voice,
"Let's get some proposal going! All we do is talk!" Mr. A swallowed
and said:

Well, what about this one? An Indian who is not present at this meeting
suggested that we think about forming an old folks' home for Indians.
We all know some very old Indians who can't care for themselves very
well anymore, and maybe we could help them out. Those oldtimers
won't go into welfare homes, because they aren't used to the food and
they aren't used to the people. But maybe if there was a little home for
them run by Indians themselves, they'd be more willing to go there when
they need help. What do you think about that idea?

There were several assenting replies from the group. One man said,
"This sounds like a good deal. If we could get a home for the aged
Indians, then it would be the same kind of environment that they're
used to. You know, it doesn't make any difference where we go—we're
still Indians." Another participant suggested that the members "talk to
some aged Indians and see what kind of a place they would like to have
to go to." Another asked, "How'll we go about doing something like
this? How could OEO help us?" The assistant director explained that
perhaps such a program could be pursued under Title V (the Migrant
Section) of the Economic Opportunity Act. "If this were the case," he

explained, "then the home for the aged would have to be on the reservation." The Indians objected to this, and one of them said, "Oh no! The Indian agent people on the reservation usually give us the run-around when we try and get some program going through. We would rather have this home right here in Topeka, not on the reservation." The group all agreed with him. A woman added, "We want a program of our very own!" The assistant director explained that if this was the case, then the home for the aged would probably be funded under Title II of the Economic Opportunity Act (Community Action Proposal) and therefore 10 percent local share would have to be provided. The Indians wanted to know what that meant, and the assistant director explained that the community would be obliged to pay 10 percent of the project cost either with cash or services. "I don't think it would be difficult to get the 10 percent local share for such a good project." "Hey," interjected one of the participants, "what about Medicare? What about the welfare people? Is there any way that they could tie their payments in with this?" The assistant director suggested that it might be a good idea to get someone from the State Welfare Department to come to their next meeting and talk to them about that. Mr. A asked, somewhat incredulously, "Is that possible?" The assistant director said that indeed it was. Mr. A then commented, "I'm a heck of a chairman—I don't know anything. But give me time, and I'll know more in the future." The assistant director inquired, "Would you like me to arrange a speaker from welfare for your next meeting?" Mr. A replied that they would, but added, "Let's make sure that we all agree on this first." One of the group members suggested that "we vote on the issue," and Mr. A turned to the assistant director for help on how to run the voting procedure. After a brief conference, Mr. A then called for a motion, called for a second, got both, and then called for the vote, which was unanimously affirmative. The members seemed pleased with this, and one of them remarked, "History has been made, that was the first vote we've ever had!"

The question about the Indian home for the aged came up again, and someone suggested that the proposal to investigate developing such a home be put into a motion. This time Mr. A carried off the procedure without the assistant director's advice. The motion was passed unanimously, and the Indians' first community action project was officially on the drawing board.

Mr. A began to adjourn the meeting without setting a date for the next meeting. As in the last meeting, he met with objections from some of the participants who wanted to know when they would get together again. It was agreed that they should meet, as they seemed routinely to be doing now, every two weeks. The date for the next scheduled meeting was December 14, and one Indian man laughingly commented, "That's a good time to have a meeting. In fact, we could even have a meeting on Christmas Eve, then, like those guys in the white shirts who work in the big office buildings, we could have that real 'organized' feeling!" (Everybody laughed.)

Mr. A adjourned the meeting and several of the members remained to make small talk and drink more coffee. He mentioned to the group that he was "getting a hold of a little book about how to run meetings," because he "didn't know what the hell was happening." In a later interview, he reflected:

> Sometimes during those early meetings I felt kind of lost about what to do while standing up there. I wanted our meetings to be informal, because that's the way it's got to be with the Indians who come to the meetings. Sometimes I would think that if we had a little more order in the meetings, and if I knew how to handle all those motions and things like that, things would go a lot smoother and maybe we'd get a lot more done. I don't mean that we should get real fancy, like they do at those board meetings, but just so we'd have a little more order. When I'm standing up in front of that group, I like to think I know what I'm doing, and where the meeting's going.

After some experience, Mr. A, in common with most of the indigenous leaders of the TNCs, was inadvertently leaning toward increased formalization of his meetings.

About fifteen minutes after the meeting adjourned, all the remaining members began to leave. Mr. A started out the door. As he stepped into the cold night air, he shivered and said, "Man, it's cold out here! Or maybe," he added with a jerk of his thumb back toward the Indian Mission, "it's because I get so sweated up about this chairman job."

WE'RE SHOOTING FOR THE MOON

Mr. A had motivated 22 people, 11 men and 11 women, to come to the Mission on a freezing December night for the ninth meeting of the Indian committee. He searched through a pile of papers on the table. He apologized to the group for not being able to find the minutes and said, "There are so many things to do to keep this show on the road that sometimes I forget things." He then called the meeting to order, and introduced the guest speaker for the evening, the director of the State Welfare Department. The official began explaining what the Medicare program would mean to the Indians. He spoke directly, unpedantically, and left plenty of time for questions. The Indians made a number of pointed inquiries, all of which were straightforwardly answered. Several of the questions related directly to the interaction between Medicare and the proposed Indian home for the aged. Mr. A, a number of times, contributed information about other homes for the aged in the Topeka community, and the way they were operating, indicating that he had, previous to tonight's meeting, done a considerable amount of background work. Questioning came to an end, and Mr. A suggested to the group that they "write down questions on pieces of paper if you don't feel like asking them out loud." In an earlier interview, he had mentioned that "I know a lot of Indians who just don't think it's right to sound off in public and a lot of others who are just scared to do so because they don't have the right words." He added, "If you have any other questions that come up after this meeting, then write them down and give them to me and I'll go down to this man's office and get the answers for you."

A woman asked the welfare official, "Will you answer some questions about welfare tonight?" He responded that he would. An Indian man outlined for the official a specific case that he thought had been handled unjustly. The official agreed, "There seems to be a basis for a grievance there, and I would suggest that you inaugurate a grievance procedure." Mr. A picked up the official's statement, asking "Can we here in this committee represent the Indians in a grievance case or an appeal case to your office?" The official felt that that would be a good idea. Mr. A looked at the rest of the group and, nodding approvingly, said, "You see, maybe we've got something here." Turning again to the official, he repeated, almost as if he wanted to make sure he had heard correctly, "So then, you'll recognize us if we represent our people?" "Yes indeed! I'm convinced that if the poor represent themselves, then they can get more done," the official reaffirmed. "By God," exclaimed Mr. A, "maybe working through this OEO organization *is* going to give us a bigger say in things!" He turned back to the official and said, "Well, it might not be very long before we have something on your desk!"

Mr. A later indicated that this had been one of the high points of his experience with the TOEO:

> I got the feeling that maybe some doors would open to us, that we wouldn't be pushed around all the time and we could have a real say about things. I think probably I had more faith in the OEO at that moment than I had at any other time. I figured that the OEO was going to give us a chance to get together with agency officials the same way that we used to be able to get together with that juvenile judge—to be listened to as people, and not as numbers. I thought that with OEO with us, and us with OEO, we might have the stuff to get past the smart aleck clerks by the front doors of the agencies, and get a chance to talk as equals with the men behind the big desks. Yeah, I guess I was really full of hope at that time.

After the welfare official had finished answering the questions, he was thanked and applauded, and he left.

Mr. A again looked through the pile of papers on the table and pulled out several newspaper clippings about OEO programs, local and national. As he passed them out to members, he commented, "I cut these out because I think we ought to have an idea of just how big this program is. I think it's important that we see that although the OEO has been getting a lot of bad publicity around the nation, there are still good parts of the program that maybe we can latch onto." Mr. A, as further revealed by his newspaper clipping searches for OEO information, was becoming quite deeply involved as a TNC leader. He had attended the board meeting and the Leadership Training Sessions, had volunteered to serve on the Health Study Committee, and was recommended by the TOEO to serve on the community's Legal Aid Advisory Committee. He spent several hours a week of his off-the-job time consulting with the assistant director about the local program, and "talking it up with Indian families." He had asked the other indigenous leaders to "refer any problems that Indians in your neighborhoods might have to me, so that I can see what I can do about it for them," and he had, in fact, gone with one Indian who had been referred to him to the Veterans Administration in order to "help the guy get through the tangle of red tape for his Veterans Administration benefits."

It was with this hope and enthusiasm that Mr. A now brought the attention of the members to the business of the old age home proposed at the last committee meeting. He called upon the assistant director to report "what the TOEO has discovered about ways that we might fund the old age home." The assistant director told the group that he had written several letters to government officials but hadn't received any definite answers yet. He suggested that the Indians set up a subcommittee and come to the OEO office for further discussion of the details of the proposal. Mr. A agreed, and thought that the "subcommittee should have among its members at least one older person who understands the problems of the aged, and one younger person who can see the long-range problem." He called for volunteers for the subcommittee and got none. He asked one woman, who "didn't have time." He then asked a man, who responded, "This would be a good deal, this old age home. But how far would OEO go into it? How long is this OEO going to last? There seems to be a lot of conflict around the nation about OEO, and I wonder if it's going to be around next year? There're all kinds of things we ought to consider about an old age home. We've got to worry about staff. It takes a lot of money, probably at least a hundred thousand dollars." Mr. A cut in somewhat impatiently, and said, "That's true, but this is like any fight—you've got to hit first, even though you don't know what the outcome will be." The man responded, "You know, this is a very long-range program, and we just can't get this going next week!" A couple of the other participants verbally agreed. Another added, "Even if we were able to get this off the ground, who would we get to go to the home for the aged?" Mr. A commented, "I know there are lots of problems with this proposal, and I know that we really don't know too much about the direction we're going in. But we've got to plant the seed before we get the tree!"

A woman asked, "Would this be a segregated place?" Mr. A responded, "We don't mean it to be. What we talked about was providing a place where old Indians could go, especially those who probably wouldn't go anywhere at all." "Besides," he joshed, "I don't think anybody else could stand the tom-tom music!" The group laughed mildly, and a man asked, "Where are you going to get the 10 percent local share to fund this thing?" Mr. A responded, "Where do you get this *you* stuff? This is *us*, not just me. I don't know where we are going to get the 10 percent yet, but OEO has got some feelers out for us." Mr. A called upon the assistant director again to explain to the group "the procedure that will be necessary for applying for a program like an old age home." After giving a careful and detailed explanation of the procedure, the assistant director commented, "It'd be at least a year before you'd be able to begin operation of such a home." The group reacted very negatively to this, and there were comments about the length of time involved. "Here we go again," muttered one man, "another one of those pie-in-the-sky deals."

A woman asked, "Is this going to be a rest home or an old folks home?" Mr. A replied, now a bit nervously, "What do you keep asking me for? It's going to be whatever *we* decide it to be." "Man," he sighed, "this sure gets complicated!" The assistant director again urged that the group "appoint a subcommittee to look further into the possibilities for the old age home." Mr. A again called for volunteers, and again there was no response. A long pause followed, finally broken by Mr. A's saying, softly and with resignation, "Well, if we can't get anybody, we might as well forget this thing." He then quickly added, a little louder, "Well, we'll all let it hang until the next meeting. You know what I think is wrong? I think we're shooting for the moon here, and maybe that's one of the problems with some of these OEO projects. I wish there was something that we could get done right away!"

Mr. A suggested to the group that it might be time to adjourn (it was 9:40 p.m.). The tenth gathering of the Indians was scheduled for late January. Mr. A looked around the group for a moment, then said, "I guess this meeting is adjourned."

Most of the participants left immediately after adjournment. Six or seven members remained to have coffee and socialize a bit. Mr. A appeared depressed and commented that "the group seems undecided about the possibility of the old age home." In a later interview, Mr. A reflected:

> That was a very tough meeting for me. When the guy from Welfare was talking, and it looked as though our committee might be able to represent Indians who needed help in dealing with that agency, I was very excited about being the chairman and what we could do for our people. Later on in that very same damned meeting, when the people started getting so doubtful about even *trying* to get the old age program going, I began to get disappointed. It's the same damn thing we always see—we quit before we even start. Then it seemed to me like the people during that meeting started giving me a bad time. The guy from Welfare has no trouble at all, but I start catching hell about the fact that the old age home idea is going to take so long and it's so complicated. For a while there I began to get the feeling that some of my own buddies were "putting me on." Toward the end there I got the rotten feeling that I was losing touch with the group, that they saw me as being way across the room, just another agency official. I can tell you this—I don't like that feeling!

After about ten minutes of conversation following this ninth meeting, Mr. A walked out of the Mission and over to his parked car. As he got in, he commented to his wife, "Damn it, I have to work harder at this than I do at my own job!"

The following day, an article appeared in one of the local newspapers, reporting the events of the meeting of the Indian Committee. In the article, mention was made of a point that had been discussed by the State Welfare Department official and Mr. A—the relative merits of providing cash versus grocery orders for needy persons. To Mr. A was attributed a comment that indicated that it would be better for Indians to receive grocery orders rather than money because the Indians have a tendency to spend all their money on beer and leave nothing for food. Mr. A felt that he had "been misquoted, and what I said was given the wrong slant. That article sure got me into a lot of trouble with the Indians! A couple of them said to me, 'Who the hell do you think you are—some big wheel now because you're an OEO officer? You think you're better than us now, so you can say things about us!' When you take the job as a committee chairman, you're on the firing line, that's for sure!"

THE "CHIEF" IS ABSENT

During the month of January, Mr. A attended TOEO sponsored Leadership Training Sessions for TNC officers. He began taking an active part in these meetings, asking questions, offering suggestions, making and seconding motions on various agenda items. At one of these meetings, he became particularly interested in the Neighborhood Aide Program proposed by two other TNCs and sponsored by the TOEO. He saw the possibility of an Indian Neighborhood Aide, working on a full-time basis "doing a lot of good to help Indians meet their needs and approach the agencies." He emphasized the point that "the Neighborhood Aide who works for the Indians has to be an Indian, someone they know and they can get along with, or else none of them will open their doors."

A few days before the scheduled January meeting of the Indian Committee, Mr. A had to leave town to attend the funeral of an out-of-state relative. Before he had left the area, he instructed the vice chairperson of the committee to conduct this tenth meeting in his absence. By 8:00 p.m. of the meeting night, only four Indians had arrived, including the vice chairperson. The door to the Indian Mission was locked, and a phone call had been made to get someone with a key. By the time the key arrived—at 8:30—no Indians remained but the vice chairman himself, along with the assistant director and two non-Indians. The vice chairperson suggested that "we cancel this meeting, and get together when Mr. A returns."

Upon his return, Mr. A reported that he had "contacted several Indian families before leaving, and told them to go ahead and have the meeting anyway. It's funny. It seems as though Indians come to depend upon one leader, and although they might give him a bad time when he's standing up there in front of them, they won't get together without him." He immediately contacted the participants in the committee, and rescheduled a meeting for the end of February.

Mr. A attended two more Leadership Training Sessions while preparing for his February meeting. At the first one, when the committee officers collectively decided that they should elect from among themselves a chair, vice chair and secretary and thus establish a Committee of Neighborhood Officers, Mr. A was nominated, along with three others, for the top position. In response to the nomination, he said, "I'm afraid I'm going to have an awful lot going for me in the future, and I'm probably going to have to miss a few meetings. I am honored that you nominated me, and that you have confidence in me, but I'm going to have to decline." He reported later, "That's all I'd have had to do—become an officer of the officers. Then my people would really have given me a bad time about becoming an organization man!"

At the second of the Leadership Training Meetings, Mr. A became interested in a Medicare Alert Program that the TOEO was trying to get under way. He became angry at one point with "all this talking about the thing. Let's get it off the ground! Let's get it going in a hurry! Why do we always dilly-dally around so much? One of the biggest faults with this whole program is that there's too much talk and not enough action!" At the same meeting, when asked if he would serve on a panel of committee officers who would make themselves available to explain to various civic organizations what the TOEO was doing, he replied, "I'm still afraid to voice my own opinions when talking to some strange group. I'm afraid that my opinions won't say what the people I represent really think." He nonetheless agreed to be on the panel and did actually have contact with some civic groups. He explained in a later interview, "I didn't get on the panel just because I wanted to sell OEO to people. I knew that most, if not all, of the Indians were still very skeptical about OEO, and if I was going to represent them it wouldn't be right for me to blow the OEO horn. I got on the panel because I thought it was a good chance to show other people in the community that Indians are interested in all kinds of things and maybe to help break down the rotten picture that they have of us."

Toward the end of the Leadership meeting, all of the officers talked about the degree of interest within their committees. Mr. A, with some force, said, "When we first started our meetings, we discussed and cussed a lot. Now, interest seems to be falling off. Unless we can get something that develops in the quick future, we're not going to hold the interest of the members much longer." The other officers agreed that they were having the same kind of difficulty, and one of them suggested that "maybe we can get some social workers out to help us get more interest." Mr. A laughed and replied, "I'm afraid that my people don't have a very good view of social workers. They have seen too many people come out to 'help' the Indians who think that they're experts on Indian life because they have read a couple of Zane Grey novels! But this Neighborhood Aide Program, maybe that's different. If we can get an Indian Neighborhood Aide, one who lives right out there with us, then maybe that will be a different story." In a later interview, he said:

> I really believed that getting an Indian Neighborhood Aide would make a lot of difference to the Indian Committee. I don't mean just because a full-time Indian Neighborhood Aide who knew his way around could be

a big help to the Indians, but also because it would prove to them that the OEO really could accomplish something for the Indian, and I mean specifically for the Indian.

I talked this Neighborhood Aide idea up with an awful lot of people, and I pretty much put it on the line that this was going to show us all that OEO really had the stuff—that it was able to get something concrete for us. Quite a few of the people who I talked to said, "Aw, come on, they'll never hire an Indian," and I argued with them, and told them that they would! In a way I was giving my word to the people that an Indian would be hired and that I was willing to put my faith in the OEO organization that this would be accomplished. I wish to hell that I would have kept my big mouth shut!

MR. A'S LAST COMMITTEE MEETING

At the February meeting, the eleventh of the Indian group, there were 21 women, 10 men, and 5 children. Mr. A had said that he had "campaigned like hell" to get a good turnout. He seemed more nervous than he usually was before the meetings. Possibly it was because the assistant director of the TOEO was not able to attend, but more probably it was because he had been "getting a lot of guff" from the Indians he talked to about OEO. He had searched for a list of the procedures for carrying out a meeting, but couldn't find one and decided to "fake it out." He called the meeting to order and instructed the secretary to read the minutes.

He then turned to the business at hand, and said, "Many of you have come to this meeting wanting OEO to help you with problems. The government won't duplicate programs already in effect. They can't do what is already being done by another agency, like the Welfare Department or the Indian Agency. OEO's primary target is to run interference between you and other agencies. At least that's the way I see our committee here. Then there may also be some other special programs that we can go into with OEO money. Actually, I guess the biggest benefit that you get from OEO participation is what you learn by being a part of it . . . " A woman interrupted him, "I don't see no sense to it. Why call us here if there is nothing in it for us right away?" Another woman said, "It seems like we always have to go through a hundred steps and fill out a hundred forms before we can get help. Is this going to be another one of those deals?" One of the men spoke up, "Sometimes the kind of help an Indian can get through the Indian agencies isn't as much as other people get through other agencies. I think our problem is that we don't know the right people. Maybe it will help us to go through this OEO outfit." Mr. A agreed, "Now you're talking! That's what got me interested in OEO, and if it works, that's what's going to keep us all interested! And remember, this isn't like welfare, they aren't going to give us anything. We've got to get it for ourselves! That's a big difference. By coming together into groups like this, by getting a voice for ourselves, and by having the force of OEO behind us, maybe we can get a lot more done!"

One of the participants asked Mr. A about the progress of the proposed "old folks home for Indians." Mr. A answered, with disappointment in his voice, "I guess we were just shooting for the moon there. We have to get 10 percent of the funding, and that's just out of reach for us. I guess everything fell through—there was too much complication." One man murmured, "I told you so," but otherwise the group remained silent. Mr. A continued to run through the reports on programs that he had observed or discovered through his participation in other OEO activities. He told the group about job placements for youths, the Head Start Program, small business loans, and the Legal Aid Program. He paused for a moment and said, "I know that we would all like a program where all we'd have to do is turn in our names and have everything done for us, but that's not the way it's going to work here. We've got to decide upon what we need, and then go after some of the available programs." A woman remarked, "Yeah, that's okay! But all these programs take so long to get going! What can we get going now?" Mr. A then continued describing to the group the local OEO-sponsored Job Corps, work-study programs, day-care center, and the Neighborhood Aide Program. One of the men challenged him. "Those programs all sound very good, but will they put bread on the table?" A woman angrily broke in, "This program sounds too good to be true. I don't believe it. I really don't think this OEA [sic] would help me out the door. They wouldn't give me anything!" Mr. A answered, "Come to an Economic Opportunity Board meeting some time and see how many people are interested in this program, and a lot of them are from the agencies too—they all want to try and help us out, or I should say, help us to help ourselves." He continued, apparently growing angry, "Why are you getting mad at me! This isn't my program you know. If you don't like something, let's do something about it, but don't give me a bad time!" Mr. A commented in a later interview:

> At that point in the meeting I began to feel like I was another person. By that I mean I knew exactly how the people who were giving me a bad time felt, and damn it, I agreed with them. I know and understand why they were interested in getting something done now, particularly with regard to jobs and the comforts of life. I could see now that they were beginning to sharpshoot me with questions, and I thought to myself, "I should be out there with them, not standing up here." But I kept trying

to answer their questions, and I kept defending OEO. I did this even though I could understand the meaning of the questions that they asked better than I could understand the meaning of the answers I gave them!

Mr. A was beginning sharply to feel the marginality of his indigenous leader role. It was a difficult conflict for him to resolve, primarily because, as he subsequently reported, "The people seemed to be forcing me to make a choice. It seemed to me that they were saying, 'Either you're with us or you're against us—either you're an OEO officer or you're an Indian, you can't be both.' I wasn't sure what I was going to do."

It was now 9:15 p.m., and Mr. A suggested that they show the film they had scheduled for this eleventh meeting. It was a documentary, dramatizing the victory that the South Dakota Indians had concerning land rights. The moral of the film, according to Mr. A's introductory remarks, was "what Indians can do if they get together and really try." The film was started, and as it progressed, more than half the audience got up and left. After its completion, Mr. A commented, "I guess some of them left because the hour was late, but I'm sure a lot of them left because they don't like to see that Indians who got together and fought could do things for themselves. I think they'd rather have things given to them. They couldn't watch that and sympathize with those Indians without admitting they were wrong themselves."

Mr. A saw no reason for formally adjourning the meeting, and while the film was being put away and the projector boxed up, he talked with a few of the participants. "I'm wondering," he said thoughtfully, "if it wouldn't be better to form an Indian group outside the OEO, built around social and cultural interests—like the Pow-Wow Clubs. Maybe that would work to get the Indians together, and then we could tie in with OEO. I'm not sure what to do. All I know is that I'm getting tired of being a target!"

THE CHIEF RESIGNS

Shortly before the twelfth meeting of the Indian TNC, scheduled in March, Mr. A informed the assistant director of the TOEO that he had "taken an evening construction job, which will make it difficult for me to continue serving as an OEO officer." The assistant director in a later interview commented, "Mr. A really doesn't want to work at an evening job, but he has to take what he can right now. The job may not last too long, and maybe he will be able to let the vice chairman run the show until he gets a daytime job that he'll like better." This eventuality, however, did not materialize. At the March meeting of the Indian Committee, no one showed up but the assistant director and a few agency representatives. No Indians, not even the vice chairman, came to the Mission. The meeting was cancelled by the assistant director.

Mr. A still had not officially resigned as chairperson of the Indian Committee, nor did he intend to, until, near the first of April, he discovered that the administrators of the Neighborhood Aide Program had not hired one of the Indians whom he had encouraged to apply, but a man whom he perceived to be "not an Indian, an outsider." Mr. A became furious when he learned of it, and felt that the Indians had been "given a raw deal again." He felt that he had "given his word to the people" that an Indian would be hired for the job, which would prove that "OEO was really interested in the Indian." He was bombarded with "I told you so's" from the members of the committee and was personally attacked by some of his friends for "having sold out to the agencies." He talked with the TOEO assistant director and was informed that the program administrators had "the primary responsibility for the hiring, and there's not much we can do about it." He went to visit the supervisor of the Neighborhood Aides, and ended up becoming even more angry because of what he perceived as a "holier than thou attitude" on the part of the supervisor. He then attempted to talk with the top official in the delegate agency sponsoring the Neighborhood Aide Program, but said he was told "the official is out of town." Mr. A said that he had "seen him go into his office just a little while before," and as far as he was concerned, "that was the last straw." By the time that the Economic Opportunity Board met on the evening of April 6, the president of the board had in hand Mr. A's letter of resignation. The board accepted it and instructed the secretary to send Mr. A a letter of commendation for his "diligent and sincere labors on our behalf."

CONCLUSION

As chairperson of a War on Poverty Indian target neighborhood committee, Mr. A experienced intense role marginality. He was an indigenous leader, elected by his peers to represent them in community poverty intervention efforts. He was to be a bridge between the community's low-income Indians and its OEO-funded antipoverty organization. That organization, and the board of directors that guided it, consisted primarily of middle-class Anglos. The Indians for whom Mr. A was to speak historically had been inadequately served or frankly exploited by Anglo-dominated federal agencies. They were understandably skeptical of the intentions and capabilities of the anti-poverty effort. They had little reason to trust those endeavors as well-meaning.

Mr. A's Indian tribe, the Prairie Potawatomi, had culturally espoused the view that people ought not flagrantly pursue leadership positions. An individual did not deliberately stand out from and thereby embarrass his or her brothers and sisters. So that all could survive, the tribe was more important than the individual. In addition to that cultural orientation, many of the Prairie Potawatomi had by hard lesson adopted a seemingly subservient status toward federally imposed leadership. However, that stance included strategies for maintaining, even if no more than "putting on" agency officials, some sense of personal dignity.

The War on Poverty legislation, at least on paper, insisted that the poor should have a significant part in shaping poverty intervention programs at the community level. The poor were to have "maximum feasible participation" in those efforts. Indigenous leaders among the poor were to be found, developed, and encouraged. They were to enact marginal roles between the poor and nonpoor. In that context, Mr. A was elected by his peers to be chair of the TOEO Indian Target Neighborhood Committee.

The feelings of role marginality as an indigenous leader were more than Mr. A could tolerate. A person of considerable ability, his attempts were characterized by dedication, imagination, and enthusiastic energy. He consistently was assaulted by the conflicting expectations of his Indian followers and those of the Anglo-dominated federal program. Most particularly, he found the program unable to generate the immediate "bread and butter" results his neighbors wanted. The War on Poverty was geared more toward long-term interventions. Increasingly, Mr. A's followers typified him as having become a federal bureaucrat, as having "sold out" his people for his own gain. In the end, he resigned as an indigenous leader. As he illustratively put it, he no longer could "walk the tightrope" between his followers and the poverty agency.

Where was the creativity, the autonomy, in Mr. A's role enactment? He quit the marginality of the indigenous leader role. Can abandoning a role be a creative and autonomous act? Indeed it can. Mr. A attempted as best he could to "walk the tightrope" between conflicting expectations for his behavior as a leader. The situation made success in that effort nearly impossible. He could have resolved the marginality by becoming "TOEO's man." If he had done so, he would have been rewarded—by increased recognition from the Anglo community and probably a paying job in the program. He could have resolved the marginality by becoming an activist rather than an advocate for his followers. If he had done so, he would have been rewarded—by increased recognition from his Indian neighbors for being, as one of them stated, a "war chief." Mr. A considered both of those alternatives and rejected them. In his judgment, the first option would have divorced him from the people he wanted to serve and of whom he was part. The second would have divorced him and his followers from the federal antipoverty program as constituted. Consequently, he elected a third option. He resigned. Role marginality is very difficult and painful to maintain. Mr. A concluded that if he could not be a successful "bridge," he would not be a bridge at all. That choice was by no means the easy way out. He had to suffer the expressed disappointment both of TOEO officials and of his Indian followers. He personally expressed feelings of failure. But he concluded that it was the best decision, and he acted accordingly. He perceived himself to be a competent and autonomous individual. When the indigenous leader role defied his competence and encroached upon his autonomy, he discarded it.

Role marginality is situated in complicated social settings and involves multiple pushes and pulls in behavioral expectations from diverse groups of people. It cuts across a broad and often personally troublesome network of social, cultural, and emotional elements. Though it causes the enactors problems, role marginality is neither unusual nor aberrant. To the contrary, it is commonplace among individuals deliberately or accidentally involved in sociocultural change. Despite the discomfort that can be associated with it, role marginality provides individuals with the opportunity for considerable autonomy and freedom. The enactor usually is not wedded to the expectations of one particular group of others. Typically, a "bridging" role is not well defined. There is no clear role to take; it has to be made. If the situation is not overwhelming, and the enactor can endure the ambiguities and contradictions, he or she can autonomously shape and define the marginal role.

12

TRANSFORMING AN ACCUSTOMED ROLE
Priests in a Protest Movement and
Felons in a Parole System

As indicated in Chapters 9 and 10, people enact some roles that are "dominant" in their role sets. The enactment of those roles demands an extensive commitment of time and energy. It is not unusual for dominant role enactments, for example, those that are associated with profession or occupation, to span the major portion of adults' lifetimes. Sometimes the dominant roles to which people have become accustomed are transformed by choice or by situational necessity. The transformation process often is difficult.

The long-standing dominant roles people enact become part of their self-concepts (Turner, 1978; Karp and Yoels, 1979; Becker, 1960; Stone, 1962; Stryker, 1980; Hewitt, 1979; McCall and Simmons, 1966). If those roles are transformed, severe dislocations of self-concept can result (Turner, 1976; Zurcher, 1977). The enactors must at least temporarily modify the manner in which they perceive themselves.

Two examples of dominant role transformation are discussed in this chapter—"dissident" priests and paroled felons. The priests had occupied that status for many years, but increasingly they found the situationally defined role expectations associated with the priestly status to

---

This chapter draws upon two unpublished papers, "The Self-Concepts of Dissident Priests" and "The Self-Concepts of Ex-Felons." The first I wrote with Louis Schneider and Ralph Nemir; the second with Rosemary J. Erickson and Waymon J. Crow. Some

212 of the 448 Catholic priests in the San

be unacceptable to them. They became part of a social movement intended to change the Catholic church. The felons had for several years enacted the dominant role of "prisoner." When at last achieving the parole from prison they sought, they found themselves released to an alien "straight" social world.

I was involved in analyzing the informal interviews that had been conducted with the study of dissident priests. My own background included eighteen years of educational training by Catholic priests and nuns, so I was familiar with that clerical role. I had not been a felon, nor had I any such direct experience with criminal justice organizations. However, I worked with former felons in the study of parolees and through them became acquainted with the parole system.

Although the relation between self-concept and role enactment has been alluded to in previous chapters, it will now become more obvious. In the following chapter (Chapter 13), the theoretical aspects of that relation will be fully discussed.

THE DISSIDENT PRIESTS

During the fall of 1968, 68 of the 448 Catholic priests in the San Antonio, Texas, archdiocese signed a petition calling for the resignation of the archbishop of San Antonio. They protested what they saw as the archbishop's conservative and authoritarian leadership style. By signing the petition, the "dissident" priests (as they were called in the media) had taken a stand that transformed their clerical role from acquiescence to activism within the church hierarchy.

Of the 68 petition signatories, 30 agreed to be interviewed about their participation in the protest. Because of the public controversy, it was not possible to interview as a control group any of the "nondissident" San Antonio priests, those who had not signed the petition. However, a comparison group of 20 such priests was available in nearby Austin, Texas. At the median, the dissident priests were 33.5 and the nondissidents 46 years of age.

During the interviews, it was possible to administer the Twenty Statements Test (TST) to 24 of the dissident and all 20 of the nondissident priests. The TST asks respondents to answer the question, "Who

of the material has been published with Louis Schneider in "Toward Understanding the Catholic Crisis: Observations on Dissident Priests in Texas," *Journal for the Scientific Study of Religion* 9 (Fall 1970): 197–209; and with Rosemary J. Erickson, Waymon J. Crow, and Archie V. Connett in *Paroled But Not Free* (New York: Human Sciences Press, 1973). Used by permission.

Table 9   TST Responses (%) for the Dissident and
            Nondissident Priests

	A	B	C	D
Dissidents (N = 24)	2.0	14.0	64.0	20.0
Nondissidents (N = 20)	2.4	44.7	27.4	25.4

am I?" twenty times consecutively on a lined sheet of paper. The TST assumes that respondents will reveal, among other aspects of their self-concepts, those that are role related.

The scoring of the TST has been guided by several different protocols (Kuhn, 1960; McPartland and Cumming, 1958; Schwirian, 1964; Spitzer et al., 1973; McPartland, 1965). In this study, the TST responses were scored according to the protocol outlined by McPartland et al. (1961), who suggest four major categories of TST responses: "A" statements refer to the individual as a physical entity (I am 6 feet tall; I weigh 170 pounds); "B" statements identify the role expectations of the individual within established statuses (I am a vice president; I am a sophomore); "C" statements reflect the individual's feelings about and evaluation of particular roles (I am an anxious pilot; I am a concerned citizen). "D" statements indicate that the individual searched for an identity beyond socially grounded roles (I am one with the universe; I am part of all reality).

Results

As shown in Table 9, the dissident priests overall had a markedly lower percentage of B responses and a markedly higher percentage of C responses than the nondissidents.

Table 10 presents the "modal" TST responses for the dissident and the nondissident priests. A respondent's modal TST response is determined by whichever scoring category, A, B, C, or D, contains the largest number of responses (Hartley, 1968a, 1968b; McPartland, 1965). B mode, for example, means that the majority of the individual's TST responses fell into the B category. As the table reveals, the dissident priests had a much lower percentage of B modes, and a much higher percentage of C modes, than the nondissident priests.

Table 10   Modal TST Categories (%) for the Dissident and Nondissident Priests

	A Mode	B Mode	C Mode	D Mode
Dissidents (N = 24)	0.0	4.0	83.0	13.0
Nondissidents (N = 20)	0.0	50.0	25.0	25.0

The interviews revealed that the dissidents had, prior to their having become discontent with the actions of their archbishop, fully enacted the traditional priestly role. Even the youngest of them had been a priest for ten years; most of them had been priests for fifteen or more years. Though they tended to be liberal in their political and theological views, they had not by any means been malcontents. However, tumultuous events in the 1960s, including the civil rights and antiwar movements, had influenced them to question the role of priest in efforts to solve contemporary societal problems. They decided that the expectation for priestly obedience to church authority, when that authority arbitrarily enforced conservative social policies, was not consistent with their personal inclinations or spiritual obligations. So they autonomously transformed the dominant role they had so long enacted and to which they had so long been accustomed.

The signing of the petition calling for the replacement of the archbishop was a powerful symbol of the dissidents' attempt to transform the priestly role. That act not only modified their enactments of the role, but hazarded their membership in the church, the organization in which the role was embedded. They in effect were engaged in mutiny, and were threatened with excommunication. They were on the edge of being removed from, or perhaps having completely to reject, the dominant role they had so long enacted and that had become so central a part of their self-concepts.

The potential or actual loss of a dominant role, whether by choice or because of circumstances, causes a person to examine, evaluate, and eventually redefine his or her self-concept (Mead, 1934; Kuhn and McPartland, 1954). The TSTs of the dissident priests reflected that dislocation. Most of their responses to the question, "Who am I?" were agonizingly reflective and emotionally profound, as illustrated by the following evaluative C responses several of the dissidents recorded:

- I am a confused man.
- I am frustrated with the church.

- I am lonely.
- I am in need of the help and consultation of others.
- I am less trusting than I was in past years.
- I am worried.
- I am unsure of my ability.
- I am reevaluating my beliefs.
- I am becoming more withdrawn.
- I am uneasy in my self-image.
- I am useless to many people.
- I am abrupt sometimes.
- I am not very organized.

The responses indicated that the dissidents, having chosen to transform their priestly dominant role, were evaluating not only the new direction that the role might take but also the conceptions of self that had been linked to that role.

The TST responses of the nondissident priests were quite different from those of the dissidents. They were mostly B-type responses, not evaluative of the priestly role, of other social roles linked with being a priest, or of a self-concept significantly based in enactment of the traditional role of priest. They were emotionally neutral. The following examples from several of the nondissidents are representative:

- I am a Roman Catholic priest.
- I am President of the Council of Churches.
- I am an Assistant Pastor.
- I am a Kiwanian.
- I am a hospital chaplain.
- I am a spiritual advisor to groups and organizations.
- I am a Rector.
- I am a Chaplain in the United States Army Reserve.
- I am a Monsignor.
- I am an ordained Catholic priest.
- I am a Pastor.

The responses indicated that the nondissidents, content with and not wanting to transform their priestly dominant role, felt at ease with and defined themselves in terms of that role.

The difference in median age between the dissident and nondissident priests did not account for the variation in their TST responses. The responses of the older and younger priests in each of the two groups (divided at the median age) were compared and found to be not significantly different. The predominance of evaluative C responses among the dissidents and of role-based B responses among the nondissidents plausibly could be attributed to a decision to transform (make) the dominant priest role or to continue to enact (take) it in its traditional form. Both the making and the taking of the priestly role reflected an autonomous decision by the priests. One of these options was not necessarily more creative than the other. But making the role, transforming it after so many years of taking it, was a disconcerting and painful process necessitating a reassessment of self-concept.

THE FELONS

People who have been convicted of felonious criminal acts usually are sentenced to several years in "hard joints," maximum-security state or federal prisons. During their incarceration, the felons live in total institutions (see Chapters 2 and 3). Though prisons by design are not pleasant, the role expectations for the prisoners typically are clear and detailed. Prison society has an elaborate but straightforward formal and informal stratification of statuses, based on such factors as the individual's type of crime, length of sentence, time already spent in prison, history of convictions, ethnicity, physical characteristics, and sexual orientation (Glaser, 1964; Baum and Wheeler, 1969; Clemmer, 1958; Studt et al., 1968; Wheeler, 1969).

Felons who are not frankly insane or wholly sociopathic do what they can to be paroled from prison. For a variety of reasons, they want to transform their role as imprisoned felon to that of paroled felon. If they are successful, the role transformation is not an easy one. The role is more sharply defined in prison than in the parole system. Irwin (1970: 117), himself an ex-felon, has commented on the challenges to accustomed role and to self-concept experienced by the parolee when released to the "straight" world:

> Not only does the world seem strange; the self loses its distinctiveness. Not only does the person find the new setting strange and unpredictable, and not only does he experience anxiety and disappointment from his inability to function normally in this strange setting, but he loses a grip on his profounder meanings, his values, goals, conceptions of himself.
>
> In this situation, planned, purposeful action becomes extremely difficult. Such action requires a definite sense of self, a relatively clear idea of one's relation to other things, and some sense of one's direction or goal. All of these tend to become unravelled in a radical shift of settings.

In August 1970, as part of a larger interview procedure, we administered the TST to a sample of 60 male paroled felons. Of the respond-

Table 11   Modal TST Categories (%) for the Paroled Felons

	A Mode	B Mode	C Mode	D Mode
Paroled felons (N = 60)	0.0	3.0	77.0	20.0

ents, 30 were randomly sampled from the population of 592 paroled felons living in San Diego County during August 1970 (Sample I). The remaining 30 respondents were randomly sampled from among all of the adult male felons newly paroled to San Diego County during August and September 1970 (Sample II). The average time since parole was 2 years for Sample I and 2 months for Sample II. The samples were not significantly different in demographic characteristics, types of crimes committed, and length of time served in prison (generally 5 or more years). Nor were Samples I and II combined significantly different in those characteristics from the parolee population in San Diego County.

The interviews were conducted by ex-felons in order to neutralize the "front gate game" often played by parolees. That "game" involves giving socially desirable responses to "straight" officials in order to enhance getting and continuing parole. All the interviews were tape-recorded.

Results

As shown in Table 11, the parolees were predominantly C mode in their TST responses. They manifested intense feelings of uncertainty, loneliness, and anxiety. They were searchingly reflective about and evaluative of their social roles. Length of time on parole (whether Sample I or Sample II), ethnicity, type of crime, age, marital status, and educational level made no significant difference in that outcome.

The responses, as illustrated by the following examples from several of the parolee respondents, revealed the difficulties of transforming the imprisoned felon to paroled felon role and the accompanying challenges to self-concept:

- I am on the outside and don't know if I can make it.
- I am scared about being able to stay straight.
- I am on parole and ain't sure what to do now.
- I am more used to prison than the streets.
- I am not going back to the joint if I can help it.

- I am lost, man.
- I am looking for a job.
- I am sorry that my family don't want me anymore.
- I am sick of being told I am a con.
- I am wondering if anybody really cares.
- I am working in a shitty job.
- I am not sure what to do anymore.
- I am wishing things were better on the outside.
- I am glad I have a PO [parole officer] who is not an asshole.

The parolees had purposefully and successfully enacted the imprisoned felon role so that they could be awarded parole. They had created the circumstances for role transformation. Once on the outside, they found the transformation difficult to enact. They usually encountered the stigma of being a "con," flimsy support systems for the paroled felon role, and little training for enacting the transformation. The prisoner status had, despite its obvious limitations, situationally given them some sense of self. The parolee status was so ambiguous that it blurred identity; they had not been prepared for it. The parolees paradoxically were free but not free. They were on the outside, but at best unevenly accepted by others in that world.

The following interview further illustrated the stresses associated with the role transformation:

Leonard Montgomery is 35 years of age. He served over 13 years without parole in California state prisons.

Leonard was reared by his mother and attended high school through the second year. He is happily married now, and has children. Though he was employed for a while after his release, he was laid off and has not been able to find new work; so he is receiving welfare assistance. He had been on parole for about six months when interviewed.

           *   *   *

The first days out were just great, really, because I had been away for 13 years and to get out and be able to walk around was great. Even after 6½ months, I'm still sort of gung ho. I'll be standing, just enjoying being out in the streets, being able to look up in the air, or at the stars or watching the planes go by. I hadn't been able to do this for a long time.

People who haven't been locked up can't understand what I see in it because it's a thing they take for granted. You know, it's there all the time, it hasn't been taken away from them. It's a gas, bein' out, and I enjoy it and I intend on stayin' out.

It was a lot for me to get used to. It was almost like the first few days in the penitentiary, but not quite that bad. I don't mean it was bad bein' out—it was beautiful—but you know how you feel when you're new to something. It's almost like being reborn. There are things you have to learn all over again, and things you have to learn. There was a lot of time between '56 and '70, and everything here was new to me, really, it was all new. New and beautiful.

My wife divorced me about two years after I got busted. But all the time I was locked up, I kept in touch with the kids, and then when I got a date and went to Chino—I had a 90-day pass. I think this is a terrific idea. I came home and looked for a job, and I got back and talked with my family. And me and my wife found out that although there are things there that had been smothered, they were still there. We decided to give it another try, and it's working out beautiful . . .

Before I got out, I wondered whether or not I could make it, you know. I always felt before I got out that if I got out, I would be able to make it. But then after I got out, I guess I was a little hesitant at being really sure. The joint didn't give me any help, but my family did.

Well, after I first got out I explained to my family that it was going to take time for me to adjust to them and for them to adjust to me. I gave them a small rundown on my little moods and the personality I have. This is just something that happens after you do so much time. I'm gonna have to take time to get rid of it. And they understand, and we get along. At times I'm awfully quick-tempered, not that I'm violent, but I'll say something that's unpleasant. But this is not really me, and they understand . . .

I made my mistake, but I'm going to make it now. I'm going to make it with my family—with their understanding, love, and willingness to help.

Leonard Montgomery (the name is fictitious) accomplished the role transition; he was about to be discharged from parole. Many of the other respondents in the study were returned to prison for parole violations or for subsequent criminal convictions. Leonard, unlike those parolees who became recidivists, had developed a combination of family encouragement, educational prison experience, and sense of autonomy that enhanced his efforts at role transformation.

People usually need the support of significant others to endure the stresses of role transformation. Family, friends, and role models can provide that support. A clarity or resiliency of self-concept can also facilitate the transformation. Choosing to transform a role is a creative and sometimes courageous act; implementing the transformation is very difficult to do alone.

CONCLUSION

The priests and the felons had elected to attempt transformation of the dominant roles they had long enacted and that were historically supported by the powerful organizations in which those roles were embedded. The priests wanted to broaden their ministerial role better to ameliorate what they saw as the important social problems of the time. The felons wanted to be parolees rather than prisoners. After successfully having taken actions to inaugurate their role transformations, both the priests and the felons suffered severe social dislocations. The priests found themselves labeled as "dissidents," cut adrift from the traditional clerical role that they had enacted within the church. The felons found themselves ambiguously labeled as "ex-cons," cut adrift from the unpleasant but predictable behavioral expectations they had known in prison.

The priests and the felons obviously had, as distinct groups of individuals, different reasons for undertaking role transformation. The priests felt that elements of the church hierarchy had unduly constricted the ministerial role and even rendered it irrelevant. They were by value orientation committed to a pastoral function that they perceived to have become organizationally impeded. The felons simply wanted to get out of prison, some because they wanted to "go straight," some because imprisonment was so repulsive, a few because they wanted to "hustle" (successfully) on the streets again. Those who wanted to "go straight" were faced most squarely with the challenges of role transformation, but all of the parolees had one way or another to deal with that transformation.

The dissident priests and the paroled felons for diverse reasons willfully had transformed accustomed dominant roles. However, since dominant roles (of any kind) are central components of self-concept, both the priests' and the felons' TSTs generally revealed intense reflection, evaluation, concern, and emotion about "who" they were and "who" they should become. Though their social situations differed markedly, the priests and felons alike were searching for the other end of their role transformations.

The priests and the felons had distinctive difficulties in effecting their role transformations. The priests wanted to broaden their ministerial role within the clerical hierarchy; they were not inclined to leave the church organization. The felons wanted to modify their role from prisoner to parolee; they wanted to be released from the prison organization. They knew that being a "parolee" kept them in the criminal justice system of which prison was a part, but that they would be "outside the walls." The priests encountered rejection from others within the church organization in which they sought role transformation. The felons were not rejected by others in the criminal justice system, but they usually were not accepted by others in the "straight" world to which they had been paroled.

Both the priests and the parolees needed support in their role transformations. The priests' clerical vows had for the most part detached them from family and precluded wives or children. The felons' long terms in prison had for the most part eroded their marriage and family ties. Those who had such support, or the support of other people significant to them, were better able to enact the role transformations.

The priests and felons are vivid examples of role transformation. But the circumstances of everyday life include many attempts at such transformation, although they may not be so dramatic as the cases of dissident priests and paroled felons. For example, individuals who choose to become "alcholics" rather than "drunks," to become "divorcees" rather than "spouses," to become "wage earners" rather than "housewives," and to change long-enacted occupations engage the difficulties of role transformation. People who become "retirees," willfully or not, experience that sort of transformation.

Roles exist in a social context, and involve behavioral expectations defined in part by organizational structure and in part by human interaction within those structures. People can to a greater or lesser extent autonomously shape those roles, depending on the rigidity of the structures and interactions. All role enactments reflect the actors' perceptions of the expectations of other people. Compared with the role situations discussed in the preceding chapters, creatively and successfully transforming a dominant role perhaps depends most fully on the unreserved and close support of significant others, whether they be family members, spouses, friends, therapists, counselors, or admired role models.

13

A FRAMEWORK FOR
ANALYZING ROLE ENACTMENT

In Chapter 1, I followed Heiss (1981a: 95) in defining roles as the behavioral expectations for what a person "should" do when occupying a position (status) in a specific social setting. The sources of the "should" included expectations associated with recognized roles in established social structures or associated with acknowledged cultural values, emergent roles in informal or atypical situations, and the person's own self-concept and inclinations.

Roles are learned as a central part of the process of socialization. The socialization messages can range from those that are quite elaborate and formally taught to those that are quite simple and incidentally taught in ad hoc situations (Heiss, 1981a: 106-107).

As part of the routine of everyday life, people accumulate extensive role repertoires. Sometimes components of those repertoires conflict; sometimes they complement each other. Whenever they can, people integrate and balance the components in a manner that best articulates with the way they perceive, evaluate, and feel about themselves and the roles. That perception, evaluation, and feeling is importantly influ-

---

This chapter draws in part from my previously published papers, "Ephemeral Roles, Voluntary Action, and Voluntary Associations," *Journal of Voluntary Action Research* 7 (Summer/Fall 1978): 65-74; and "Role Selection: The Influence of Internalized Vocabularies of Motive," *Symbolic Interaction* 2 (Fall 1979): 45-62. Used by permission.

enced by the responses they get from individuals with whom they socially interact.

I have assumed, along with the symbolic interactionists, that human beings by nature are active in their social environments. The "motive" for accumulating and integrating role repertoires is based in that tendency and is shaped, as a vocabulary of motive, by the necessity for people to explain, justify, or make sense of their behavior to themselves and to significant others (those whose appraisals they consider important) with whom they interact.

The case examples in Chapters 2 through 12 have been intended to illustrate how people actively and autonomously work to integrate their role repertoires in a wide variety of social settings. Depending on the situation and the contents of their own self-concepts, they conformed to the role expectations of others, reacted to what they perceived to be conflicts in the expectations, or created the expectations. They assimilated roles in a total institution, developed informal roles in a formal organization, dealt with unacceptable roles, modified routine roles, filled role voids, enjoyed ephemeral roles, developed role balance, reacted to disruption of role balance, resolved role marginality, and transformed accustomed roles.

My emphasis on autonomy in role conformity, conflict, and creativity is not meant to suggest a vacuous "individualism" (Hall, 1983). Though I agree that people by nature are active in their environments, their perceptions of themselves, including perceptions of autonomy and individuality, are learned from social interactions. Autonomy and individuality are elements in vocabularies of motive, albeit crucial ones. They represent people's arriving at understandable, acceptable terms between themselves and the groups, organizations, and other societal or cultural structures that constitute their social worlds.

Discussion

ANALYZING ROLE ENACTMENT

In this chapter, I will consider four key components as being central for analyzing role enactment: person, self-concept, identity, and social setting. I will expand and connect those components by referring to several other role-related elements that have been apparent in the previous chapters: the "I," as processor, organizer, and "feeler" of social experiences; the "Me," as social object; self-esteem; self-consistency; attribution; role repertoire; role balance; taking and making roles; negotiation; impression management; conforming to, resolving conflict in, and creating roles; expressing emotion; significant others; and group, organizational, cultural, historical, and power-based expectations for "appropriate" role behavior. Finally, I will argue that an "internalized vocabulary of motive" theoretically links person, self-concept, identity, and social setting and that the vocabulary is essential to understanding role enactment. The components and elements are summarized in Figure 1. They do not constitute an exhaustive consideration of the dynamics of role enactment or of the symbolic interactionist treatment of those dynamics. There are other books and articles that undertake that comprehensive task (for example, Biddle and Thomas, 1966; Heiss, 1981a, 1981b; Goslin, 1969; Kando, 1977; Hewitt, 1976; Rose, 1962; Charon, 1979; Blumer, 1969; Meltzer et al., 1975; Manis and Meltzer, 1972; Stone and Farberman, 1981). I emphasize those aspects of role enactment that I see as exemplary of the individual's autonomous encounters with behavioral expectations.

The Person

Turner (1978: 2) has suggested that, sociologically considered, a "person"

is a human being who has acquired status and engages in social interaction (Hoult, 1969: 237). . . . In the broadest sense the person consists of all the roles in an individual's repertoire, with some qualification about how well each is played. . . . The person is best described in terms of the roles that are still played when not called for and that color the way in which other roles are played.

Becoming a person involves a socialization process that begins at birth and continues throughout adult life. Individuals routinely encounter a series of behavioral expectations that others have for them. As children, they enact those roles, in appropriate social settings, without much reflection. As time goes on, and as they accumulate role repertoires, individuals become more selective in their role enactments. Their role taking is guided by more sophisticated and autonomous perceptions of others' behavioral expectations and by the set of expectations they now have for themselves. They are able to draw upon a synthesis of previous role experiences that "transcends the situation," gives them discretionary choice, and "mutes the effect of the positive and negative sanctions that regulate the situationally indicated role enactment" (Turner, 1978: 13). From among the roles in their repertoire and the new ones they confront, individuals purposefully elect some as central to and dominant in their definition of self. They "merge role and person selectively so as to maximize autonomy and positive self-evaluation" (Turner, 1978: 14).

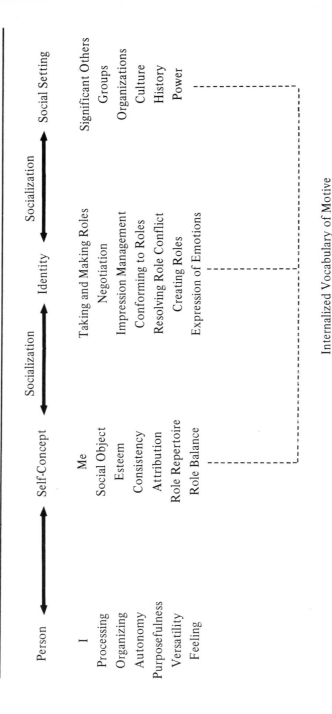

Person	Self-Concept	Socialization	Identity	Socialization	Social Setting
I	Me		Taking and Making Roles		Significant Others
Processing	Social Object		Negotiation		Groups
Organizing	Esteem		Impression Management		Organizations
Autonomy	Consistency		Conforming to Roles		Culture
Purposefulness	Attribution		Resolving Role Conflict		History
Versatility	Role Repertoire		Creating Roles		Power
Feeling	Role Balance		Expression of Emotions		

Internalized Vocabulary of Motive

Figure 1 Some Important Components for Analyzing Role Enactment

It can be said that the notion of "person" incorporates the "I" that Mead (1934) thought represented the impulses and inclinations of individuals and the unique way they organized their social experiences. The term also parallels what Allport (1961) calls the "proprium"—the active, unifying, synthesizing, and creative attributes of the individual. The proprium includes role enactments that are freely chosen and enjoyed by individuals as part of their "persons," despite the fact that those enactments might at first have been no more than conformity to the expectations of others. Through this process, which Allport calls "functional autonomy," individuals convert conformity to autonomy. Finally, the notion of "person" includes the assumption, as White (1959) suggests, that healthy human beings competently engage and organize their social experiences, including role enactments. They "feel" those experiences, and assess their competence in them both cognitively and emotionally.

Self-Concept

The "person" has a "self-concept," a conscious and selective organization of role-related values, expectations, and perceptions that

> form a workable anchorage for social interaction. Typically, self-conception is a vague but vitally felt idea of what I am like in my best moments, of what I am striving toward and have some encouragement to believe I may achieve, or what I can do when the situation supplies incentive for unqualified effort. The individual function of self-conception is to supply stable and workable direction to action by providing a criterion for selective attention to the social consequences and reflections of the individual's behavior [Turner, 1968b: 105; see also Stone, 1962: 104].

The notion of "self-concept" incorporates Mead's (1934) characterization of the "Me"—a socially conventional accommodation of the expectations of other people and of institutionalized roles. Whereas the term "person" highlights the subjective processes by which individuals organize their social experiences, the term "self-concept" highlights the manner in which individuals make social objects of themselves. They think about themselves as individuals acting in a particular social setting, interpret the reactions of others to their behavior in that setting, and evaluate both their own and others' performances. They conduct that objectification and evaluation in a manner consistent with their accumulated role repertoires and with their self-esteem, the degree of positive assessment they have accorded themselves.

The hashers (Chapter 5) and the airplane passengers (Chapter 6) were pressured to enact roles that included behaviors not consistent with their self-concepts. The community destruction caused by a tornado dislocated the way the volunteers in the disaster work crew (Chapter 7) perceived themselves and their social world. The Naval Reservists had established a consistent and enjoyable balance of satisfactions from enactment of their civilian dominant roles and Navy ephemeral role (Chapter 9), but had that balance disrupted by an unexpected military exercise (Chapter 10). The priests and felons (Chapter 12) had become discontent with the roles that had long been dominant in their self-concepts. Their expected behavior had become institutionalized, but those expectations no longer were consistent with how they perceived themselves.

The airplane passengers "fought the system." They discovered and implemented strategies by which they could exert their autonomy and maintain their privacy. They avoided, stretched, or modified the bureaucratic rules so as to provide the greatest degree of personal freedom and choice. The volunteer work crew members created a small, temporary social system and lodged themselves in it until the routine of everyday community life was restored. The hashers and Naval Reservists elected behaviors that, though serving their own autonomy, involved making scapegoats of others in the social setting they experienced as demeaning or disturbing. The priests and felons decided to transform their accustomed roles. The priests became part of a protest movement; the felons became parolees. The transformation shattered their self-concepts. They became painfully reflective of themselves as social objects and actively sought ways they could incorporate the transformed roles into their self-concepts and sought settings in which the role enactments would be acceptable to significant others.

Role-related challenges to self-concept usually are dealt with vigorously, for example, by attribution of responsibility or hostile reaction to those perceived to be the source of the challenges, by energetic attempts to evade the challenges while remaining in the setting, or by withdrawal from the setting and perhaps finding one that is compatible.

Identity

"Identity" is the extension of self-concept squarely into a social setting. Stone (1962: 93) notes that individuals' identities are determined when they are situated in a specific social situation and are acknowledged by others as members/participants in acceptable role enactments (see also Turner, 1978: 2; Nye, 1976: 23).

Following their inclinations to be autonomous, people attempt to negotiate their situation-specific identities, including the expression of feelings called for in the situation. They try to effect a compromise between how they want to present themselves and the presentation they perceive others to expect of them. They "manage" that impression (Goffman, 1959), usually hoping to shape the situation more than it shapes them. If the situation permits, they work to make rather than take roles. The recruits in boot camp (Chapter 2) had little opportunity to negotiate their identity. It was rigidly dictated in the socialization setting of a total institution. However, they could "play" or conform to the expected role effectively while at the same time not letting it dominate their self-concepts or merging it with their "persons." Aboard ship (Chapter 3), the sailors used the informal organization as a mechanism to negotiate an identity that was a compromise between what they wanted to be and what the formal organization expected them to be. They were able to make as well as to take the sailor role. The identities of the players and fans at the football game (Chapter 4), including their emotional performances, were orchestrated in an elaborately staged setting. But they had chosen to enact the roles of player or fan. They "managed" their identities and the associated emotions in a manner that was acceptable to themselves and to others in the setting. The participants in the friendly poker game (Chapter 8) creatively negotiated identities as enactors of a situation-specific ephemeral role. The negotiation of that identity, and the impression management associated with it, was a thoroughly enjoyable part of their role enactment. The poverty program indigenous leader (Chapter 11) experienced an identity made distressing by intense role marginality. He attempted to bridge the expectations of diverse groups of individuals important to him. When he concluded that the bridging was impossible, he quit the program and eliminated the leader identity.

Social Setting

The social setting, including roles mandated by organizational, cultural, historical, and power imperatives, is the locus in which the "person," "self-concept," and "identities" are developed. Individuals engage those settings, are socialized within them, and strive to effect a conciliation between the expectations they have for themselves and that significant others have for them. All of the illustrations in this book have demonstrated, from the symbolic interactionist perspective, the crucial nature of such settings. The settings differed in degree of power, and included a variety of groups, organizations, and cultural values. Some of them permitted more latitude for autonomy and role making than others. The recruit training center (Chapter 2) provided virtually no latitude; the volunteer work crew (Chapter 7) provided virtually complete latitude. The hashers (Chapter 5) were affected by their culturally based assumptions about males and work. The indigenous leader (Chapter 11) was influenced by his culturally based understanding of being a "chief." Regardless of the degree of opportunity for autonomy, the participants in all the illustrative settings were able to find some way to temper role conformity with creativity or innovatively to resolve role conflict. Nonetheless, in all the settings the "persons," "self-concepts," "identities," and behavior of the participants were affected by the social situation. All of the settings either attempted to socialize the feelings of the participants or to elicit the appropriate expressions of emotion. It is not possible to analyze or understand role enactment adequately unless the social structure of the setting, the inclinations of the individual, the interactions of the participants, and the emergent aspects of the specific social setting are considered.

LINKING PERSON, SELF-CONCEPT, IDENTITY, AND SOCIAL SETTING

Why do we select a particular role for enactment? Why do we conform to some roles and modify or create others? What influences our choices of strategy for resolving role conflict or marginality? Why do we accept some identities and reject others? The circumstances of the social settings and the socialization processes in which we find ourselves instrumentally affect the character of our role selections and enactments. But what is there within us that influences the particular role choices?

Heiss (1981a) notes that a role can become internalized as "a guiding principle, a gestalt, perhaps a 'deep structure'" that shapes our behavior in many different settings. Brim (1958, 1968) observes that we develop a few "extended" roles that influence our other role choices and enactments. Bandura's (1977) work on "creative modeling" suggests that we assemble amalgams of role behaviors that provide a cognitive map for our enacting other roles. Heiss (1981a), Stryker (1981), McCall and Simmons (1966), Sherohman (1977), and Travisano (1981) conclude that we arrange our role repertoires in hierarchies. We prefer to enact some of those roles more than others; some are more dominant than others. Those higher in the preferential hierarchy are closely merged with person, are central to self-concept, and are enacted in a wide variety of settings. Homans (1961) implies that we make central to ourselves and frequently enact roles that we experience as rewarding in our interactions with others.

Sarbin and Allen (1968) suggest that role enactments vary in the extent to which they involve our organic systems. A casual role, such as being a customer in a supermarket, demands limited organismic response—a few words and gestures. At the other end of the continuum, a role can demand profound organismic response, involving all of our physical and emotional energies—for example, fully enacting the role of one under a voodoo curse or possessed by the devil. The football players and fans (Chapter 4) were expected, in the game setting, to display considerable organismic involvement (that is, emotion) in their role performances. Many of the fans and players not only displayed that involvement, but acutely felt and situationally committed themselves to it. In contrast, the airplane passengers (Chapter 6) studiously avoided involving much of themselves in the passenger role. They did what they could to distance themselves from the passenger role expected by the airlines.

Turner (1978) proposes several circumstances that determine when we are likely to merge "person" with role, including: others identifying us with a particular role; the degree of our discretion in enacting the role; the positive evaluation of the role by others; our ability to enact the role adequately; the amount of time and effort we invest in the role enactment; the sacrifices we make in order to enact the role; the publicity accorded the role; the degree of our unresolved role strain; and the benefits we gain from the role enactment. The roles that we merge with our persons significantly influence our subsequent role selections and enactments.

Throughout this book, and especially in Chapters 8, 9, and 12 (Naval Reservists, priests, and parolees), I have indicated that some roles are more dominant than others for individuals. The dominant roles, for example, affected their choice of ephemeral roles. But something else is operating in those illustrations and in the explanations of the authors whose views I have briefly (and incompletely) summarized above. It is clear that people incorporate a few roles deeply into their persons and self-concepts. It is clear that the dominant roles serve as a point of reference for subsequent role selections, including the kinds of conformity, creativity, and conflict resolution that will be elected. What, from the symbolic interactionist perspective, conceptually links together person, self-concept, identity, and social setting in the role enactment process? It is useful and, I believe, accurate to assume that healthy human beings by nature are inclined to be autonomous, to organize their role repertoires, and to establish role hierarchies whenever they can. I suggest that understanding those assumptions, and the relations among person, self-concept, identity, and social setting can be facilitated by considering the notion of "internalized vocabulary of motive."

Vocabularies of Motive

Mills (1940) implies that people are obliged to verbalize their motives, including reasons for particular role selections and enactments, when significant others in a specific setting challenge their choices as being unclear, incompletely enacted, unfamiliar, unexpected, inappropriate, deviant, or ineptly novice (see also Burke, 1962, 1965, 1969; Foote, 1951; Scott and Lyman, 1968; Hewitt and Hall, 1973; Stokes and Hewitt, 1976). Those challenges and queries are not unusual or infrequent. They are part of the routine of everyday life in which interacting individuals attempt to make sense of each others' behavior. By direct and indirect question, comment, gesture, or other kinds of cues, people solicit and provide meaning to role enactments. Stone (1977) notes that personal acts, including role performances, inevitably involve actors in an "internal conversation" that is a composite of their own inclinations and their perceptions of others' queries about the inclinations. Perinbanayagam (1977) argues that individuals attempt to develop "persuasive vocabularies" of motive that reconcile their subjective perceptions of themselves and what they interpret as others' perceptions of their behavior.

As depicted in Figure 1, vocabularies of motive are elicited in specific social settings, particularly when individuals are negotiating their situated identities with significant others. The hashers (Chapter 5), for example, had to explain to inquiring friends in social gatherings why they were enacting the seemingly demeaning hasher role. Their expressed justifications, their "accounts" (Scott and Lyman, 1968) for enacting the hasher role, were consistent with their perceptions of a dominant role by which they defined themselves—college student. Being a hasher, they explained, enabled them to continue enacting the student role. It was a temporary means to a desirable end.

Internalized Vocabularies of Motive

Vocabulary of motive items, though situationally based and developed, can become internalized by those who express them. They can generate or expand dominant roles and reinforce or modify self-concepts.

For example, imagine that a Naval Reservist (Chapter 9) is challenged by his nonmilitary friends for having chosen to enact the Reservist ephemeral role. His peers cannot understand why he would want to do that; it does not fit with their expectations for him. In their view, nobody volunteers for the military; they become involved only if drafted. He responds to the queries by stating that being a Naval Reservist permits him to be a "well-rounded" individual. The Reserve role is quite different from the other roles he enacts, and constitutes one satisfying component in a repertoire of partially satisfying roles. Assume that he has never thought of being "well-rounded" as important, but his friends' challenge has caused him to pronounce that vocabulary of motive item. He internalizes the notion of being "well-rounded," makes it part of how he perceives himself (his self-concept). His view of himself as "well-rounded," or wanting to be, now influences his new choices for role selection and enactment. Whenever it is feasible he wants the roles he chooses to contribute to his becoming or remaining "well-rounded." That vocabulary of motive item, initially expressed in response to a call for clarification from significant others, has become "functionally autonomous" (Allport, 1961). It is now a part of the unique way he organizes his role repertoire.

Consider another Naval Reservist, one whose previous socialization (including past internalized vocabularies of motive) has influenced her to elect being a "social science researcher" among the roles dominant in her self-concept. Assume that she is challenged by peers to explain why she is actively involved in the Naval Reserve. Are not social scientists typically opposed to the military, her friends ask. Why then would she enact the Reservist role? She responds by saying that she is a researcher and that participation in the Reserve has provided her with otherwise unavailable opportunities to conduct studies that have contributed to social science theory. The vocabulary of motive item she presented to her inquiring peers did not generate or modify the "social science researcher" role dominant in her self-concept, but it validated and reinforced that role.

Suppose that a fan at a college football game (Chapter 4) was outlandishly dressed in the school colors, was waving a huge banner, and was vociferously cheering at every play. He is challenged by a friend about that role enactment. He answers by proclaiming he is "showing team spirit"—the emotions he has embraced as appropriate and satisfying. Figure 2 summarizes the internalized vocabulary of motive process.

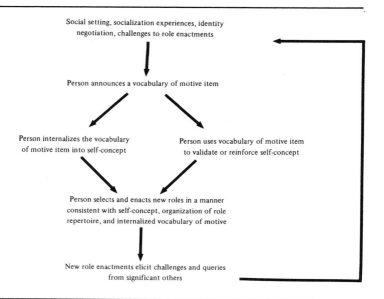

Figure 2   Summary of the Internalized Vocabulary of Motive Process

Why do some roles become dominant, and, correspondingly, why do some vocabulary of motive items become internalized into individuals' self-concepts? The symbolic interactionist perspective suggests that people by nature actively and autonomously organize their role enactments, and the meaning of those enactments, into coherent and hierarchical repertoires. They are inclined to "make" the roles and the associated justifications for role enactment. The symbolic interactionist perspective also suggests that the specific social settings in which individuals are situated along with significant others generate emergent and shared understandings for appropriate role enactment. The individuals are inclined to "take" the roles and the associated justifications for role enactment that they determine will work best in the setting. A major theoretical and empirical strength of the symbolic interactionist perspective is its attention to individual autonomy, social determinism, and the dialectic relation between them. In the reality of everyday life, people both shape their role enactments and are shaped by them.

In order to analyze whether a role will become dominant in, or whether a vocabulary of motive item will be incorporated into, an individual's self-concept, one must know about the individual's style of autonomy, the kinds of socialization processes experienced, and the characteristics of the specific social setting. Why, for example, didn't Mr. A, the poverty program indigenous leader (Chapter 11), internalize being a "bridge" between the poor and the poverty intervention organization? "Bridging" was a vocabulary of motive item used by the indigenous leaders when they had to explain to their followers' persistent inquiries about why they were not being total or successful activists for the poor. Mr. A repeatedly offered the "bridging" item when challenged by the participants in his target neighborhood committee. Despite his earnest efforts, the painful marginality of the indigenous leader role was more than he wanted to endure. Equally important, the manner in which the indigenous leader role was structured in the intervention setting made the "bridging" task very difficult to accomplish. Mr. A's self-concept included the perception that he was a competent individual and an American Indian. He did not internalize the "bridging" vocabulary item because he was prevented from competently enacting the role it purported to justify. Furthermore, he discovered that "bridging" meant his increasingly becoming defined by significant others as having "sold out" his Indian identity. The indigenous leader role and the "bridging" vocabulary of motive item that rationalized it became unacceptable to him. They were not consistent with nor could they be balanced with other roles and motive vocabularies he had made part of his self-concept. He quit the role and rejected the item. Understanding that outcome necessitated knowing something of how Mr. A perceived himself, his leadership-related socialization experiences, and the characteristics of the leadership setting.

THE TWENTY STATEMENTS TEST
AS AN INDICATOR

In Chapter 12, I described how the Twenty Statements Test (TST) had been used to assess role-related aspects of the priests' and the parolees' self-concepts. The TST asks respondents to answer the question "Who am I?" twenty times, and can be scored by assigning the responses to one of four categories: physical, social, reflective, and oceanic (Zurcher, 1977: 47). These four categories are identical to the A, B, C, and D classifications described in Chapter 12, but the descriptive terms will be more useful than letters in the following discussion.

The kinds of statements elicited by the TST provide some indication of individuals' self-concepts, dominant roles, and internalized vocabularies of motive. The physical responses suggest self-perceptions, but do not usually give much information about dominant roles or vocabularies of motive (unless the individual is a body builder, a contestant in a beauty pageant, or in some other way strongly links physical characteristics to a particular social role). However, the volunteers in the disaster work crew (Chapter 7) might, during the first day on the job, have given such physical responses as "I am sweating" and "I am stiff and sore." In doing so, they would have revealed that they had, as an initial reaction to disaster-disrupted roles, temporarily fallen back on rudimentary physical self-definitions. The next day, they might have revealed that they had made "work crew member" (a social response) a dominant role even if only for a brief time.

Social responses to the TST are especially informative about dominant roles. "I am a Naval recruit" would have revealed that the respondent had, as ideally expected in the training center setting (Chapter 2), situationally made the "boot" role dominant in his or her self-concept. "I am a Shellback" would have indicated that a role in the ship's informal organization (Chapter 3) was central to the respondent's self-concept. "I am a football fan" (Chapter 4) would have suggested that the respondent made that role central enough to his or her self-concept to accommodate the required staging of emotion for the game. "I am a poker player" (Chapter 8) would have shown the importance of that ephemeral role in the respondent's role repertoire.

The contents of internalized vocabularies of motive are most fully revealed by reflective TST responses. Those responses are self-assessing and evaluative, even painfully so. They often involve justifications, rationalizations, feelings, and other sorts of accounts (to self and to significant others) for role enactments, as the following hypothetical responses would have indicated: "I am a disgusted hasher" (Chapter 5); "I am a reluctant airplane passenger" (Chapter 6); "I am only a part-time Naval officer" (Chapter 9); "I am a sailor, not a Marine" (Chapter 10); "I am trying to be a 'bridge' between the poor and the nonpoor" (Chapter 11); "I am a concerned priest" (Chapter 12); "I am a reformed felon (Chapter 12). All of those responses would explain to inquiring others why the individual was enacting what seemed to them to be a problematic role.

Oceanic responses to the TST can indirectly be informative about dominant roles and internalized vocabularies of motive. A dissident priest (Chapter 12) might have responded, "I am part of the Mystical Body of Christ," thereby suggesting an orientation of self beyond earthbound church expectations. A parolee might have responded, "I am a decent human being in the eyes of Allah," thereby suggesting an orientation of self beyond officials in the earthbound criminal justice system. It is likely that the priest and the felon gave those responses to the significant others who inquired why they had decided to be a dissident priest or a paroled felon. The responses were part of the impression management and negotiated identity that necessitated an expressed vocabulary of motive item. That expression probably was consistent with their self-concepts or was perceived by them as appropriate to the social setting, providing an opportunity to justify the transformation of accustomed roles.

CONCLUSION

Throughout this book, I have assumed with symbolic interactionists that "autonomy" was a natural inclination of healthy human beings and that "role creativity," "role conformity," and "resolution of role conflict" were choices individuals made whenever possible in specific social settings. I do not renege on those assumptions. However, I must emphasize that "autonomy," "creativity," "conformity," and "role conflict" (along with its preferred resolutions) are culturally and situationally influenced. Indeed those terms *themselves* can be items in individuals' internalized vocabularies of motive.

The meaning of autonomy to someone living in India is not the same as its meaning to someone living in the United States. Role creativity, conformity, and conflict resolution are not the same to the Californian as to the Zambian. I espouse the view that those inclinations cut across cultural and societal boundaries, but advise that they are modified by situational differences within those boundaries. Any analysis of role enactment must first examine the underlying local assumptions about the nature of human beings and society, and then the situation-specific individual behavioral expectations. A military Reservist in Israel will have a different interpretation of that role than a Reservist in the United States. Fan-tan card players in China will have a different understanding of that role than poker players in the United States. The human inclination to be autonomous and creative regarding role enactments is pervasive but culturally interpreted. The vocabularies of motive elicited from individuals about their role enactments are couched in culturally accepted terms.

14

STUDYING ROLES
IN NATURAL SETTINGS

In Chapter 1, I suggested that the study of social roles is best informed by the researcher's "being there," that is, by his or her presence in the natural, nonlaboratory settings where the roles are enacted. The researcher is able to assess firsthand the character of the specific setting, the kinds of "persons," "self-concepts," and behavioral expectations individuals bring to it, and the situated negotiations they undertake to establish understandable or acceptable identities within it.

In this chapter, I offer some suggestions for studying role enactments in natural settings. They are drawn from the illustrations presented in Chapters 2 through 12, and therefore focus on qualitative research techniques that reveal how individuals autonomously conform to roles, create them, and resolve role conflicts. I hope the suggestions, as well as the illustrations, will encourage you to conduct investigations of the role conformity, conflict, and creativity that permeate the social settings in your own everyday lives.

This chapter is not a comprehensive treatment of the varieties of qualitative research procedures. There are many books that offer such treatments, including the following, which have influenced my discussion and which I recommend to you for further reading (the complete citations are in the bibliography): Lofland (1971, 1976), Schatzman and Strauss (1973), Bogdan and Taylor (1975), Glaser and Strauss (1967), Adams and Preiss (1960), Habenstein (1970), McCall and Simmons (1966), Filstead (1970), Spradley and McCurdy (1972), Webb et al. (1966), Schwartz and Jacobs (1979), Johnson (1975), Shaffir et al. (1980), Speier (1973).

CHOOSING A ROLE ENACTMENT SETTING FOR STUDY

Settings in which role conformity, conflict, and creativity can be examined virtually surround you. Chapters 2 through 12 show something of the diversity of such settings and of the kinds of roles within them. Often the situations are so commonplace that they are overlooked, as the proverbial goldfish overlooks its bowl. Think of the myriad role settings associated with these routine societal functions: education, work, family, marriage, friendship, neighboring, leisure, politics, economics, law, religion, sports, transportation, communications, medicine, and sustenance (food, housing, clothing).

Take a moment to jot down the roles you enacted during a single day, for example, yesterday. Assess the conformity, conflict, and creativity involved in those enactments. You will be impressed by their number and diversity. When you get up tomorrow morning, begin listing each of the roles you enact, and how you enact them, as you engage different settings throughout the day. It is likely that your list will grow so large, and the effort of recording them so cumbersome, that you will find the task exhausting. Instead of considering all your role enactments, try focusing on where and how you enact one particular role in a day or perhaps over a week's time (driving your car, riding your bicycle, eating your lunch, being a student in classes, being a date, being a jogger). Even that will be taxing; the single role is enmeshed in a network of physical circumstances, feelings, social situations, behavioral expectations, and interactions with others. You will discover dozens of different facets of the enactment upon which you could concentrate—for example, the role-related interactions between you as a bicyclist and the motorists driving on the same street, your lunch-eating behavior with different groups of people, ranging from close friends to job interviewers, your jogging behavior when alone on a trail and when on a track crowded with other joggers.

The exercise of examining your own role enactments in natural settings not only informs you about the abundant opportunities for studying roles, but alerts you to how subjectivity can influence your perspective as a researcher. You attempt to make an object of yourself, to understand your role enactments as if they were separate from you. It is difficult to do, but not impossible. You have to resist the inclination to evaluate rather than to catalogue your enactments. When you stop to examine a role you are enacting in a particular setting, the enactment probably will be modified by your observation of it. The nature of your interaction with others in the setting is altered, at least inside your head. Although the subjectivity to some extent gets in your way, it gives you a richer and more detailed understanding of the role enactment. As I shall point out again later, some degree of subjectivity is unavoidable, and actually desirable, in the qualitative study of roles in natural settings.

The opportunities for study you see when examining your own role enactment are vastly increased when considering other people's enactments. Among all of the possibilities, which role and setting should you choose for your research? Four essential factors ought guide your decision: your own interests, access to the setting, feasibility of completing the project, and usefulness of the findings.

Your Own Interests

The more a role topic interests you, the more productive your study of it will be. Collecting, organizing, analyzing, and reporting natural field data demand considerable time, energy, and concentration. Boredom will make those tasks agonizing and futile. When picking a topic, it is best to follow your own inclinations. The projects that generated the illustrations presented in Chapter 2 through 12 all interested me very much. Though the research processes often were difficult in those projects, I was never hindered by boredom or by the feeling that I was "putting in my time."

Access to the Setting

Obviously, you cannot study roles in a natural setting unless you have access to it. If you are interested in the role of the prisoner awaiting execution, you would have difficulty getting access to death row. If you are interested in the role of the hostage during captivity, you would have difficulty "being there." Those are important but unusual roles. The call of the unusual can be unduly seductive to novice researchers. They mistakenly think that roles routinely enacted in everyday life are not worth examining. They conclude, for example, that it unquestionably would be better to study the role of nude hockey player than the role of grocery clerk, although they are interested in both topics. When they cannot find any nude hockey players, they decide not to do any research at all.

Occasionally, you will unexpectedly be squarely situated in a setting that includes unusual role enactments. While you are waiting in line to make a deposit, the bank is robbed. While you and many others are frolicking in the surf along a popular beach, the lifeguard screams, "Shark!" The crowded elevator in which you are riding gets stuck between floors for two hours. I did not anticipate being a volunteer in a disaster work crew (Chapter 7) or a Naval Reservist in a Marine field exercise (Chapter 10). I found myself in those settings, and took advantage of the opportunity to study the role enactments within them.

The many roles you routinely enact give you the opportunity to study the enactments of others in the same settings. My being a boot (Chapter 2), a sailor aboard ship (Chapter 3), an airline passenger (Chapter 6), a poker player (Chapter 8), and a Naval Reservist (Chapter 9) gave me access to those settings. I was there as a member, and was able to record what I observed. In other instances, you will need help in getting access. I would not have been able to go "behind the scenes" to study the emotional roles of football fan and player if I had not been invited by the director of athletics to be a "visiting coach." It was not possible for me to be a hasher (Chapter 5) myself, but two of my undergraduate students were. They had access to the setting, and I through them. Before I could examine the role of indigenous leader in a poverty program (Chapter 11), I had to get permission from the program administrators and its board of directors to enter the setting. Furthermore, if Mr. A had not been willing to be observed and interviewed, and to support my presence in the setting, I would have gathered no data. The dissident priests and the paroled felons (Chapter 12) would have been unapproachable for research purposes without the cooperation of key intermediaries. Priest friends helped us get access to the dissidents. Parole officials and ex-felon friends helped us get access to the parolees.

When you are not already part of, or cannot readily become part of, the setting in which you want to study role enactments, you usually can depend on setting-situated "gatekeepers" to help you get access.

Feasibility of Completing the Project

It does little good to be interested in a particular role enactment and to have access to the setting in which that role operates unless you gather enough data to make sense out of what is going on. There will be times when you begin a project and circumstances will terminate your observation. The enactors you are studying might become uneasy with your research and ask you to leave the setting. You might "burn out" and decide to quit. Those eventualities are not predictable, and ought not discourage you from beginning a project. But before you begin you should have a reasonable appraisal of the long-term tolerance the role enactors will have of your observation, and of your own tolerance for enduring the inevitable stresses of field research. If you have serious doubts about respondent acceptance or your own endurance, it would be wise not to begin the project.

All researchers prefer to be funded for their projects. Dollars facilitate the task, and accord it more professional prestige. If you can get a grant for your study, or become part of a project that has such funding, by all means do so. However, qualitative studies generally are less favored for funding than quantitative studies. That unfortunate fact should not discourage you. Among the studies reported in Chapters 2 through 12, only the research on the poverty program indigenous leaders and parolees were funded by government grants. Some of the other projects were assisted, in the writing stage, by very small university grants. You or your faculty supervisors probably can get such awards. If that is not possible, do not be put off. Funding is less important to the project than your ability to expend the necessary time and energy.

The Usefulness of the Findings

Do not choose a research setting, even if access if easy, that will yield insufficient data. You are interested in the fullness of role enactments. You should be able to get pertinent information about person, self-concept, identity, and the characteristics of the setting.

You must ask yourself who cares about what you discover in your project. Perhaps it will be your professor, who has assigned you the task and will give you a grade. Perhaps you want to publish your findings or present them at professional meetings, thus contributing to the accumulation of social science knowledge. Perhaps you want to complete the project for your own satisfaction or because you see it as an important part of your training. All of these reasons are sound. You should have confidence that your findings will serve some purpose or you will be wasting the respondents' time and your own, and will have exhausted a research access for a serious scholar.

ATTENDING TO THEORY
AND PREVIOUS RESEARCH

Qualitative studies of role enactments, like all social science research, are legitimized by their contributions to theory and their corresponding links to previous research. As I have suggested above, you plausibly can complete such a study because your professor expects it, because it is part of your academic training, or because it interests you. However, your findings will best serve social science if they are theoretical contributions (your professor probably will insist upon your attempting that outcome).

There are many social science theories that are pertinent to research on social roles. In this book, I have emphasized symbolic interactionism and some of the psychological theories that stress individual autonomy in role enactment. The particular theory you select to guide your research is less important than the fact that you should elect one or some. If you do not, then you should attempt, as your data develop, to generate theoretical contributions that emerge from or are "grounded" in your findings (Glaser and Strauss, 1967). My studies of Naval recruits and sailors aboard ship were based on theories concerning total institutions and formal organizations. The analysis of football fans and players drew upon the dramaturgical perspective in symbolic interactionism. The hasher study was lodged in theory about the resolution of role conflict. The airplane passenger research generated theoretical considerations about people pipelines and encapsulated groups. The disaster work crew was analyzed according to theories of psychological and social stability and discontinuity. The concept of "ephemeral role" was broadened in the research on the friendly poker game. Psychological balance theory guided my analysis of the Naval Reservist role and its disruption. The study of the poverty program indigenous leader was set in theoretical perspectives about role marginality. The priests and parolees were considered in the light of theories of self-concept and social change. Theory, whether guiding your research or emerging from it, organizes your data and makes them useful to other social scientists.

Your findings, regardless of their theoretical relevance, can be useful in another way. They can provide information to practitioners who are responsible for the amelioration of social problems. For example, as a result of the studies presented in this book, recruits in boot camp and sailors aboard ship were perceived in a different light by Navy supervisors. City officials were informed about the importance of volunteer work crews in disaster recovery. Senior Naval officers were alerted to the role complexity of Naval Reservists. Poverty program managers were shown the difficulties encountered by indigenous leaders. Church leaders and parole officials were instructed about the reactions of priests and felons to voluntary role transformation. If your research contributes to social science theory, well and good. If it improves the way people are treated in organizational settings, all the better.

ETHICAL CONSIDERATIONS WHEN STUDYING ROLES IN NATURAL SETTINGS

The U.S. Department of Health and Human Services has published guidelines for the conduct of research involving human subjects. The administrative office coordinating campus research and the library in your university probably will have them on file. The guidelines primarily are concerned with protecting the privacy and safety of respondents in survey studies and subjects in laboratory experiments, but they also apply to qualitative research projects. You ought to read the guidelines before you begin your study, even if it is small, involves no funds, or is a class assignment (also see Sjoberg, 1967). In the context of those guidelines, you should consider the ethical aspects of your research intentions discussed below.

Entering a Setting Specifically for the Purpose of Studying Role Enactments

When you deliberately enter a natural setting to study a role enactment, you might or might not enact the role. If it is a large group, for example, a crowd at a rock concert, you can "blend in" as an observer, not enact the role of audience member, and probably not have to explain to anyone that you are studying that role. If it is a small group, you can identify yourself as a researcher and observe the interactions of others without becoming directly involved (keep in mind that "researcher" involves a role enactment). The other people in the small group setting will want to know why you are doing the study and what in general you are looking for. They also will want to know something about your qualifications. You should provide that information honestly and straightforwardly in terms that are meaningful to them. Go easy on the social science jargon, unless you know they are familiar with it. Be brief. They usually will not want elaborate descriptions of your research design, just enough to be able to make sense of your being in their setting. For example, in response to their inquiries I told the poverty program leaders and followers that I was "interested in how neighborhood groups developed and what they accomplished." I explained to the Naval Reservists that I wanted "to assess their satisfactions and dissatisfactions with Reserve participation and how that participation compared with their civilian jobs." The dissident priests were told that we were "studying how the church and its clergy were affected by social change." The paroled felons were informed that we "wanted to know firsthand what they experienced on parole." Most of those respondents wanted to know nothing more than what was said in those brief statements. Some had further questions, and were answered, but never in a way that would prime them to give the "right" responses to the research queries. You are not obliged to explain your theoretical orientations, hypotheses, or expected results. To do so could bias the respondents and confound your findings.

Perhaps you will choose to enter the natural setting, for the purpose of studying a role, by presenting yourself as someone who wants to enact or is enacting that role. You might intend to fake the enactment in order to gather data. Maybe you really do want to enact the role, but want to study it at the same time. Either way, you must not lie to others about your being a researcher. Whether you are obliged to volunteer that information if not asked has been debated at length. What you do depends on the setting and your sense of ethics. Most certainly if you are asked questions about your intentions, you must answer honestly. If, for example, you join a religious chanting group because you want to study the member role, it would be unethical for you to state that you are a convert who has no other reason for being there. Your honesty may cost you access to the group, but so be it.

You might conclude that such honesty would automatically eliminate any opportunity to study roles that are considered "deviant" by other people—such as pot smokers, draft evaders, punk rockers, sexual swingers, pornography customers, nudists. Not necessarily. Sometimes individuals who enact "deviant" roles welcome or at least tolerate the competent study of their behavior. If so, should you enact the role? That is a decision you must make according to your own values and beliefs. However, you ought not to enact a felonious role in order to gather data or maintain access to the setting. Nor should you enact a role that would encourage or support others in doing violence to people and their property.

The natural settings that contained the Naval Reservist, indigenous leader, dissident priest, and paroled felon roles were deliberately entered for the purpose of research. The participants knew that a social scientist was interested in studying their role enactments and they voluntarily gave their consent. They were assured of confidentiality and anonymity. In the Reservist study, I enacted the role I was studying. In the indigenous leader, the priest, and the parolee studies, I did not.

None of the illustrations in Chapters 2 through 12 involved intentionally illegal or violent role behaviors (except in the sense that college football and the military are in the violence business). Some of the parolees told us about activities that might have been infractions of parole regulations. Before we began the study, we made it clear that we would not report those infractions. The parole officials whose cooperation gave us access to the research agreed. They wanted to learn about the problems experienced by parolees, knew that we would not obtain useful responses unless we could guarantee confidentiality, and in any event did not want us mucking about as amateur parole officers. You will frequently discover that agencies interested in finding out how better to serve their clients want that sort of information from your role study and nothing more.

Deciding to Study a Role Enactment
After You Are in the Setting
and Have Enacted It

Since people enact many roles in many settings, it is likely that those of us who have social science training will at some time or another become so intrigued by a role/setting that we decide to study it. We might be like the proverbial goldfish, but we are fascinated by and have the ability to answer researchable questions about the other goldfish, the water, the miniature figures propped up in the gravel, the confines of the bowl, and who and what we see outside the bowl.

The roles you are enacting and subsequently decide to study can be routine or unusual, part of everyday life, or associated with some infrequent event. I did not plan in advance to examine the roles of Navy boot, sailor aboard ship, airplane passenger, disaster work crew member, or poker player. After enacting those roles for a while (and in the case of the hasher after my students had enacted the role) I thought it important to study them.

Ethically, what must you say to the other role enactors in a natural setting that for you has become a research site? You did not enter that setting for research purposes. You enacted the role because it was enjoyable, because you were thrust into it, or simply because you were there. Your initial reasons for being in the setting have not been misrepresented. But you have now decided to stand back from the role, to make researchable objects of yourself and others in the setting. Should you announce to the others that you have changed from participant to participant-researcher? For example, should I have stood up in the airplane and said that I was observing the passenger role? Should I have turned to the other disaster work crew members and proclaimed that I was studying our behavior? Was I obliged to tell my poker-playing colleagues that I was systematically attending to our emphemeral role? In my judgment, the answer to those questions is no (a conclusion that certainly can be questioned and is worth considerable classroom discussion). I was a passenger, a crew member, a poker player, and wanted to be. I did not want to change the nature of the interactions in a way that would modify my role enactment or that of others in the setting. However, I believe that if you are in a small, private setting rather than a large, public one, you ought when finished share your interpretations with the other role enactors and solicit their corrections, and, if you intend to distribute your analysis to a broader audience, get their concurrence to do so. They surely will offset your misinterpretations and consequently make your study better. It is likely that they will support the dissemination of your findings, but if they do not you might have to "bite the bullet" and junk your research.

Fortunately for me, the work crew members and the poker players agreed to critique my analysis and concurred with publishing the findings. Whenever feasible, sharing your final interpretations with the enactors is a good idea even if they knew from the onset that you were a researcher, although in that situation they have already at least by implication concurred with your intention to disseminate the findings. The Marine-mobilized Naval Reservists and the poverty program participants were aware that I was a social scientist gathering data. When at the end of the studies I showed them my findings, they offered very useful validations and corrections.

Reporting the Findings

The oral or written presentation of your findings should protect the anonymity of the role enactors you have studied, and should not violate any promises of confidentiality you made to them. Occasionally, a respondent will want or will give you permission to be identified in your reports, and it can be useful to do so. Usually, however, you will be obliged to disguise quotes by attributing them to pseudonyms, by editing or paraphrasing them to eliminate identifying remarks, or by combining the quotes of several role enactors into a single illustrative statement. You should clearly indicate when the quotes are paraphrased or combined, so the reader or listener will know that they are not verbatim but do convey the message.

Sometimes you will need to disguise the setting as well as the respondents in order to protect the integrity of both. You can use pseudonyms, eliminate descriptive material, or merge the findings from several settings into a representative composite (indicating to your audience that you have done so).

All of the studies used for illustrations in this book yielded findings that were published as books or articles. The recruit training center, the ship, the sorority house, the airlines, the location of the poker game, and the Marine field exercise were not specifically identified nor were the respondents in those settings. However, I did provide enough descriptive information to indicate the representativeness of the settings and the roles studied. I suggest that you do the same, being careful not to abandon your responsibility to protect anonymity and confidentiality. The football game was identified as the University of Texas Longhorns versus the University of Arkansas Razorbacks, and the coaches as Darrell Royal and Frank Broyles; the quoted players and fans were not identified. The location of the disaster work crew, the dissident priests, and the paroled felons were revealed respectively as Topeka, Kansas; San Antonio, Texas; and San Diego, California. None of the respondents in those settings was identified. Recall that I assigned each of the disaster work crew members a label that summarized his role in the crew (Chapter 7). If the setting lends to it, that is an effective procedure for reporting the analysis of role enactments. The responses of the surveyed Naval Reservists were presented as aggregate data, but the sampling frame for the study was fully described (including locations and pay grades sampled). The direct quotes I used were attributed to individuals not by name but by the rank they held. "Mr. A" was obviously a pseudonym for the indigenous leader, though the poverty program was identified as being in Topeka, Kansas. The differences in the procedures I used indicate that there are a variety of ways you can protect the privacy of your respondents while at the same time giving your audience a sense of the generality of your findings.

Usually, you have a responsibility to tell your respondents something of what you have discovered about them. That is particularly important if you have committed yourself to do so as a condition for your having access to the setting. You can give them a written summary of the results or show them copies of the publications (assuming you have not already shared those documents with them for validation and concurrence). You probably will not be able to reach all the respondents. There was no way I could reach all of the boots, sailors, and airplane passengers I observed. I did not know who most of them were. But you will be able to contact many if not all of the enactors you most closely observed, and should do so. If they are not interested in seeing the findings, they will tell you so.

RESEARCH PROCEDURES

Observing Role Enactments in Natural Settings

Whether you enter a natural setting for the purpose of studying a role enactment or decide to study that role while enacting it, you will be using the qualitative research technique of systematic observation. You must decide how fully you will enact, or will continue to enact, the studied role. Essentially, you will choose some sort of balance between enacting the role of researcher and enacting the researched role, between being an observer and being a participant. Gold (1958) has identified four categories to which researchers in natural settings can be assigned, depending on the degree to which they emphasize the observer or the participant role. The "complete participant" fully enacts the role he or she is studying, and is not known (at least during the period of study) as a researcher to the other enactors in the setting. The "participant-as-observer" fully enacts the role, but the other enactors know that he or she is a researcher. The "observer-as-participant" is a known researcher, enacts the studied role incidentally, and is in the setting briefly, perhaps only long enough to interview the other enactors one time. The "complete observer" is known as a reseacher, but does not enact the studied role. He or she observes it, and nothing more.

I was a complete participant in the recruit training center, ship, football game, airplane, volunteer work crew, and poker game settings. I was a participant-as-observer in the Naval Reserve Drill and Marine field exercise settings. In the hasher, poverty program, dissident priest, and paroled felon settings, I was a complete observer.

As those examples illustrated, you not only have a variety of settings in which you can study role enactments, but a variety of ways to balance your enactment of the studied role with your systematic observation. Your choice will be influenced by how you came into contact with the role, the kind of access you have for gathering useful data, and your own inclinations for enacting the role you want to study. The more fully you enact the studied role, the greater the chance that you will "go native," as the anthropologists have put it. You become so committed to the role that you will lose your research detachment. Your own feelings will dominate your perception. If you decide to be a complete participant, and continue being interested in accumulating data about the role, you must steadily remind yourself that you are first a researcher and second an enactor of the studied role. That stance can be particularly difficult if you are examining a role enacted by people who are hurting and who you would like to help. You might be faced with the difficult task of determining whether your own enactment of the studied role or the research you report about it will better serve the disadvantaged others.

Will your systematic observation influence the interactions and role enactments of others in the setting? Yes, no matter what balance you have effected between enacting the role of researcher and the studied role. Even if you are a complete participant and the others in the setting do not know you are a researcher, you are an additional and contributing element to the interaction processes. Even if you are a complete observer, known to be a researcher, and make every effort to distance yourself from the studied role, your presence in the setting changes the interaction processes. That's the bad news. The good news is that your systematic observation, whether known or not, though affecting the setting, probably does not affect it very much. If you are a complete participant, you can be careful not to assume an influential position or call too much attention to yourself in the setting. If you are a participant-as-observer, an observer-as-participant, or a complete observer, the enactors you are studying probably will quickly take you for granted in the setting. In fact, you might even become a little dismayed by their nonchalance about you.

Whatever your mode of participation, you need to get as full a sampling of observations within the setting and among other relevant settings as possible. The role enactment you are studying can vary with the time of day, the day of the week, the kinds of events taking place within the setting, the shifting nature of the social interactions, and the orientations of the different enactors. It would not have been possible to get a thorough understanding of the role conflict experienced by the hashers, and the way they dealt with the conflict, if they had not been observed in the kitchen, in the dining room, during different meal-times, on weekday and weekend work shifts, and during special social events involving meals. I sampled the boot and sailor roles on a 24-hour, 7-day a week basis within the total institutions, and the passenger role in a variety of airplanes, airlines, schedules, and itineraries. Had I observed the disaster work crew role only on the first day of its 3-day existence, I would not have seen the way the enactment evolved. I would have missed the richness of the socialization process for new players if I had not attended a long and consecutive series of games with the poker group. Similarly, I would not have understood the complicated nature of the indigenous leader's role marginality had I been unable to observe the enactment in many of the poverty program settings thoughout a period of several months.

You will not always be able to sample the times, days, events, and enactors in a natural setting as completely as you would like. Your access to the setting, your resources, and your own schedule may not permit it. Do the best you can, realizing that the less you have observed in the setting the more cautious you must be in your interpretations.

Interviewing and Questionnaires

It is possible and sometimes necessary for you to study a role enactment in a natural setting without asking any of the others in the setting even a single question. For example, you might not be able to interview any of the bystanders at the scene of a grisly automobile accident even though you are interested in the bystander role. You might not want to impose on mourners at a funeral even though you are systematically observing the mourner role.

You can accumulate a considerable amount of useful data about identity negotiations and role enactments just by carefully watching and listening in the setting. You can also provide an extensive description of the setting without asking anyone about it. But you would be disadvantaged in learning about the self-concepts and role repertoires of the enactors unless you interview them. It is hard to assess what is role creativity, conformity, or conflict for the enactors, and with what degree of autonomy they are engaging the roles, unless you talk with them.

Interviewing need not be formal and structured. You do not have to sit the respondent down and lead him or her through a set of fixed items on a questionnaire. Although that approach has merit for standardization and objectivity, it is not usually appropriate for use in natural field studies—especially if you have elected to be a complete participant in the setting.

It is a good idea to write down for yourself the queries you have for the enactors. The queries will then be in your mind. You can informally make them, and others that occur to you as you interact in the setting, whenever it is most appropriate.

For example, we had the following kinds of questions in mind when we informally interviewed the hashers:

- What do you think of the job of hasher? Advantages? Disadvantages?
- When is the job most enjoyable? Least enjoyable?
- Why did you choose being a hasher as a part-time job?
- Do you intend to continue being a hasher while you are a student?
- What do you think of the members in this sorority?
- What is the attitude of the members toward the hashers? How do they treat the hashers?
- How do the hashers and the members get along?
- Have you worked as a hasher in any other sorority? If so, how do the jobs compare?

- What is your idea of a "good" sorority house for which to work as a hasher? A "bad" sorority house?
- Do you volunteer to do extra work tasks, beyond the hasher role, for the members?
- Do you represent the sorority in intramural sports or in any other way on campus?
- Do you or any of the hashers date sorority members in this house or from other houses?
- Would you recommend the job of hasher to a friend?

The questions that guided our informal interviews with sorority members included the following:

- What do you think of the job of sorority hasher for a college male?
- What do you think of the hashers in your sorority?
- What is your idea of a "good" hasher? A "bad" hasher?
- How do the members and the hashers get along?
- What are the names of the hashers that work in your sorority house?
- How does the hasher crew in your house compare with the crews of other houses?
- Do you ever find it difficult to get a hasher to do what you ask him to do?
- Do you think sorority members should date hashers? Have you ever dated a hasher?
- Do you have a "turnabout" day (a day each year when the sorority members wait on the hashers)? If so, tell me about it. Do you think turnabout days are a good idea?

Our informal interviews with sorority house mothers and cooks included the following questions:

- What do you think of the job of hasher for a college male?
- What is your idea of a "good" hasher employee? A "bad" hasher employee?
- Do you have any work or disciplinary problems with the hashers?
- How do the sorority members and hashers get along with each other?
- What is your opinion about members dating hashers? Is there a formal or informal house rule about such dating?
- What is the employment turnover rate for hashers in your sorority house?
- Have you worked in other sorority houses? If so, how do the hashers in this house compare with those in the others? Are there any differences among the houses with which you are familiar in the way that the hashers and members get along with each other?

As is typical in informal interviewing, those questions were not always asked in the order listed, and routinely were expanded with probes for further respondent elaboration on pertinent points. The questions were "open-ended"—the respondents could formulate their own answers. They were not, as in questionnaires using "closed-ended" items, expected to select one answer from among several alternatives provided by the researcher. Notice that the hashers, sorority members, house mothers, and cooks in many instances were asked essentially the same questions, all of which sought data on role conflict. When you are studying social roles in natural settings, you should attempt informally to interview the different actors in the setting, and compare their perspectives on the enactment aspects that interest you.

You do not always have to ask direct questions in order to conduct an effective interview with your respondents. Sometimes such questions can be threatening to the respondents or disruptive to the social setting. Instead of asking a question, you can simply make a declarative statement that elicits discussion from your respondents about aspects of their role enactments in which you are interested—a procedure that Snow et al. (forthcoming) have called "interviewing by comment." For example, if you are studying the role transition experienced by recently divorced women, and you are sitting with some of them in the first session of a small counseling group, it would be clumsy to ask, "Are you nervous about this?" It would be better to state, "I'm sure nervous about this" (assuming you are a complete participant and do feel nervous) or "Everybody seems so nervous about this." Then wait and see what the other enactors will add to your declaration.

Data from your observations and informal interviewing can be merged, or "triangulated" (Denzin, 1970), and perhaps also triangulated with data you have gathered by more structured methods. In addition to our observations of and interviews with hashers, sorority members, house mothers, and cooks, we administered a structured questionnaire to a sample of students in order to assess the relative prestige they assigned to hasher as a part-time job. I not only observed but informally interviewed enactors in the recruit training center, the ship, the football game, the airplane, the volunteer work crew, the Naval Reserve centers, and the Marine field exercise. The Naval Reservist study involved the administration of a structured questionnaire to a large sample of respondents. The questionnaire items had been developed from information I gathered by informal interview and participant observation. In the indigenous leader study, I used both formal and informal interviewing and, though Chapter 11 does not report data from it, I also used a structured questionnaire. The Twenty Statements Test given to the priests and parolees is a structured instrument, but provides opportunity for open-ended responses. The TST data were triangulated with data from informal interviews with the priests and with data from both formal and informal interviews with the parolees.

As you can see, there are several combinations of observational, interview, and questionnaire techniques that you can employ in your study of role enactments. If possible, use more than one technique so that you can triangulate your findings, thereby enhancing their reliability. But do not overburden the setting with more research techniques than you need to get useful data. If you do, you will have transformed a natural into a laboratory setting and the people in the setting will primarily enact the "subject" role.

In natural field studies, you might depend on "gatekeepers" to get you access to the setting, individuals who enable you to observe and interview the participants. Those gatekeepers usually will become key "informants" (a term used by anthropologists) in your study. You will depend on informants to instruct and validate your observations. I did that with Mr. A, the poverty program indigenous leader. Without his cooperation, I would not have been able to observe the meetings of the Indian target neighborhood committee and his leadership role in it. During my observation, I interviewed Mr. A in part with the intent of checking on my interpretations, and in part to obtain data on his leadership role. I told him that fact. Informants can become friends; they might expect you to conform to a friendship role. In the interest of your research, you will have to make it clear to informants that friendship, if it happens, will not interfere with your commitment to gather useful data on role enactments. They will almost always understand and support your position.

Recording, Field Notes, Documents, and Files

While you are studying a role enactment in a natural setting, you will be bombarded by pertinent information that you do not want to forget. You will somehow have to make a record of that information. Audio and video recordings are the most accurate but least sensitive techniques. The tapes or disks capture statements and interactions with precision and permit you to replay the episodes repeatedly for the purpose of analysis. However, these techniques can be disruptive if openly used in the setting. At least initially, your respondents will perform for them. Most likely, the enactors will not want the machines in the setting. If the devices are hidden, ethical issues arise. Recording machines were not used in any of the illustrative projects presented in Chapters 2 through 12, with the exception of the parolee study. Interviews with the parolees were openly audio-recorded, but only after the project was explained to them, their anonymity guaranteed, and their permission obtained.

Typically, researchers studying roles in natural settings depend on taking notes to record what they perceive to be important quotes, events, interactions, characteristics of the enactors, and characteristics of the settings. Schatzman and Strauss (1973: 99) have suggested that field notes be kept under three categories: observational notes (concerning what you have seen and heard); theoretical notes (pinpointing observations that have specific relevance to the theory that is guiding or emerging from your study); and methodological notes (messages to yourself about other role/setting aspects for further investigation). Lofland (1971) has advised that field notes should also contain comments about your own feelings and reactions. That is particularly important when you are enacting the role you are studying. As Lofland (1971: 106) succinctly puts it, "The field notes are not only for recording the setting; they are for 'recording' the observer as well." In all of the illustrative studies involving me as a complete observer, I used note categories similar to those suggested by Lofland and by Schatzman and Strauss, and I advise you to do the same. For purposes of insight, validity, and reliability, you should "triangulate" what you have seen and heard with your theoretical perspectives, your methodological inclinations, and what you have felt about the role enactment. Look again at the study of emotional role behavior among fans and football players for an example of the results of that procedure.

Your observational notes on role behavior should chronologically follow the events and enactments in the setting as they occur. Episodes of enactor autonomy and of role conformity, conflict, or creativity will develop as interactive processes over time. The relations among the enactors and the significance of "others" in the setting will be more or less fluid, but they will always appear in a sequential pattern. Role socialization and reactions to it will be continuous events, making sense only if considered in their continuity. You must capture the particulars of those processes in your notes.

Do not let your close attention to the social interactions cause you to forget about taking notes describing the institutionalized social structures and the physical characteristics of the setting. Those characteristics importantly influence the nature of the interactions. Consider how incomplete my study of the informal sailor role would have been if I had not described the formal organization of the ship. Try to understand the hashers' creating role "bits" without knowing about the kitchen/dining room arrangement in the sorority. Attempt to see the relevance of "people pipelines" without the description of the airports and airplanes in which the pipelines operated.

Taking too many notes is no problem; taking too few is a waste of research access. Jot down everything you think is important at the moment, and capture as much detail about the setting, interactions, and role enactments as possible. Be guided by your research questions and your other interests in the topic, but record observations you think might productively take you beyond those boundaries. You can refine your notes and eliminate the dross later. My notes on the indigenous leader filled fifteen large binders. I used only a small portion of that material when writing the report, but I could not have predicted what portion I would in the end find most salient.

If you are less than a complete participant in the setting, it probably will be no problem to take notes openly and continuously. The enactors know you are a researcher and usually expect you to act like one, particularly when you are conducting interviews. Notes were openly and easily taken in the studies of the indigenous leader, priests, and parolees.

If you are a complete participant, you might or might not be able to write down your observations when they actually occur. I was able to do so in the ship, football game, airplane, and Naval Reservist studies. Other people in those settings were for one reason or another writing things down, so I did not stand out. In the recruit training center, disaster work crew, and poker game settings, I had to jot down notes only when I could do so privately. Open note taking would have been disruptive. I could have taken notes during the Marine field exercise without being obtrusive—the other enactors knew I was a researcher interested in the military—but the pace of the role-related activities in which I too was involved was so hectic that I could not stop to do so.

When you are a complete participant, and if your note taking would get in the way of the interactions or activities, you can snatch moments here and there hurriedly to record some observations. Visiting the restroom, making a phone call, going to your car to retrieve something, getting a cup of coffee, taking a "break" from the action, and other such real or contrived events can be used as recording opportunities. Do not abuse those situations. If you make ten trips to the restroom during a four-hour encounter group you are studying, the other enactors will wonder, and are likely to ask, if you have a problem.

Circumstances probably will afford you longer periods for summarizing your observations while you are in the field. Typically, you will be able to do so in the evening—whenever it is that the activities abate or you go "home" from the setting.

When you are a known researcher in the setting, you can carry large notebooks around with you. When you are a complete participant and cannot take notes openly, you should have a pocket-sized memo pad to use at fortuitous moments. But do not worry about being fancy if you observe something worth recording and are without a pad. Use anything that works: paper bags, cocktail napkins, pieces of newspaper, matchbook covers, envelopes, paper towels, whatever the setting provides. Some of my notes about the airplane passengers were on used boarding passes and ticket envelopes; some about the Marine field exercise on pieces of a pistol target; some about the disaster work crew on a piece of wallpaper that I found in the street. Preferably, use a mechanical pencil. A stick pencil most surely will break at the wrong time. Ink can smear and will not write on many materials you grab when you have no note paper. I obliterated about twenty pages of notes, written in felt-point pen, when I fell in a swamp during the Marine field exercises.

At the conclusion of each period of observation, you should review your notes, expand them, and file them into folders. The folders can represent time segments in a chronological sequence, categories of events, kinds of interactions, theoretical notes, methodological notes, or whatever you decide best organizes your data and facilitates your analysis. I had 88 folders (many of them multiple) for my study of the Topeka poverty program. The indigenous leader part of that research included the following folders:

- background for the inception of the target neighborhood committee
- physical description of the TNC meeting place
- evidence of neighborhood participation in the TNC
- emergence of a leader
- elections
- participants' expressed goals for the TNC
- programs selected by the TNC
- evidence of marginality in the leadership role
- leader attitudes, and changes in attitudes, toward the poverty program and the Topeka Office of Economic Opportunity staff
- leadership behavior, and changes in that behavior
- evidence of increasing or decreasing involvement in the Topeka poverty program
- issues of power, control, and competence in the leadership role
- indices of autonomy in enactment of the leader role
- interactions with other target neighborhood committee leaders
- followers' attitudes toward the leader, and changes in those attitudes
- followers' behaviors toward the leader, and changes in those behaviors
- TNC stages of development

As you can discern from your reading of Chapter 11 about the indigenous leader, those file folder categories helped me organize my observations. But some of the categories overlapped. That will happen to you; do not be concerned. File folders should work for you, not you for them. When you undertake your final analysis of the data and write the results, take the information you want from any file folder regardless of its label. There is nothing sacred about file categories. If you have the luxury of grant money, you can make multiple copies of your notes and cross-file them in more than one appropriate folder. But remember that some of the best qualitative research in the literature was done without dollars to permit cross-filing and other such niceties (not, however, without care, insight, and purposeful expenditure of time and energy).

Keep your eye out for any documents in or about the setting that bear on the role enactments you are studying: minutes of meetings; agendas; organizational charts; schedules of activities; job descriptions; statements of organizational goals, policies, and operating procedures; newspaper articles; court records; and the like. Those documents can save you much note taking and interviewing and can tell you much about the institutionalized aspects of the interactions. Having copies of the "Plan of the Day" published each day in the recruit training center and aboard ship, for example, informed me quickly and accurately about the organizational routine in which the boot and sailor roles were enacted.

Analyzing the Data

Novice researchers typically are puzzled about what role to study, how to get access to the setting, how to make a study theoretically sound, and how to gather and record data efficiently. Assuming that you have solved those puzzles (probably with the help of your professors—that is what professors are for), you then face an inevitable problem. How in the world do you analyze, make sense of, and write up the mound of observational, theoretical, methodological, and personal reflection notes that you have accumulated? Do not despair; experienced researchers often encounter the same problem.

In Chapter 13, I stressed the importance of using, and offered an example of, a conceptual framework for analyzing role enactment. Briefly look at that chapter again, especially at Figure 1. Remember that it is just one framework and includes a limited number of variables. Perhaps it will not do the job with your data. Analytical schemes are nothing more than devices, like tire irons. If the tool fits, use it. If not, select another. That a framework appears in print and has academic blessing means only that it is an alternative for your consideration.

You can base your own conceptual framework on established social science theory, on theoretical notions that have emerged from your data, or a combination of both those sources. Perhaps you have clearly established a framework in your mind before you began the study. Perhaps you have developed it as you conducted your observation in the natural setting. Whatever procedure you used, having a conceptual framework (even if only a temporary, "working" framework) to guide you facilitates, indeed makes possible, the useful analysis of your data. Your obligation as a social scientist is not just to report your qualitative data as a good journalist would do, but to impose your interpretations on the collected body of social science theory.

If you have organized your data into file categories patterned after the components in your conceptual framework, you have a leg up on the analysis. You can proceed with the analysis according to those categories, a synthesis of several of them, or new ones that emerge as you review the material. Obviously, the best approach is to consider that the analysis of qualitative data gathered in natural settings is not an "end of the project" task. While you are gathering the data, take some time to write working papers about what you have discovered so far. In the Naval Reserve and indigenous leader studies, I wrote a summary paper at least once a month, based on the data I had in hand. Whether or not those papers were publishable, they definitely made my final analysis more manageable. I did not do that with the poker study. Consequently, I paced the floor on many occasions, wondering what I should do with the data. (Your discerning eye will have noticed that the original poker paper was not published until 1970; I gathered the data during 1966-1968. That accurately indicates a lot of floor pacing.)

Analyses of role enactments in natural settings often yield conclusions couched in typologies or processes. The typologies emphasize the kinds of enactments (for example, ephemeral poker roles, disaster roles, recruit roles, sailor roles, and Naval Reservist roles). The processes emphasize emergent role enactments (for example, hasher resolution of role conflict, distancing from the airplane passenger role, Naval Reservist reactions to disruption of role balance, and priest and parolee transformation of accustomed roles). In the symbolic interactionist framework the types and processes of role enactment are empirically and analytically intertwined, as I trust the examples in Chapters 2 through 12 have shown.

The analysis of the roles you have chosen to study ought to generate both typologies of enactment and an understanding of the social processes influencing the enactment. The meaning of the enactment to the person, how it relates to self-concept, the autonomous choices of role conformity, creativity, and conflict resolution, the situated negotiation of identity, and the institutionalized social forms and physical characteristics of the setting should guide your analysis (if you are using the framework presented in Chapter 13, Figure 1).

The paramount rules for your analysis and the resulting written report of your social science observations simply should be: make it concise, accurate, and readable; make it useful (theoretically and practically); do justice to the data your respondents have given you; be consistent with your own perspectives. Analyzing and reporting qualitative data are similar to the way a lawyer prepares an argumentative brief for the court (although I do not suggest that lawyers are social scientists or that their methods and ethics ought to be emulated). You make the best scientific case you can for your interpretations, always inviting and expecting constructive criticism from other researchers. Since your field investigation probably suffers from limited generality of findings, your report should be structured to provoke replication of the study in other settings. If other researchers agree with you, celebrate. If they do not, use their conflicting findings to inform your further research.

PUBLISHING YOUR FINDINGS

Your analysis of the qualitative data will result in some kind of written document about role enactment in a natural setting. It probably will be a paper that you will use to satisfy a class assignment or, if longer, and much more elaborate, as a master's thesis or doctoral dissertation.

If you have done a good job with the analysis, you should consider disseminating your findings more broadly. Qualitative studies usually are based on limited samples; the greater the number of soundly conducted, well-written case studies available, the greater the likelihood that corrective comparisons can be made. Before you distribute your findings, you should consult your professor(s) about the advisability of doing so. You want your work to be a contribution to and not a distraction from the literature.

Using the U.S. Mail

One quick and uncomplicated way of getting findings in the hands of potentially interested people is to send machine-duplicated copies of your paper to those social scientists whose works you cited. Use your own bibliography as a guide. More often than not, those scholars appreciate seeing what you have discovered and how you have used their work.

Oral Presentation

Another dissemination strategy is to present your paper at a social science convention. Pick an appropriate session for your paper, one that focuses on the substantive, theoretical, or methodological contribution you have made about role enactment. Follow the instructions for submitting your paper to the session chairperson for consideration. Do not submit a paper that is more than fifteen double-spaced manuscript pages, even though your report probably was longer than that. Summarize the major findings so that you can present them within the time limits specified by the session chairperson (usually fifteen to twenty minutes). You can bring copies of your full report to the session and make them available to people in the audience who want to see more of your study. If your paper is selected for the session (or even before you submit it), present it formally to a group of classmates/faculty members for critique and discussion.

Publishing in Journals

Submitting a manuscript based on your findings to a social science journal for publication consideration simultaneously can be a frustrating and rewarding experience. If assessed by the editor to be of sufficient quality, your paper will be reviewed by referees—social scientists who are quite familiar with research on your topic. That process typically takes several long months. Having a paper rejected is no disgrace; most journals have about an 80 percent rejection rate. Use the referees' comments to improve your work. Should the editor and reviewers judge your paper to have publication potential, they probably will want you to revise the manuscript and resubmit it for further consideration. Fewer than 1 percent of the papers submitted to journals are accepted without revision. Unless the editor's demands are unreasonable or unfounded, always take advantage of the invitation to revise and resubmit. The odds for the acceptance of a revision are reasonably encouraging (roughly a 50/50 chance), and you have the advantage of being guided by specific editorial suggestions/expectations.

Some Reasons Papers Are Rejected

You can enhance the possibility of having your paper on role enactments in natural settings accepted for publication by avoiding some common mistakes. I offer the following list of errors for your perusal, based primarily on my experience as editor of *The Journal of Applied Behavioral Science* (Zurcher, 1981: 454-457) and as consulting editor to several other journals.

- The manuscript represents a premature effort. It suggests a research project that should be done, but does not carry the task to completion. As provocative as those papers might be, they usually are not accepted for publication. They often are entitled "a pilot study" or "an exploratory study."
- There is no review of the literature or it is inadequate. The author has missed major studies that bear directly on the research. This is not to say that the literature review ought to be just an academic exercise. Readers have a right to expect that the author will inform them of pertinent related work and how it fits with the findings presented in the paper.
- The paper is atheoretical; it lacks social science relevance. The analysis of the data is not guided by an adequate conceptual framework, whether that framework is based in established theory or has emerged from the data. Qualitative research typically is used to generate rather than to test hypotheses. The paper does not generate hypotheses, inform theory, or stimulate further research.
- The qualitative research was not rigorously conducted. The author gives the impression that he or she has not consulted some of the recent texts on qualitative methods before undertaking the study. The field techniques employed are so loose that the findings, no matter how interesting, would be dismissed by readers as invalid or unreliable. Sometimes the author has used sound qualitative research methods, but does not report them fully enough in the paper. The reader needs to know how the author actually proceeded in gathering and analyzing the data.
- The author overgeneralizes findings based on a limited sample or a single case. Qualitative researchers, given their inclination to focus on "micro"

rather than "macro" social phenomena and to study them in depth, must be especially cautious about undue extrapolations.

- The paper is distractingly written. The syntax and grammar are so poorly constructed that they interfere with the ideas in the narrative. Journal reviewers rightly are distressed by obtuse writing. They get few rewards for the hard and time-consuming job of being a referee. It is reasonable for them to expect that the papers they are to assess will be clear presentations, both stylistically and in appearance. They should not have to translate or dig for what the author is attempting to say.
- The paper's findings represent nothing new. The research and the writing might be well formulated, but the results are already conventional wisdom. This does not necessarily include sound replications of research already in the literature.
- The author has not read the journal's statement of editorial purpose, its instructions for the preparation and submission of papers, or looked at its most recent issues. Consequently, the author submits a paper on a topic not within the journal's purview, or, if the topic is suitable, submits a manuscript that does not conform to the journal's format.

What Journal to Choose

Some journals are more likely than others to publish papers reporting qualitative studies of role enactment in natural settings, assuming high quality of course. Those journals include: *Symbolic Interaction; Qualitative Sociology; Urban Life; Deviant Behavior; Human Organization; Sociological Quarterly; Social Forces; Social Problems; Sociological Spectrum; Sociological Inquiry; Sociological Focus; Journal of Social Issues; Journal of Popular Culture; Sociological Perspectives; Work and Occupations; Journal of Applied Behavioral Science; Small Group Behavior; International Review of Sport Sociology; Journal of Marriage and the Family;* and *Human Relations.* Several of the specialty journals in social work, psychology, and political science will consider qualitative papers on role enactment if the roles are pertinent to them—for example: *Journal of Gerontology; Journal of Community Psychology; Journal of Voluntary Action Research; Social Casework;* and *Sociology and Social Welfare.*

Your library will probably have several publications that list social science journals and detail the kinds of articles they prefer. You can also browse through the current journal issues displayed in the library stacks and see for yourself.

Watch for announcements of special issues of journals that are being prepared. Your role enactment paper might be just what the editor is looking for. Also try to find out if someone is assembling an anthology of not previously published papers for which your manuscript might be appropriate.

Publishing a Book

Perhaps your manuscript is extensive enough and good enough to be published as a book. Unless it has a high probability of being widely adopted as a text for classroom use or of capturing a large "trade" (popular) audience, most publishers these days will not be interested in your study of role enactments in natural settings. Check with the publishers' representatives who regularly come to your campus to solicit book orders, or visit them at the book displays at social science conventions. Prepare a three- or four-page summary of the manuscript, including a chapter outline, the special contribution the book will make, the intended audience for it, and the names of other books with which it will compete. Send the summary, and a copy of your curriculum vitae, to some publishers you think will be interested. They will let you know if they want to see the entire manuscript.

University presses are usually interested in publishing books based on outstanding qualitative studies or role enactments in natural settings. Your library will have a list of those presses. Among commercial publishers, a few have had or do have a pertinent monograph series, for example: Sage Publications; Wadsworth Publishing Company; Aldine Publishing Company; Human Sciences Press; Praeger Publishers; Gage Publishing Limited; D. C. Heath and Company; Charles C Thomas, Publishers; JAI Press, Inc.; and Hemisphere Publishing Company.

A Note on Keeping Your Notes

Do not throw away your field notes, even after you have completed your analysis, written your report, and published your findings (I wish I always had followed that advice myself). Other researchers might be interested in seeing them. Equally importantly, you might have occasion to mine them again for further insights or for comparison with new data you have gathered or when you have gone back to the same setting to take another look. I did that with the Reserve center, ship, and Reservist studies. The hasher, volunteer work crew, poker, and indigenous leader studies were replicated by other researchers; I was able to use my notes to answer inquiries from them when they began their studies. Furthermore, as the years pass in your social science career, you will find it interesting if not a bit disconcerting to read what the social role of researcher, what "being there," meant to you in "the old days."

References

Abrahamsson, Bengt
    1977 Bureaucracy or Participation. Beverly Hills, CA: Sage.
Adams, Richard N. and Jack J. Preiss (eds.)
    1960 Human Organization Research. Homewood, IL: Dorsey.
Adler, Peter
    1981 Momentum: A Theory of Social Action. Beverly Hills, CA: Sage.
Adler, Peter and Patricia A. Adler
    1978 "The role of momentum in sport." Urban Life 7 (July): 153-176.
    1982 "The car pool: an uninvestigated setting for early childhood socialization."
        Presented at the annual meetings of the American Sociological Association,
        San Francisco.
Adorno, Theodore W., Else Frenkel-Brunswik, Daniel J. Levinson, and R. Nevitt
    Sanford
    1950 The Authoritarian Personality. New York: Harper & Row.
Allport, Gordon W.
    1954 The Nature of Prejudice. Reading, MA: Addison-Wesley.
    1955 Becoming: Basic Considerations for a Psychology of Personality. New Haven,
        CT: Yale University Press.
    1961 Pattern and Growth in Personality. New York: Holt, Rinehart & Winston.
Altheide, David and John M. Johnson
    1980 Bureaucratic Propaganda. Boston: Allyn & Bacon.
Anonymous
    1946a "Informal social organization in the army." American Journal of Sociology 51
        (March): 365-370.
    1946b "The making of an infantryman." American Journal of Sociology 51 (March):
        376-379.
Argyris, Chris
    1957 Personality and Organization. New York: Harper & Row.
    1964 Integrating the Individual and the Organization. New York: John Wiley.
Atkinson, John W. and David Birch
    1978 An Introduction to Motivation. New York: Van Nostrand.
Bachman, Jerald G., John D. Blair, and David R. Segal
    1977 The All-Volunteer Force: A Study of Ideology in the Military. Ann Arbor:
        University of Michigan Press.
Bandura, Albert
    1977 Social Learning Theory. Englewood Cliffs, NJ: Prentice-Hall.
Baum, M. and Stanton Wheeler
    1969 "Becoming an inmate," pp. 87-120 in S. Wheeler (ed.) Controlling Delinquents.
        New York: John Wiley.

Becker, Howard S.
    1951 "The professional dance musician and his audience." American Journal of
         Sociology 57 (September): 136-144.
    1960 "Notes on the concept of commitment." American Journal of Sociology 66
         (July): 32-40.
Berger, Peter L. and Thomas Luckman
    1967 The Social Construction of Reality. Garden City, NY: Doubleday.
Bergler, Edmund
    1957 The Psychology of Gambling. New York: Hill & Wang.
Berkman, Paul
    1946 "Life aboard an armed guard ship." American Journal of Sociology 51 (March):
         380-388.
Bernstein, Haskell C.
    1975 "Boredom and the ready-made life." Social Research 42 (Autumn): 512-537.
Biddle, Bruce J. and Edwin J. Thomas
    1966 Role Theory: Concepts and Research. New   York: John Wiley.
Blau, Peter M.
    1963 The Dynamics of Bureaucracy. Chicago: University of Chicago   Press.
Blauner, Robert
    1964 "Work, self and manhood: some reflections on technology and identity." Pre-
         sented at the annual meeting of the American Sociological Association,
         Montreal.
Bloch, Herbert A.
    1951 "The sociology of gambling." American Journal of Sociology 57 (November):
         215-221.
Blumer, Herbert
    1969 Symbolic Interaction: Perspective and Method. Englewood Cliffs, NJ:
         Prentice-Hall.
Bogdan, Robert and Steven J. Taylor
    1975 Introduction to Qualitative Research Methods. New York: John Wiley.
Brim, Orville G.
    1958 "Family structure and sex role learning by children: a further analysis of Helen
         Koch's data." Sociometry 21 (March): 1-16.
    1968 "Adult socialization," pp. 183-226 in J. A. Clausen (ed.) Socialization and
         Society. Boston: Little, Brown.
Brim, Orville G. and Stanton Wheeler
    1966 Socialization After Childhood. New York: John Wiley.
Brissett, Dennis and Charles Edgley
    1975 Life as Theatre: A Dramaturgical Sourcebook. Chicago: Aldine.
Brotz, Howard and Everett K. Wilson
    1946 "Characteristics of military society." American Journal of Sociology 51
         (March): 371-378.
Burchard, Waldo
    1954 "Role conflict of military chaplains." American Sociological Review 19
         (August): 528-535.
Burke, Kenneth
    1962 A Grammar of Motives and Rhetoric of Motives. New York: World.
    1965 Permanence and Change. Indianapolis: Bobbs-Merrill.
    1969 A Rhetoric of Motives. Berkeley: University of California Press.
Burns, Tom
    1953 "Friends, enemies and the polite fiction." American Sociological Review 18
         (December): 654-662.

Bush, Diane Mitsch and Roberta G. Simmons
  1981 "Socialization processes over the life course," pp. 133-164 in M. Rosenberg and R. H. Turner (eds.) Social Psychology: Sociological Perspectives. New York: Basic Books.
Caillois, Roger
  1961 Man, Play and Games. New York: Macmillan.
Charon, Joel M.
  1979 Symbolic Interactionism: An Introduction, an Interpretation, an Integration. Englewood Cliffs, NJ: Prentice-Hall.
Chertkoff, Jerome and James K. Esser
  1976 "A review of experiments in explicit bargaining." Journal of Experimental Social Psychology 12 (September): 464-486.
Cicourel, Aaron V.
  1968 The Social Organization of Juvenile Justice. New York: John Wiley.
Clanton, Gordon
  1978 "The social construction of emotions." Department of Sociology, San Diego State University. (unpublished)
Clanton, Gordon and Lynn G. Smith
  1977 Jealousy. Englewood Cliffs, NJ: Prentice-Hall.
Clausen, John A. (ed.)
  1968 Socialization and Society. Boston: Little, Brown.
Clemmer, David
  1958 The Prison Community. New York: Holt, Rinehart & Winston.
Clifton, James A.
  1965 "Culture change, structural stability and factionalism in the Prairie Potawatomi Reservation community." Midcontinent American Studies Journal 6 (Fall): 101-122.
Clifton, James A. and Barry Isaac
  1964 "The Kansas Prairie Potawatomi: on the nature of a contemporary Indian community." Transactions of the Kansas Academy of Science 67, 1: 1-24.
Cooley, Charles H.
  1902 Human Nature and the Social Order. New York: Scribner.
Coser, Rose L.
  1961 "Insulation from observability and types of social conformity." American Sociological Review 26 (February): 28-39.
Coulson, Margaret
  1972 "Role: a redundant concept in sociology? Some educational considerations," pp. 107-128 in J. A. Jackson (ed.) Role. Cambridge: Cambridge University Press.
Cousins, Albert N.
  1951 "Social equilibrium and the psychodramic mechanisms" Social Forces 30 (December): 202-209.
Crawshaw, Ralph
  1953 "Reactions to disaster." Archives of General Psychiatry 9 (August): 156-162.
Crespi, Irving
  1956 "The social significance of card playing as a leisure time activity." American Sociological Review 21 (December): 717-721.
Cummings, Larry L. and Ali M. El Salmi
  1970 "The impact of role diversity, job level, and organizational size on managerial satisfaction." Administrative Science Quarterly 15 (March): 1-10.
Dalton, Melvin
  1959 Men Who Manage. New York: John Wiley.

Daniels, Arlene Kaplan
   1970 "Development of the scapegoat in sensitivity training sessions," pp. 234-249 in
       T. Shibutani (ed.) Human Nature and Collective Behavior. Englewood Cliffs,
       NJ: Prentice-Hall.
Davidson, Helen M., Frank Riessman, and Edna Meyers
   1962 "Personality characteristics attributed to the worker." Journal of Social Psy-
       chology 57 (June): 155-160.
Davis, Fred
   1959 "The cabdriver and his fare: facets of a fleeting relationship." American Jour-
       nal of Sociology 65 (September): 158-165.
Davis, Morris and Sol Levine
   1967 "Towards a sociology of public transit." Social Problems 15 (Summer): 84-91.
Deegan, Mary Jo and Michael Stein
   1978 "American drama and ritual: Nebraska football." International Review of
       Sport Sociology 13: 31-44.
Denzin, Norman J.
   1970 The Research Act. Chicago: Aldine.
Dewey, John
   1922 Human Nature and Conduct. New York: Holt, Rinehart & Winston.
Dickie-Clark, H. F.
   1966 "The marginal situation: a contribution to marginality theory." Social Forces
       44 (March): 363-369.
Dornbusch, Sanford
   1955 "The military academy as an assimilating institution." Social Forces 33 (May):
       316-321.
Dorsey, Michael A. and Murray Meisels
   1969 "Personal space and self protection." Journal of Personality and Social Psy-
       chology 11 (February): 93-97.
Douglas, Jack D. and John M. Johnson
   1977 Existential Sociology. Cambridge: Cambridge University Press.
Drabek, Thomas E. and John S. Stephenson III
   1971 "When disaster strikes." Journal of Applied Social Psychology 1 (April/June):
       187-203.
Dubin, Robert
   1968 Human Relations in Administration. Englewood Cliffs, NJ: Prentice-Hall.
Durkheim, Emile
   1947 The Division of Labor in Society (G. Simpson, trans.). New York: Macmillan.
Edwards, Ward
   1955 "The prediction of decisions among bets." Journal of Experimental Psychology
       50 (September): 201-214.
Elias, Norbert and Eric Dunning
   1970 "The quest for excitement in unexciting societies," in G. Luschen (ed.) The
       Cross-Cultural Analysis of Sport and Games. Champaign, IL: Stipes.
Elkin, Frederick
   1946 "The soldier's language." American Journal of Sociology 51 (March): 414-422.
Erickson, Kai T.
   1957 "Patient role and social uncertainty: a dilemma of the mentally ill." Psychiatry
       20: 263-274.
   1962 "Notes on the sociology of deviance." Social Problems 9 (Spring): 307-314.

Erikson, Erik
1950 Childhood and Society. New York: Norton.
Farberman, Harvey
1979 "A review symposium: Anselm L. Strauss—negotiations: varieties, contexts, processes and social order." Symbolic Interaction 2 (Fall): 153-159.
Ferguson, John David
1980 "Emotions in the sociology of sport." Presented at the annual meeting of the Society for the Study of Symbolic Interaction, New York.
Festinger, Leon
1957 A Theory of Cognitive Dissonance. Stanford, CA: Stanford University Press.
Filstead, William J. (Ed.)
1970 Qualitative Methodology. Chicago: Markham.
Foote, Nelson
1951 "Identification as the basis for a theory of motivation." American Sociological Review 46 (February): 14-21.
Form, William H. and Sigmund Nosow
1958 Community in Disaster. New York: Harper & Row.
Frazer, James G.
1957 The Golden Bough, Vol. II. London: Macmillan. (Reprint of the 1937 edition.)
Freud, Anna
1946 The Ego and Mechanisms of Defense. New York: International Universities Press.
Gardner, Burleigh B. and William Foote Whyte
1945 "The man in the middle: position and problems of the foreman." Applied Anthropology 4 (Spring): 1-28.
Garfinkle, Harold
1956 "Conditions of successful degradation ceremonies." American Journal of Sociology 61 (March): 420-424.
1967 Studies in Ethnomethodology. Englewood Cliffs, NJ: Prentice-Hall.
Gecas, Viktor
1981 "Contexts of socialization," pp. 165-199 in M. Rosenberg and R. H. Turner (eds.) Social Psychology: Sociological Perspectives. New York: Basic Books.
Glaser, Barney G. and Anselm L. Strauss
1966 Awareness of Dying. Chicago: Aldine.
1967 The Discovery of Grounded Theory. Chicago: Aldine.
Glaser, Daniel
1964 The Effectiveness of a Prison and Parole System. New York: Bobbs-Merrill.
Glass, Albert J.
1959 "Psychological aspects of disaster." Journal of the American Medical Association 171: 222-225.
Goffman, Erving
1956 "Embarrassment and social organization." American Journal of Sociology 62 (November): 264-271.
1957 "Alienation from interaction." Human Relations 10, 1: 47-60.
1959 The Presentation of Self in Everyday Life. Garden City, NY: Doubleday.
1961a Asylums. New York: Doubleday.
1961b Encounters: Two Studies in the Sociology of Interaction. Indianapolis: Bobbs-Merrill.
1963 Behavior in Public Places. New York: Macmillan.

1967 Interaction Ritual. Chicago: Aldine.

Gold, Raymond L.
1958 "Roles in sociological field observations." Social Forces 36 (March): 217-223.

Goldman, Nancy
1973a "The changing role of women in the armed forces." American Journal of Sociology 78 (January): 892-911.
1973b "The utilization of women in the military." Annals of the American Academy of Political and Social Science 406: 107-116.

Goode, William S.
1960 "A theory of role strain." American Sociological Review 25 (August): 483-496.

Goslin, David A.
1969 Handbook of Socialization Theory and Research. Chicago: Rand McNally.

Gouldner, Alvin
1957 "Cosmopolitans and locals: toward an analysis of latent social roles." Administrative Science Quarterly 2 (December): 281-306.

Gross, Edward and Gregory P. Stone
1964 "Embarrassment and the analysis of role requirements." American Journal of Sociology 70 (July): 1-15.

Gross, Neal, Ward Mason, and Alexander McEachern
1958 Explorations in Role Analysis. New York: John Wiley.

Gusfield, Joseph
1963 Symbolic Crusade: Status Politics and the American Temperance Movement. Urbana: University of Illinois Press.

Habenstein, Robert W.
1970 Pathways to Data: Field Methods for Studying Ongoing Social Organizations. Chicago: Aldine.

Habermas, Jurgen
1969 Toward a Rational Society. Boston: Beacon.

Hall, Peter
1983 "Individualism and social problems: a critique and an alternative." Journal of Applied Behavioral Science 19 (January/February/March): 128-134.

Handel, Warren H.
1979 "Normative expectations and the emergence of meanings as solutions to problems: convergence of structural and interactionist views." American Journal of Sociology 84 (January): 855-881.

Hartley, Wynona
1968a "Self concept and social functioning of former mental patients." Kansas City, MO: Greater Kansas City Mental Health Foundation.
1968b "Self conception and organizational adaptation." Presented at the meeting of the Midwest Sociological Association.

Hartshorne, Eliot C.
1943 Undergraduate Society and the College Culture. Cambridge, MA: Harvard University Press.

Heider, Fritz
1958 The Psychology of Interpersonal Relations. New York: John Wiley.

Heilbrun, Alfred B.
1981 Human Sex-Role Behavior. New York: Pergamon.

Heirich, Max
1971 The Spiral of Conflict: Berkeley 1964. New York: Columbia University Press.

Heiss, Jerold
1981a "Social roles," pp. 94-129 in M. Rosenberg and R. H. Turner (eds.) Social Psychology: Sociological Perspectives. New York: Basic Books.

1981b The Social Psychology of Interaction. Englewood Cliffs, NJ: Prentice-Hall.

Henslin, James M.

1967 "Craps and magic." American Journal of Sociology 73 (November): 316-330.

Herman, Robert D.

1967a (ed.) Gambling. New York: Harper & Row.

1967b "Gambling as work: a sociological study of the race track," pp. 87-104 in R. D. Herman (ed.) Gambling. New York: Harper & Row.

Hewitt, John P.

1976 Self and Society: A Symbolic Interactionist Social Psychology. Boston: Allyn & Bacon.

1979 Self and Society (2nd ed.). Boston: Allyn & Bacon.

Hewitt, John P. and Peter M. Hall

1973 "Social problems, problematic situations and quasitheories." American Sociological Review 38 (June): 367-374.

Hill, Reuben and Donald A. Hanson

1962 "Families in disaster," pp. 124-150 in G. W. Baker and D. W. Chapman (eds.) Man and Society in Disaster. New York: Basic Books.

Hilliard, Dan C. and Louis A. Zurcher

1978 "The temporal segregation of activities and their meanings in leisure sports settings." Journal of Physical Education and Recreation 49 (October): 26-30.

Hochschild, Arlie Russell

1975 "The sociology of feeling and emotion," in M. Milman and R. M. Kanter (eds.) Another Voice. Garden City, NY: Doubleday.

1979 "Emotion work, feeling rules, and social structure." American Journal of Sociology 85 (November): 551-575.

Hollingshead, August

1946 "Adjustment to military life." American Journal of Sociology 51 (March): 439-450.

Homans, George C.

1946 "The small warship." American Sociological Review 11 (April): 294-300.

1961 Social Behavior: Its Elementary Forms. New York: Harcourt Brace Jovanovich.

Hoult, Thomas F.

1969 Dictionary of Modern Sociology. Totowa, NJ: Littlefield, Adams.

Hughes, Everett C.

1945 "Dilemmas and contradictions of status." American Journal of Sociology 50 (March): 353-359.

1949 "Social change and status protest: an essay on the marginal man." Phylon 10 (1st quarter): 58-64.

Huizinga, Johan

1955 Homo Ludens, the Play Element in Culture. Boston: Beacon.

Hummel, Ralph P.

1982 The Bureaucratic Experience. New York: St. Martin's.

Hyman, Herbert H.

1942 "The psychology of status." Archives of Psychology 38 (June): 1-94.

Irwin, John

1970 The Felon. Englewood Cliffs, NJ: Prentice-Hall.

Janis, Irving L.

1945 "Psychodynamics of adjustment to army life." Psychiatry 8 (May): 159-176.

1958 Psychological Stress. New York: John Wiley.

Janowitz, Morris

1960 The Professional Soldier. New York: Macmillan.

1964 "Converging theoretical perspectives." Sociological Quarterly 5 (Spring): 113-132.

1971 The Professional Soldier: A Social and Political Portrait. New York: Macmillan.

Janowitz, Morris and Roger Little
1959 Sociology and the Military Establishment. New York: Russell Sage.

Johnson, John M.
1975 Doing Field Research. New York: Macmillan.

Kahn, Robert L., Donald M. Wolfe, Robert P. Quinn, J. Diedrick Snoek, and Robert A. Rosenthal
1964 Organizational Stress: Studies in Role Conflict and Ambiguity. New York: John Wiley.

Kando, Thomas M.
1977 Social Interaction. St. Louis: C. V. Mosby.

Kardiner, Abraham
1941 The Traumatic Neurosis of War. Psychosomatic Medicine Monograph II-III. New York: Hober.

Karp, David A. and William C. Yoels
1979 Symbols, Selves and Society. New York: Lippincott/ Harper & Row.

Katz, Daniel and Robert L. Kahn
1966 The Social Psychology of Organizations. New York: John Wiley.

Keenan, Francis W.
1966 "The athletic contest as a tragic form of art." International Review of Sport Sociology 1: 38-53.

Kemper, Theodore D.
1978a "Toward a sociology of emotions." American Sociologist 13 (February): 30-41.

1978b A Social Interactional Theory of Emotions. New York: John Wiley.

Kerckhoff, Alan C. and Thomas C. McCormick
1955 "Marginal status and marginal personality." Social Forces 34 (October): 48-55.

Klapp, Orrin E.
1962 Heroes, Villains and Fools. Englewood Cliffs, NJ: Prentice-Hall.

1969 Collective Search for Identity. New York: Holt, Rinehart & Winston.

Kohn, Melvin L.
1971 "Bureaucratic man: a portrait and an interpretation." American Sociological Review 36 (June): 461-474.

Kolb, William L.
1942 "A critical evaluation of Mead's 'I' and 'me' concepts." Social Forces 22 (March): 291-296.

Krawczyk, Zbigniew
1973 "Sport as a factor of acculturation." International Review of Sport Sociology 9, 2: 63-75.

Krech, David, Robert S. Crutchfield, and Egerton L. Ballachey
1962 The Individual in Society. New York: McGraw-Hill.

Kreh, W. R.
1969 Citizen Sailors: The U.S. Naval Reserve in War and Peace. New York: McKay.

Kuhn, Manford H.
1960 "Self attitudes by age, sex, and professional training." Sociological/ Quarterly 9 (January): 39-55.

Kuhn, Manford H. and Thomas S. Mc Partland
1954 "Empirical investigation of self attitudes." American Sociological Review 19 (February): 68-76.

Lahr, John
1976 "The theater of sports," in M. Hart (ed.) Sport in the Sociocultural Process. Dubuque, IA: William C. Brown.
Largey, Gayle P. and David R. Watson
1972 "The sociology of odors." American Journal of Sociology 77 (May): 1021-1034.
Lauer, Robert H. and Warren H. Handel
1977 Social Psychology: The Theory and Application of Symbolic Interactionism. Boston: Houghton Mifflin.
Leon, Robert L.
1965 "Maladaptive interaction between Bureau of Indian Affairs staff and Indian clients." American Journal of Orthopsychiatry 35 (July): 723-728.
Levine, Janey, Anne Vinson, and Deborah Wood
1973 "Subway behavior," pp. 208-216 in A. Birenbaum and E. Sagarin (eds.) People in Places: The Sociology of the Familiar. New York: Praeger.
Levitin, Teresa E.
1965 "Role performance and role distance in a low status occupation: the puller." Sociological Quarterly 5 (Spring): 251-260.
Linton, Ralph
1936 The Study of Man. New York: Appleton-Century-Crofts.
Little, Roger
1971 Handbook of Military Institutions. Beverly Hills, CA: Sage.
Littrell, W. Boyd, Gideon Sjoberg, and Louis A. Zurcher
1983 Bureaucracy as a Social Problem. Greenwich, CT: JAI.
Lofland, John
1971 Analyzing Social Settings. Belmont, CA: Wadsworth.
1976 Doing Social Life: The Qualitative Study of Human Interaction in Natural Settings. New York: John Wiley.
Lovette, Leland P.
1939 Naval Customs, Traditions and Usages. Annapolis, MD: Naval Institute.
Lukacs, John
1963 "Poker and American character." Horizon 5: 56-62.
Luschen, Gunther
1967 "The interdependence of sport and culture." International Review of Sport Sociology 2: 127-141.
Maines, David R.
1977 "Social organization and symbolic interactionism," pp. 235-259 in A. Inkeles et al. (eds.) Annual Review of Sociology, Vol. 3. Palo Alto, CA: Annual Reviews.
Malinowski, Bronislaw
1948 Magic, Science and Religion. Garden City, NY: Doubleday.
Manis, Jerome G. and Bernard N. Meltzer (eds.)
1972 Symbolic Interaction: A Reader in Social Psychology. Boston: Allyn & Bacon.
Mann, Leon
1969 "Queue culture: the waiting line as a social system." American Journal of Sociology 75 (November): 340-354.
1970 "The social psychology of waiting lines." American Scientist 58 (July/August): 390-398.
Mann, Leon and K. F. Taylor
1969 "Queue counting: the effect of motives upon estimates of numbers in waiting lines." Journal of Personality and Social Psychology 12 (June): 95-103.
Martinez, Thomas M. and Robert LaFranci
1969 "Why people play poker." Transaction 6 (July/August): 30-35, 52.

Masden, K. B.
  1968 Theories of Motivation. Kent, OH: Kent State University Press.
Maslow, Abraham H.
  1954 Motivation and Personality. New York: Harper & Row.
May, Rollo
  1969 Love and Will. New York: Norton.
McCall, George J. and James L. Simmons
  1966 Identities and Interactions. New York: Macmillan.
McIntosh, P. C.
  1971 "An historical view of sport and social control." International Review of Sport
       Sociology 6: 5-16.
McLemore, S. Dale
  1970 "Simmel's 'Stranger': a critique of the concept." Pacific Sociological Review 13
       (Spring): 86-94.
McPartland, Thomas S.
  1965 Manual for the Twenty Statements Problem. Kansas City, MO: Greater Kan-
       sas City Mental Health Foundation.
McPartland, Thomas S. and John H. Cumming
  1958 "Self conception, social class and mental health." Human Organization 17
       (Fall): 24-29.
McPartland, Thomas S., John H. Cumming, and Wynona S. Garretson
  1961 "Self conception and ward behavior in two psychiatric hospitals." Sociometry
       24 (June): 111-124.
Mead, George Herbert
  1934 Mind, Self and Society. Chicago: University of Chicago Press.
Mehan, Hugh and Houston Wood
  1975 The Reality of Ethnomethodology. New York: John Wiley.
Meltzer, Bernard N.
  1972 "Mead's social psychology," pp. 4-22 in J. G. Manis and B. N. Meltzer (eds.)
       Symbolic Interaction: A Reader in Social Psychology. Boston: Allyn & Bacon.
Meltzer, Bernard N., John W. Petras, and Larry T. Reynolds
  1975 Symbolic Interactionism: Genesis, Varieties and Criticism. London: Routledge
       & Kegan Paul.
Menninger, William C.
  1952 "Psychological reactions in an emergency." American Journal of Psychiatry
       109 (August): 128-130.
Merton, Robert K.
  1940 "Bureaucratic structure and personality." Social Forces 18 (March): 560-568.
  1957 "The role set." British Journal of Sociology 8 (June): 106-120.
  1968 Social Theory and Social Structure. New York: Macmillan.
Merton, Robert K. and E. Barber
  1963 "Sociological ambivalence," pp. 91-120 in E. A. Tyriakian (ed.) Continuities in
       Social Research: Essays in Honor of Pitirim A. Sorokin. New York: Macmillan.
Merton, Robert K. and Alice S. Kitt
  1950 "Contributions to the theory of reference group behavior," in R. K. Merton
       and P. F. Lazarsfeld (eds.) Continuities in Social Research. New York:
       Macmillan.
Miller, Donald C. and William H. Form
  1964 Industrial Sociology: The Sociology of Work Organizations. New York: Harper
       & Row.

Mills, C. Wright
  1940 "Situated actions and vocabularies of motive." American Sociological Review 5 (December): 904-913.
Moore, Harry Estell
  1958 Tornadoes over Texas. Austin: University of Texas Press.
Moskos, Charles C.
  1970 The American Enlisted Men. New York: Russell Sage.
Moynihan, Daniel Patrick
  1968 Maximum Feasible Misunderstanding: Community Action in the War on Poverty. New York: Macmillan.
Murphy, Gardner
  1947 Personality: A Biosocial Approach. New York: Harper & Row.
Nash, Jeff
  1975 "Bus riding: community on wheels." Urban Life 4 (April): 99-124.
Newcomb, Theodore M.
  1949 "Role behaviors in the study of individual personality and of group." Journal of Personality 18 (September/June): 273-289.
  1950 Social Psychology. New York: Dryden.
Nye, F. Ivan
  1976 Role Structure and Analysis of the Family. Beverly Hills, CA: Sage.
Orwell, George
  1933 Down and Out in Paris and London. London: Secker & Warburg.
Park, Robert E.
  1928 "Human migration and the marginal man." American Journal of Sociology 33 (May): 881-893.
Parsons, Talcott
  1951 The Social System. London: Routledge & Kegan Paul.
  1970 Social Structure and Personality. New York: Macmillan.
Perinbanayagam, Robert S.
  1977 "The structure of motives." Symbolic Interaction 1 (Fall): 104-120.
Perry, Stewart E. and L. C. Wynne
  1959 "Role conflict, role redefinition, and social change in a clinical research organization." Social Forces 38 (October): 62-65.
Piaget, Jean
  1951 Play, Dreams and Imitations in Childhood. New York: Norton.
Quarantelli, Enrico L.
  1960 "Images of withdrawal behavior in disasters: some basic misconceptions." Social Problems 8 (Summer): 68-79.
  1977 Disasters: Theory and Research. Beverly Hills, CA: Sage.
Quarantelli, Enrico L. and Russell R. Dynes
  1977 "Responses to social crisis and disaster," pp. 23-49 in A. Inkeles et al. (eds.) Annual Review of Sociology, Vol. 3. Palo Alto, CA: Annual Reviews.
Riezler, Kurt
  1941 "Play and seriousness." Journal of Philosophy 38 (September): 505-517.
  1943 "Comment on the social psychology of shame." American Journal of Sociology 48 (January): 457-465.
Roethlisberger, Fritz J.
  1945 "The foreman: master and victim of double talk." Harvard Business Review 20 (Spring): 285-294.

Roethlisberger, Fritz J. and William J. Dickson
    1939 Management and the Worker. Cambridge: Harvard University Press.
    1964 Management and the Worker. New York: John Wiley.
Rokeach, Milton
    1960 The Open and Closed Mind. New York: Basic Books.
Rose, Arnold M.
    1946 "The social structure of the army." American Journal of Sociology 51 (March):
        361-364.
    1962 (ed.) Human Behavior and Social Process. Boston: Houghton Mifflin.
Roy, Donald
    1959-1960 "Banana time: job satisfaction and informal interaction." Human Organi-
        zation 18 (Winter): 158-168.
Rubin, Lillian
    1967 "Maximum feasible participation: the origins, implications and present status."
        Poverty and Human Resources Abstracts 2 (November/December): 5-18.
Sagarin, Edward
    1973 "Etiquette, embarrassment and forms of address," pp. 195-207 in A. Biren-
        baum and E. Sagarin (eds.) People in Places: The Sociology of the Familiar.
        New York: Praeger.
Sarbin, Theodore R. and A. V. Allen
    1968 "Role theory," pp. 488-567 in G. Lindzey and E. Aronsen (eds.) The Handbook
        of Social Psychology, Vol. 1. Reading, MA: Addison-Wesley.
Schacter, Stanley and John A. Singer
    1962 "Cognitive, social and psychological determinants of emotional states." Psy-
        chological Review 69 (November): 379-399.
Schatzman, Leonard and Anselm L. Strauss
    1973 Field Research: Strategies for a Natural Sociology. Englewood Cliffs, NJ:
        Prentice-Hall.
Scheff, Thomas J.
    1967 "Toward a sociological model of consensus." American Sociological Review 32
        (February): 32-46.
    1979 Catharsis in Healing, Ritual and Drama. Berkeley: University of California
        Press.
Schutz, Alfred
    1944 "The stranger: an essay in social psychology." American Journal of Sociology
        49 (May): 499-507.
    1967 The Phenomenology of the Social World. Evanston, IL: Northwestern Univer-
        sity Press.
Schwartz, Barry
    1968 "The social psychology of privacy." American Journal of Sociology 73 (May):
        741-752.
    1970 "Notes on the sociology of sleep." Sociological Quarterly 11 (Fall): 485-499.
Schwartz, Howard and Jerry Jacobs
    1979 Qualitative Sociology. New York: Macmillan.
Schwirian, Kent
    1964 "Variations in structure of the Kuhn-McPartland Twenty Statements Test and
        related response differences." Sociological Quarterly 5 (Winter): 59.
Scott, Marvin B.
    1963 "A note on the place of truth." Berkeley Journal of Sociology 8 (June): 35-40.
Scott, Marvin B. and Stanford M. Lyman
    1968 "Accounts." American Sociological Review 33 (February): 46-62.

Searcy, Ann
  1965a "The value of ethnohistorical reconstruction of American Indian typical per-
        sonality: the case of the Potawatomie." Transactions of the Kansas Academy
        of Science 68, 2: 274-282.
  1965b "Contemporary and traditional Prairie Potawatomie child life." K.U. Pota-
        watomie Study Research Report 7. Department of Anthropology, University
        of Kansas.
Shaffir, William B., Robert A. Stebbins, and Allan Turowetz
  1980 Fieldwork Experience: Qualitative Approaches to Social Research. New York:
        St. Martin's.
Sherif, Muzafer
  1948 An Outline of Social Psychology. New York: Harper & Row.
Sherohman, James L.
  1977 "Conceptual and methodological issues in the study of role taking accuracy."
        Symbolic Interaction 1 (Fall): 121-131.
Shibutani, Tamotsu
  1955 "Reference groups as perspectives." American Journal of Sociology 60 (May):
        562-569.
  1961 Society and Personality: An Interactionist Approach to Social Psychology.
        Englewood Cliffs, NJ: Prentice-Hall.
Shott, Susan
  1979 "Emotion and social life: a symbolic interactionist analysis." American Journal
        of Sociology 84 (May): 1317-1334.
Sieber, Sam D.
  1974 "Toward a theory of role accumulation." American Sociological Review 39
        (August): 567-578.
Simmel, Georg
  1950 "The stranger," pp. 402-406 in K. H. Wolff (trans.) The Sociology of Georg
        Simmel. New York: Macmillan.
Siu, Paul C.P.
  1952 "The sojourner." American Journal of Sociology 58 (July): 34-44.
Sjoberg, Gideon
  1967 Ethics, Politics and Social Research. Cambridge, MA: Schenckman.
Sloan, Lloyd R.
  1979 "The function and impact of sports for fans," in J. H. Goldstein (ed.) Sports,
        Games and Play: Social Psychological Viewpoints. Hillsdale, NJ: Erlbaum.
Slotkin, J. S.
  1943 "Status of the marginal man." Sociology and Social Research 28 (September):
        47-54.
Snoek, J. D.
  1966 "Role strain in diversified role sets." American Journal of Sociology 4: 363-372.
Snow, David A., Louis A. Zurcher, and Robert Peters
  1981 "Victory celebrations as theatre: a dramaturgical approach to crowd behavior."
        Symbolic Interaction 4 (Spring): 21-42.
Snow, David A., Louis A. Zurcher, and Gideon Sjoberg forthcoming "Interviewing by
        comment: an adjunct to the direct question." Qualitative Sociology.
Snyder, Eldon E. and Elmer Spreitzer
  1975 "Sociology of sport: an overview," in D. W. Ball and J. W. Loy (eds.) Sport
        and Social Order. Reading, MA: Addison-Wesley.
Sommer, Robert
  1969 Personal Space: The Behavioral Basis of Design. Englewood Cliffs, NJ:
        Prentice-Hall.

Spaulding, Charles
   1961 An Introduction to Industrial Sociology. San Francisco: Chandler.
Speier, Matthew
   1973 How to Observe Face-to-Face Communication: A Sociological Introduction.
        Pacific Palisades, CA: Goodyear.
Spence, Janet T. and Robert L. Helmreich
   1978 Masculinity and Femininity. Austin: University of Texas Press.
Spitzer, Stephan, Carl Couch, and John Stratton
   1973 The Assessment of Self. Iowa City: Escort, Sernoll.
Spradley, James P. and David W. McCurdy
   1972 The Cultural Experience: Ethnography in Complex Society. Chicago: Science
        Research Associates.
Stebbins, Robert A.
   1972 "Modesty, pride and conceit: variations in the expression of self-esteem."
        Pacific Sociological Review 15 (October): 461-481.
Steele, Paul D. and Louis A. Zurcher
   1973 "Leisure sports as ephemeral roles: an exploratory study." Pacific Sociological
        Review 16 (July): 345-356.
Stokes, Randall and John P. Hewitt
   1976 "Aligning actions." Americal Sociological Review 41 (December): 838-849.
Stone, Gregory P.
   1962 "Appearance and the self," pp. 86-118 in A. M. Rose (ed.) Human Behavior
        and Social Process. Boston: Houghton Mifflin.
   1977 "Personal acts." Symbolic Interaction 1 (Fall): 2-19.
Stone, Gregory P. and Harvey A. Farberman (eds.)
   1981 Social Psychology Through Symbolic Interaction. New York: John Wiley.
Stonequist, Everett
   1937 The Marginal Man: A Study in Personality and Culture Conflict. New York:
        Scribner.
Stouffer, Samuel A., Edward A. Suchman, Leland C. DeVinney, Shirly A. Star, and
        Robin M. Williams
   1949 The American Soldier, Vol. I: Adjustment During Army Life. Princeton: Prin-
        ceton University Press.
Strauss, Anselm L.
   1956 The Social Psychology of George Herbert Mead. Chicago: University of Chi-
        cago Press.
   1959 Mirrors and Masks. New York: Macmillan.
   1978 Negotiations: Varieties, Contexts, Processes and Social Order. San Francisco:
        Jossey-Bass.
Stryker, Sheldon
   1980 Symbolic Interactionism: A Social Structural Version. Menlo Park, CA:
        Benjamin/Cummings.
   1981 "Symbolic interactionism: themes and variations," pp. 3-29 in M. Rosenberg
        and R. H. Turner (eds.) Social Psychology: Sociological Perspectives. New
        York: Basic Books.
Studt, Elliott, Sheldon L. Messinger, and Thomas P. Wilson
   1968 C-Unit: Search for a Prison Community. New York: Russell Sage.
Sullivan, Mortimer A., Jr., Stuart A. Queen, and Ralph C. Patrick
   1958 "Participant observation as employed in the study of a military training pro-
        gram." American Sociological Review 23 (December): 660-667.

Sutton-Smith, Brian and John M. Roberts
1963 "Game involvement in adults." Journal of Social Psychology 60: 15-30.

Taylor, James B., Louis A. Zurcher, and William H. Key
1970 Tornado: A Community Responds to Disaster. Seattle: University of Washington Press.

Thomas, W. I. and Florian Znaniecki
1927 The Polish Peasant in Europe and America. New York: Knopf.

Toby, Jackson
1952 "Variables in role conflict analysis." Social Forces 30 (March): 323-327.

Travisano, Richard V.
1981 "Alternation and conversion as qualitatively different transformations," pp. 237-248 in G. P. Stone and H. A. Farberman (eds.) Social Psychology Through Symbolic Interaction. New York: John Wiley.

Turner, Ralph H.
1947 "The navy disbursing officer as a bureaucrat." American Sociological Review 12 (June): 342-348.

1956 "Role taking, role standpoint and reference group behavior." American Journal of Sociology 61 (January): 316-328.

1962 "Role taking process versus conformity," pp. 20-40 in A. Rose (ed.) Human Behavior and Social Processes. Boston: Houghton Mifflin.

1967 "Types of solidarity in the reconstituting of groups." Pacific Sociological Review 10 (Fall): 60-68.

1968a "Role: sociological aspects," pp. 522-527 in D. L. Sills (ed.) International Encyclopedia of Social Sciences, Vol. 12. New York: Macmillan.

1968b "Self-conception in social interaction," pp. 93-106 in C. Gordon and K. S. Gergen (eds.) The Self in Social Interaction. New York: John Wiley.

1970 Family Interaction. New York: John Wiley.

1976 "The real self: from institution to impulse." American Journal of Sociology 81 (March): 986-1016.

1978 "The role and the person." American Journal of Sociology 84 (July): 1-23.

Turner, Ralph H. and Lewis M. Killian
1972 Collective Behavior. Englewood Cliffs, NJ: Prentice-Hall.

Turner, Victor W.
1974 Dramas, Fields and Metaphors: Symbolic Action in Human Society. Ithaca, NY: Cornell University Press.

Tyhurst, J. S.
1951 "Individual reactions to community disaster." American Journal of Psychiatry 107 (April): 764-769.

Vogt, E. Z.
1957 "The acculturation of American Indians." Annals of the American Academy of Political and Social Science 311: 137-146.

Wallace, Anthony F.C.
1957 "Mazeway disintegration: the individual's perception of socio-cultural disorganization." Human Organization 16 (Summer): 23-27.

Warren, Roland R.
1946 "The naval reserve officer: a study in assimilation." American Sociological Review 11 (April): 202-211.

Webb, Eugene J., Donald T. Campbell, Richard D. Schwartz, and Lee Sechrest
1966 Unobtrusive Measures: Nonreactive Research in the Social Sciences. Chicago: Rand McNally.

Weber, Max
    1968 Economy and Society. New York: Irvington.
Weinberg, S. Kirson
    1944-1945 "Problems of adjustment in army units." American Journal of Sociology
        50 (January): 271-278.
Weitman, Sasha R.
    1970 "Intimacies: notes toward a theory of social inclusion and exclusion." Euro-
        pean Archives of Sociology 11, 1: 348-367.
Wheeler, Stanton
    1969 "Socialization in correctional institutions," pp. 1005-1024 in D. A. Goslin (ed.)
        Handbook of Socialization Theory and Research. Chicago: Rand McNally.
White, Robert W.
    1959 "Motivation reconsidered: the concept of competence." Psychological Review
        66 (September): 297-333.
Whyte, William Foote
    1948 Human Relations in the Restaurant Industry. New York: McGraw-Hill.
    1949 "The social structure of the restaurant." American Journal of Sociology 54
        (January): 302-310.
Williams, Robin M.
    1960 American Society: A Sociological Interpretation. New York: Knopf.
Wilson, Thomas P.
    1970 "Conceptions of interaction and forms of sociological explanation." American
        Sociological Review 35 (August): 697-710.
Withey, Stephen B.
    1962 "Reaction to uncertain threat," pp. 93-123 in G. W. Baker and D. W. Chapman
        (eds.) Man and Society in Disaster. New York: Basic Books.
Wohl, Andrzej
    1970 "Competitive sport and its social functions." International Review of Sport
        Sociology 5: 117-130.
Wolfenstein, Martha
    1957 Disaster: A Psychological Essay. New York: Macmillan.
Wolff, Michael
    1973 "Notes on the behavior of pedestrians," pp. 35-48 in A. Birenbaum and E.
        Sagarin (eds.) People in Places: The Sociology of the Familiar. New York:
        Praeger.
Wood, Margaret M.
    1934 The Stranger: A Study in Social Relationships. New York: Columbia Univer-
        sity Press.
Woolf, Henry B.
    1975 Webster's New Collegiate Dictionary. Springfield, MA: G&C Merriam.
Wray, Donald E.
    1948 "Marginal man of industry: the foreman." American Journal of Sociology 54
        (January): 298-301.
Zola, Irving Kenneth
    1964 "Observations on gambling in a lower class setting," pp. 247-260 in H. Becker
        (ed.) The Other Side. New York: Macmillan.
Zurcher, Louis A.
    1970 Poverty Warriors: The Human Experience of Planned Social Intervention.
        Austin: University of Texas Press.
    1977 The Mutable Self: A Self-Concept for Social Change. Beverly Hills, CA: Sage.

1981 "About the rejection of manuscripts submitted to the Journal of Applied Behavioral Science." Journal of Applied Behavioral Science, 16 (October/November/December): 454-457.

Zurcher, Louis A. and R. George Kirkpatrick
1976 Citizens for Decency: Anti-Pornography Crusades as Status Defense. Austin: University of Texas Press.

Zurcher, Louis A. and Arnold Meadow
1967 "On bullfights and baseball: an example of the interaction of social institutions." International Journal of Comparative Sociology 8 (March): 99-117.

Author Index

Subject Index

About the Author

Louis A. Zurcher is Ashbel-Smith Professor of Social Work and of Sociology at the University of Texas at Austin. He earned a B.A. (summa cum laude) from the University of San Francisco and an M.A. and Ph.D. in psychology from the University of Arizona at Tucson. During 1980-1981 he was Acting Dean of the School of Social Work at the University of Texas. Prior to that, he served as Dean of the Graduate School and Professor of Sociology at Virginia Polytechnic Institute and State University, and served for eleven years as Professor of Sociology, Acting Chairperson of the Department of Sociology, and Associate Graduate Dean at the University of Texas at Austin. Trained as a social psychologist, he has published thirteen books (including *The Mutable Self: A Self-Concept for Social Change*, Sage Publications, 1977) and over 100 articles spanning the fields of sociology, psychology, and social work. Dr. Zurcher currently is Editor of *The Journal of Applied Behavioral Science*. He has been active in professional associations, including the American Psychological Association, the American Sociological Association, and the Council on Social Work Education. He was president of the Association of Voluntary Action Scholars during 1979-1980. His memberships in scholastic honor societies include Phi Beta Kappa, Phi Kappa Phi, Sigma Xi, Psi Chi, and Alpha Kappa Delta. His present research interests focus on personality and social structure, particularly self-concept and social change.